# SCIENCE VISUAL RESOURCES

# EARTH SCIENCE

## An Illustrated Guide to Science

## The Diagram Group

CHELSEA HOUSE
PUBLISHERS
An imprint of Infobase Publishing

**Earth Science: An Illustrated Guide to Science**

Copyright © 2006 The Diagram Group

| | |
|---|---|
| Authors: | Simon Adams, David Lambert |
| Editors: | Gordon Lee, Jamie Stokes |
| Design: | Anthony Atherton, bounford.com, Christopher Branfield, Richard Hummerstone, Lee Lawrence, Tim Noel-Johnson, Phil Richardson |
| Illustration: | Peter Wilkinson |
| Picture research: | Neil McKenna |
| Indexer: | Martin Hargreaves |

Chelsea House
An imprint of Infobase Publishing
132 West 31st Street
New York NY 10001

For Library of Congress Cataloging-in-Publication data,
please contact the publisher.

ISBN 0-8160-6164-5

Chelsea House books are available at special discounts when purchased in bulk quantities for businesses, associations, institutions, or sales promotions. Please call our Special Sales Department in New York at 212/967-8800 or 800/322-8755.

You can find Chelsea House on the World Wide Web at
http://www.chelseahouse.com

Printed in China

CP Diagram 10 9 8 7 6 5 4 3 2 1

This book is printed on acid-free paper.

# Introduction

*Earth Science* is one of eight volumes in the **Science Visual Resources** set. It contains six sections, a comprehensive glossary, a Web site guide, and an index.

*Earth Science* is a learning tool for students and teachers. Full-color diagrams, graphs, charts, and maps on every page illustrate the essential elements of the subject, while parallel text provides key definitions and step-by-step explanations.

**Earth and space** provides an introduction to the study of our planet in the context of the solar system. Issues such as Earth's dependence on the Sun, and reciprocal influence with the Moon, are illustrated and discussed, as the elementary concerns of the earth sciences are introduced.

The concept of geologic time—a timescale staggering by the standards of human history—is expanded in **Earth's history**. Reference is made to the fossil traces of past life that enable modern paleontology to make deductions about the development of life-forms, while the land of the present-day USA is presented as a familiar point of reference in a story of unceasing change.

**Earth's rocks** introduces the elementary chemistry and physics underlying the geology of the planet, and discusses how minerals form rocks. The three major classifications of igneous, metamorphic, and sedimentary rock are examined in detail before the chapter returns to the origins of Earth's current surface alignment and mineral resources.

**Air and oceans** examines in detail Earth's unique and life-sustaining atmosphere and surface water.

**Shaping the surface** looks at the physical geography of the land and how it is naturally shaped by weather and water movement.

Finally, familiar and significant geographical features of the world are statistically compared in **Comparisons**.

# Contents

# 3 EARTH'S ROCKS

# 4 AIR AND OCEANS

# 5 SHAPING THE SURFACE

# 6 COMPARISONS

# APPENDIXES

## Key words

| | |
|---|---|
| aphelion | perihelion |
| asteroid | planet |
| comet | |
| gravity | |
| orbit | |

## Gravity and inertia

- The planet Earth tries to speed through space in a straight line. The Sun's gravitational force tries to pull Earth into the Sun. Inertia—the tendency of an object to resist a force changing its speed or direction—prevents this from happening. Instead, the captured Earth continually orbits the Sun.
- Earth orbits the Sun at a mean distance of 92,960,000 miles (149,600,000 km).
- Earth's orbital velocity is 18.5 miles per second (29.8 kmps).

## Earth's path

- Earth revolves around the Sun in a counterclockwise direction if viewed from space.
- Each year's complete revolution traces an elliptical orbit bringing Earth closest to the Sun in January and furthest away in July. The point at which a planet, comet, or asteroid most closely approaches its sun is termed *perihelion*, while the point furthest away is *aphelion*.
- At perihelion, about January 3rd, Earth comes within 91,400,000 miles (147,100,000 km) of the Sun.
- At aphelion, about July 4th, it is 94,510,000 miles (152,100,000 km) from the Sun.

# Earth's orbit

## Gravity and inertia

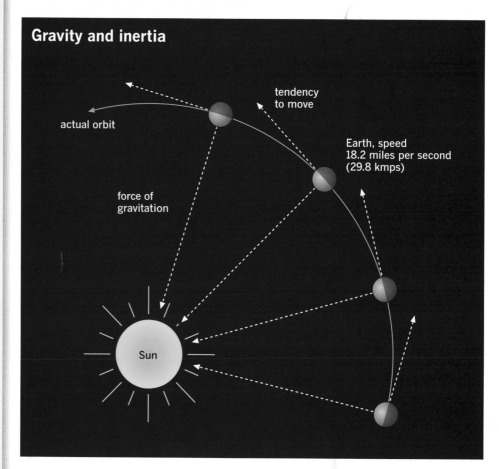

actual orbit

tendency to move

force of gravitation

Earth, speed 18.2 miles per second (29.8 kmps)

Sun

## Earth's path

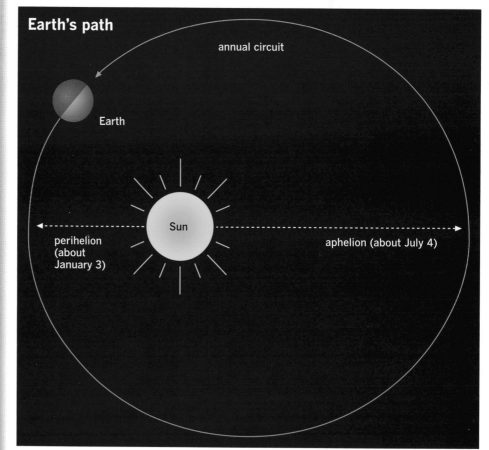

annual circuit

Earth

Sun

perihelion (about January 3)

aphelion (about July 4)

# Earth's shape and size

## Earth's size

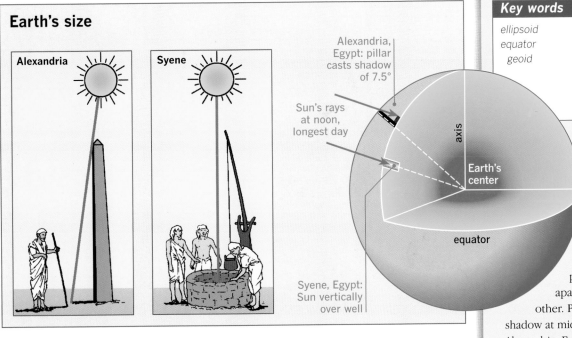

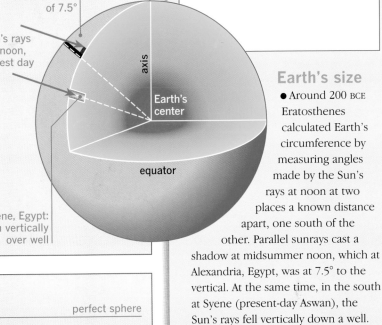

| Alexandria | Syene |

Alexandria, Egypt: pillar casts shadow of 7.5°

Sun's rays at noon, longest day

axis

Earth's center

equator

Syene, Egypt: Sun vertically over well

● Around 200 BCE Eratosthenes calculated Earth's circumference by measuring angles made by the Sun's rays at noon at two places a known distance apart, one south of the other. Parallel sunrays cast a shadow at midsummer noon, which at Alexandria, Egypt, was at 7.5° to the vertical. At the same time, in the south at Syene (present-day Aswan), the Sun's rays fell vertically down a well.

## Earth: nearly an ellipsoid

perfect sphere

polar diameter

equatorial diameter

ellipsoid

The diagram shows an *ellipsoid* against a perfect sphere. Earth is almost an ellipsoid.

● The distance from the North Pole to the South Pole of 7,900 miles (12,714 km) is 26 miles (42 km) shorter than the distance across the equator, which is 7,926 miles (12,756 km).
● The shape of Earth can be represented as a near-ellipsoid by visually exaggerating the differences between its polar and equatorial diameters.

## The geoid: Earth's actual shape

● The *geoid* is Earth's actual shape calculated to take account of its mass, elasticity, and rate of spin. It follows mean sea level in the oceans and is slightly pear-shaped, with the North Pole 18.9 miles (30 km) further from Earth's center than other places and the South Pole 25.8 miles (42 km) nearer.
● The diagram stresses Earth's pearlike shape by visually exaggerating small differences in distance from surface to center.

## The geoid

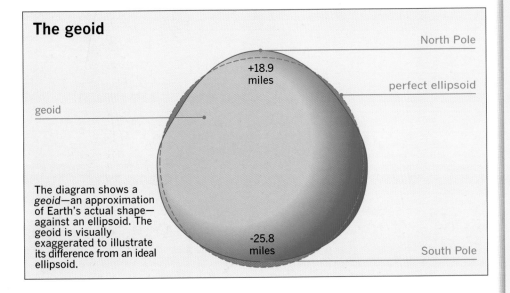

North Pole

+18.9 miles

perfect ellipsoid

geoid

-25.8 miles

South Pole

The diagram shows a *geoid*—an approximation of Earth's actual shape—against an ellipsoid. The geoid is visually exaggerated to illustrate its difference from an ideal ellipsoid.

# Day and night time zones

## Key words

*longitude*
*meridian*
*prime meridian*
*Sun*
*time zone*

## Day and night

- Earth spins like a spinning top, and completes one revolution every 24 hours. As it spins, each place on its surface moves into sunlight and daytime, and then into the Sun's shadow and night.
- When North America faces away from the Sun it is night there.
- When North America faces the Sun it is day there.

## Time zones

- The world is divided into standard time zones based on the *prime* (or *Greenwich*) *meridian* at 0° longitude.
- With local adjustments, each standard time zone is a 15 degree band east or west of the prime meridian and represents a difference in time of one hour.

### Day and night

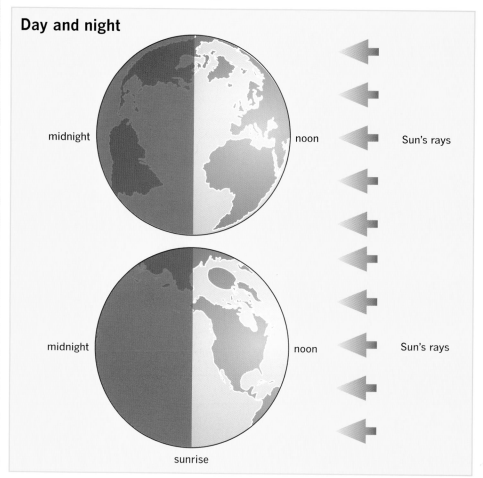

midnight — noon — Sun's rays

midnight — noon — Sun's rays

sunrise

### World time zones

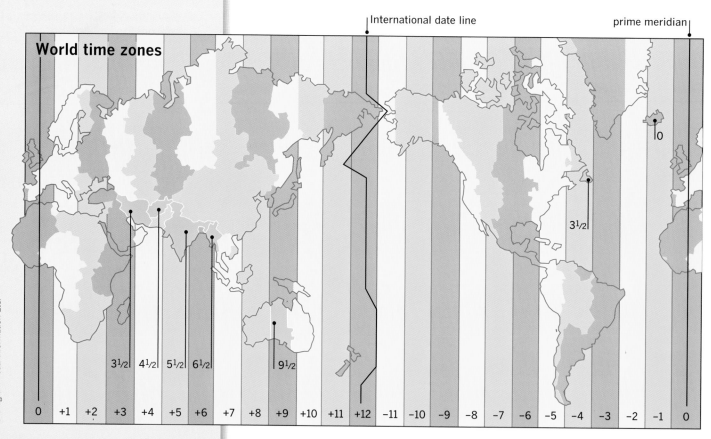

International date line

prime meridian

0

3½

3½ 4½ 5½ 6½

9½

| 0 | +1 | +2 | +3 | +4 | +5 | +6 | +7 | +8 | +9 | +10 | +11 | +12 | -11 | -10 | -9 | -8 | -7 | -6 | -5 | -4 | -3 | -2 | -1 | 0 |
|---|----|----|----|----|----|----|----|----|----|-----|-----|-----|-----|-----|----|----|----|----|----|----|----|----|----|---|

# The seasons

**Key words**

*equinox*
*solstice*

## Summer solstice
### June 21

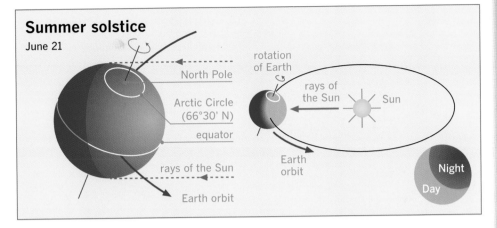

rotation of Earth

North Pole

Arctic Circle (66°30' N)

equator

rays of the Sun

Earth orbit

rays of the Sun

Sun

Earth orbit

Night

Day

## Autumnal (fall) equinox
### September 23

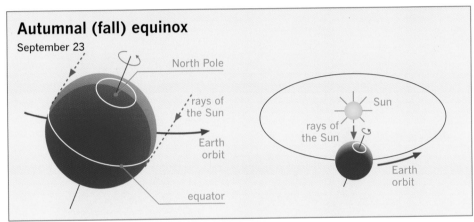

North Pole

rays of the Sun

Earth orbit

equator

Sun

rays of the Sun

Earth orbit

## Winter solstice
### December 22

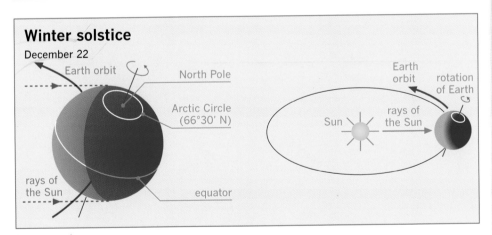

Earth orbit

North Pole

Arctic Circle (66°30' N)

rays of the Sun

equator

Earth orbit

rotation of Earth

Sun

rays of the Sun

## Vernal (spring) equinox
### March 21

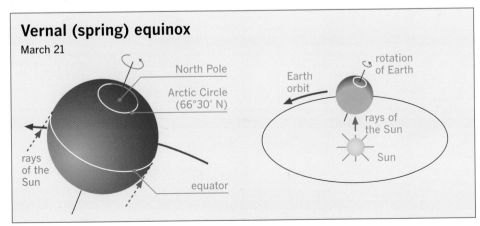

North Pole

Arctic Circle (66°30' N)

rays of the Sun

equator

rotation of Earth

Earth orbit

rays of the Sun

Sun

## Seasons

- Seasons are periods of the year with characteristic weather. Many tropical and subtropical regions have only wet and dry seasons.
- Temperate regions such as North America and Europe have four seasons: spring, summer, fall (autumn), and winter.
- Seasons result from the fact that Earth's axis of rotation is not perpendicular to the plane of its orbit around the Sun, but tilted by 23.5 degrees.
- This tilt means that Northern and Southern hemispheres receive more or less sunlight depending on whether they are tilted toward or away from the Sun.
- Seasons depend on the intensity of solar radiation, so the northern summer coincides with the southern winter and vice versa. The diagrams show seasons for the Northern Hemisphere.

## Summer

- At the summer solstice the Northern Hemisphere is tilted toward the Sun. Summer is the hottest time of year.

## Fall (autumn)

- At the autumnal equinox, the Sun is directly overhead above the equator. In the fall daytime grows shorter, crops ripen, and deciduous trees shed leaves.

## Winter

- At the winter solstice, the Northern Hemisphere is tilted away from the Sun. Winter is the coldest time of year. Daytime hours are shortest. Plant growth slows or stops.

## Spring

- At the vernal equinox, the Sun is overhead at the equator. In spring days lengthen and plants grow.

© Diagram Visual Information Ltd.

| Key words | |
|---|---|
| *Earth* | *pole* |
| *equator* | |
| *latitude* | |
| *longitude* | |
| *prime meridian* | |

## Latitude

- *Latitude* is a position on Earth's surface north (N) or south (S) of the *equator*, the imaginary line around the middle of Earth.
- Degrees of latitude are measured as angles from the center of Earth. A degree (°) of latitude is divided into 60 minutes ('). A minute is divided into 60 seconds (").
- A line joining locations with the same latitude is called a "parallel." Parallels are so called because they run parallel to the equator and to one another.
- The equator is at latitude 0°. The North and South poles lie at latitudes 90° N and S.

## Longitude

- *Longitude* is a position east (E) or west (W) of the *prime meridian*, an imaginary line on Earth's surface, passing through Greenwich, England, and joining the North and South poles.
- The prime meridian is at longitude 0°. Meridians are measured up to 180° E or W of it.
- Degrees of longitude are measured as angles from the center of Earth and divided into minutes and seconds.
- Lines of longitude are 69 miles (111 km) apart at the equator, but become closer together as their distance from it increases.

# Latitude and longitude

## Latitude

### Obtaining an angle of latitude

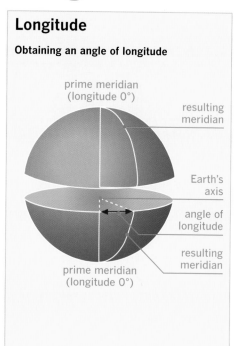

### Degrees of latitude

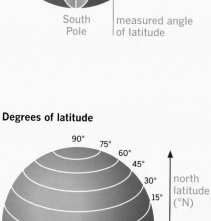

### Key latitudes

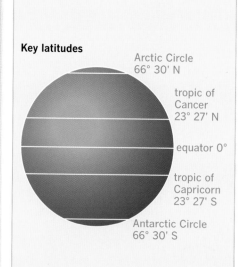

Arctic Circle 66° 30' N

tropic of Cancer 23° 27' N

equator 0°

tropic of Capricorn 23° 27' S

Antarctic Circle 66° 30' S

## Longitude

### Obtaining an angle of longitude

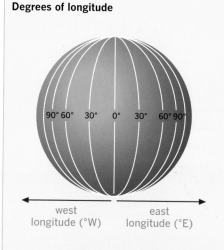

### Degrees of longitude

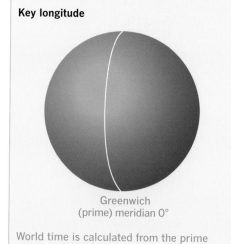

west longitude (°W)  east longitude (°E)

### Key longitude

Greenwich (prime) meridian 0°

World time is calculated from the prime meridian (0°).

# The solar system

## Planetary orbits

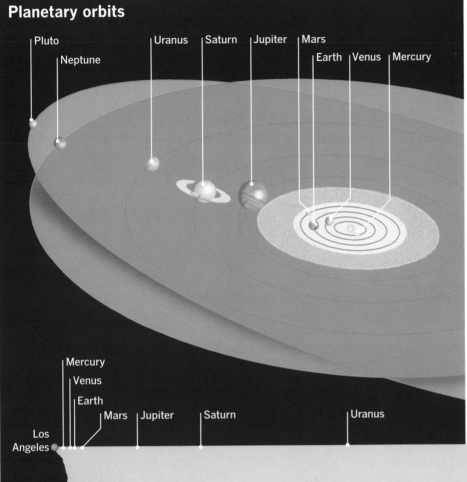

Pluto
Neptune
Uranus
Saturn
Jupiter
Mars
Earth
Venus
Mercury

Mercury
Venus
Earth
Mars
Jupiter
Saturn
Uranus

Los Angeles

Neptune

Pluto
New York

This map of part of the United States demonstrates the relative distances of the planets from the Sun if it were located in Los Angeles, California and Pluto at New York City.

### Key words

| | |
|---|---|
| asteroid | moon |
| comet | outer planet |
| gas giant | terrestrial |
| inner planet | |

## Types of planets

- The inner planets Mercury, Venus, Earth, and Mars have rocky surfaces. They are known as terrestrial or Earthlike planets.
- The outer planets Jupiter, Saturn, Uranus, and Neptune are gas giants.
- Pluto is made of rock and ice.
- The distance of the planets from the Sun varies from 28.6 million miles (45.9 million km) for Mercury at its closest to 4,609 million miles (7,375 million km) for Pluto at its farthest.

## Planets' mean distance from the Sun

| | Miles | Kilometers |
|---|---|---|
| Mercury | 36,000,000 | 57,900,000 |
| Venus | 67,200,000 | 108,100,000 |
| Earth | 93,000,000 | 149,700,000 |
| Mars | 141,600,000 | 227,900,000 |
| Jupiter | 483,800,000 | 778,600,000 |
| Saturn | 890,800,000 | 1,436,600,000 |
| Uranus | 1,784,800,000 | 2,872,600,000 |
| Neptune | 2,793,100,000 | 4,494,900,000 |
| Pluto | 3,647,200,000 | 5,869,600,000 |

# Structure of the Sun

## Key words

chromosphere    photosphere
convection       Sun
core
corona
nuclear fusion

## Core

- At the heart of the Sun nuclear fusion reactions convert hydrogen into helium.
- Temperatures reach 27,000,000°F (15,000,000°C).

## Radiative zone

- Energy produced in the core radiates toward the surface of the Sun through this region.
- This energy prevents the Sun from collapsing under the force of gravity.

## Convective zone

- Energy waves, weakened by their passage through the radiative zone, pass through this area via constantly churning *convection* currents.

## Photosphere

- The *photoshere* "surface" of the Sun is highly irregular. Temperatures vary from 7,800–16,000°F (4,300–9,000°C).

## Chromosphere

- The *chromosphere* is a highly agitated zone of thin gases rising to about 6,000 miles (9,700 km) above the photosphere. This region is constantly disrupted by solar flares, prominences, and spiricules.

## Corona

- Extending millions of miles into space the *corona* is a very thinly dispersed ball of gas.
- Atoms and molecules in this region have very high velocities and temperatures up to 7,000,000°F (4,000,000°C).

## Structural view of the Sun

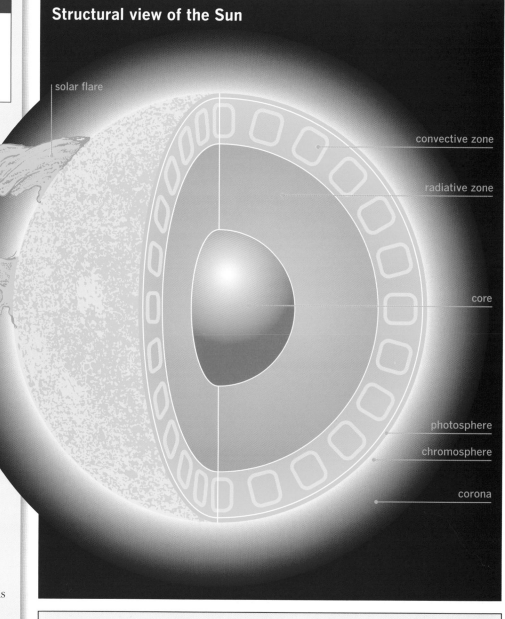

solar flare

convective zone

radiative zone

core

photosphere

chromosphere

corona

## Nuclear fusion at the Sun's core

loose hydrogen nuclei

hydrogen nuclei combined into helium atom

energy released by fusion reaction

# The Sun's energy

Key words

*nuclear
  fusion*

## Nuclear fusion

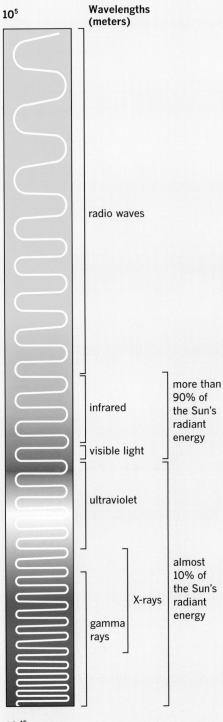

- proton
- neutron
- positron
- neutrino

**1** Hydrogen nuclei (protons) collide.

**2** Collisions throw off two positrons and neutrinos, and form two deuterons (heavy hydrogen nuclei).

**3** Each deuteron collides with a proton.

**4** Collisions form light helium nuclei.

**5** Fusion of light helium nuclei forms one stable helium nucleus and frees two protons.

**6** Fusion releases energy.

## Radiant energy

$10^5$

**Wavelengths (meters)**

radio waves

infrared

visible light

ultraviolet

X-rays

gamma rays

more than 90% of the Sun's radiant energy

almost 10% of the Sun's radiant energy

$10^{-15}$

Most of the Sun's visible light can penetrate the whole of the atmosphere right down to Earth's surface, except where cloud intervenes. However only some of the infrared radiation gets through: the rest is cut off, along with the most harmful ultraviolet radiation, by atmospheric gases.

### Nuclear fusion

- During *nuclear fusion*, hydrogen atoms fuse to produce helium.
- The mass of helium produced is less than the mass of the hydrogen that produced it.
- The mass that is "lost" is converted to energy, given off by the Sun as light, heat, and invisible forms of *radiation*.

### Radiant energy

- The Sun radiates energy through space at *wavelengths* in the electromagnetic spectrum from (very short wavelength) gamma rays to the longest longwave radio waves.
- Gamma rays, X-rays, and ultraviolet rays are shortwave penetrative forms of radiation that are potentially damaging to living tissue.
- Visible light comprises wavelengths perceived as colors ranging from violet through red.
- Infrared radiation is perceived as radiant heat.
- Microwaves resemble those used in microwave ovens.
- Radio waves from the Sun include waves shorter than those used for radio broadcasts.

# The Moon

## Key words

| | |
|---|---|
| axis | Sun |
| barycenter | |
| Earth | |
| Moon | |
| orbit | |

## Common center of mass

- Both the Moon and Earth travel around a common center of mass known as a *barycenter*.
- As Earth's mass is much greater than the Moon's, their barycenter lies within Earth's diameter.

## The Moon's path

- The Moon revolves around Earth every 27 days. It also revolves on its own *axis* once every 27 days, so the same side always faces Earth.
- As Earth revolves around the Sun, and the Moon around Earth, the Moon's path around the Sun resembles a cogwheel.

### The Moon–Earth barycenter

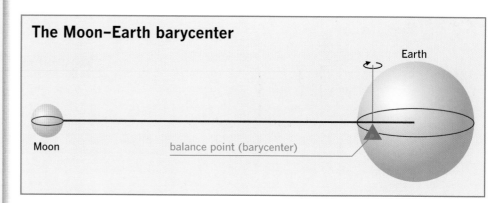

Earth

Moon

balance point (barycenter)

### The Moon's path around Earth

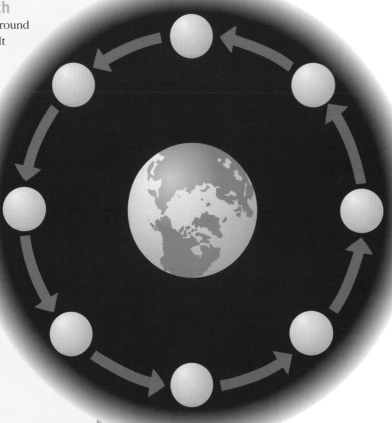

### The Moon's path around the Sun

Earth's orbit

Moon's orbit

## The Moon's phases

| | | | | | | | |
|---|---|---|---|---|---|---|---|
| New Moon | Waxing crescent Moon | Half Moon, first quarter | Waxing gibbous Moon | Full Moon | Waning gibbous Moon | Half Moon, last quarter | Waning crescent Moon |

# The Moon: surface

## Lunar seas

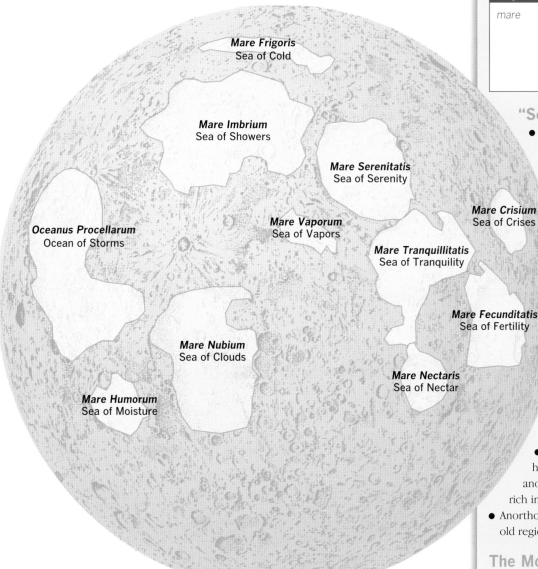

- **Mare Frigoris** — Sea of Cold
- **Mare Imbrium** — Sea of Showers
- **Mare Serenitatis** — Sea of Serenity
- **Mare Crisium** — Sea of Crises
- **Mare Vaporum** — Sea of Vapors
- **Oceanus Procellarum** — Ocean of Storms
- **Mare Tranquillitatis** — Sea of Tranquility
- **Mare Fecunditatis** — Sea of Fertility
- **Mare Nubium** — Sea of Clouds
- **Mare Nectaris** — Sea of Nectar
- **Mare Humorum** — Sea of Moisture

### Key words

*mare*

### "Seas" and mountains

- Great "seas" or *maria* (singular: *mare*) are visible on the Moon's Earth-facing side.
- These seas are in fact ancient flows of basalt lava.
- This lava welled up from the Moon's interior when asteroids ruptured the surface.
- With no atmosphere to burn up and fragment such incoming missiles, the Moon suffered a heavy bombardment while the solar system was still young.
- The Moon's cratered highlands consist mainly of anorthosite and related rocks rich in plagioclase feldspar.
- Anorthosite occurs on Earth only in old regions of continents.

### The Moon's size

- The Moon's diameter is less than one third that of Earth.
- Its mass is 81 times less that of Earth.
- Its volume is 49 times less that of Earth.

**Comparative sizes of the Moon and Earth**

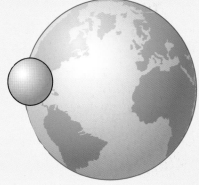

## Major lunar craters

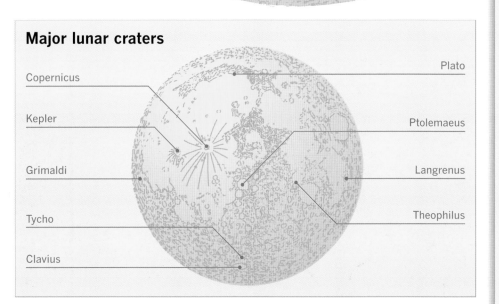

- Copernicus
- Kepler
- Grimaldi
- Tycho
- Clavius
- Plato
- Ptolemaeus
- Langrenus
- Theophilus

# The Moon: structure

### Key words

| | |
|---|---|
| asteroid | mantle |
| basalt | regolith |
| boulder | |
| core | |
| crust | |

## The Moon's structure

- Like Earth, the Moon has a core, mantle, and crust.
- Unlike Earth's mantle and crust, those of the Moon are rigid.

## Structure of a plain

- This block diagram shows features typical of a basalt lunar plain.
- Much of it is covered by *regolith*: loose debris from dust to boulders produced by old asteroid impacts.

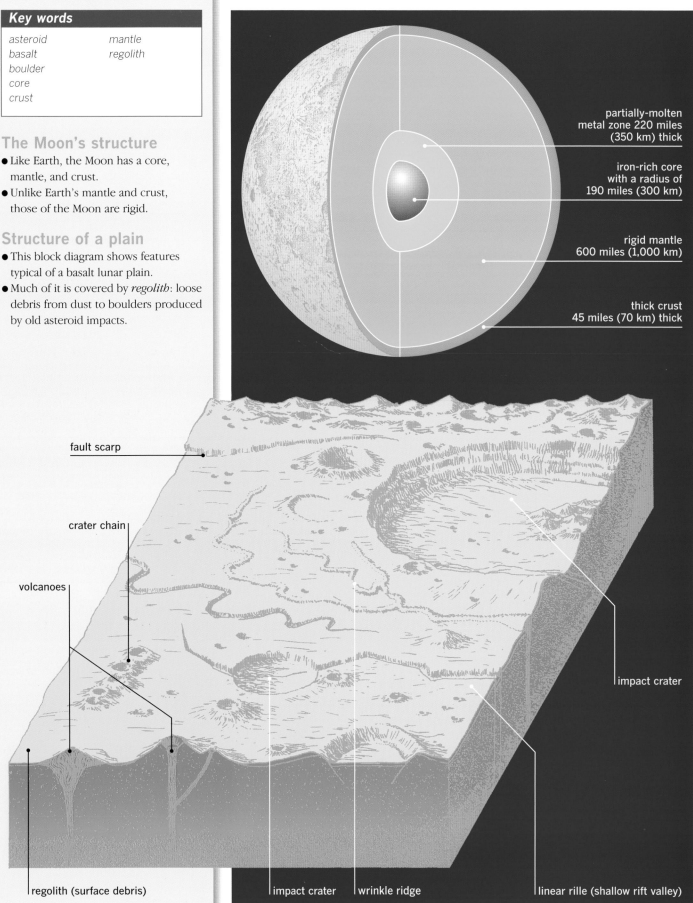

partially-molten metal zone 220 miles (350 km) thick

iron-rich core with a radius of 190 miles (300 km)

rigid mantle 600 miles (1,000 km)

thick crust 45 miles (70 km) thick

fault scarp

crater chain

volcanoes

impact crater

regolith (surface debris)

impact crater   wrinkle ridge   linear rille (shallow rift valley)

# Solar and lunar eclipses

## Solar eclipses

**Total eclipse**

area of partial eclipse: sunlight is partially blocked by the Moon

area of totality: sunlight is completely blocked by the Moon

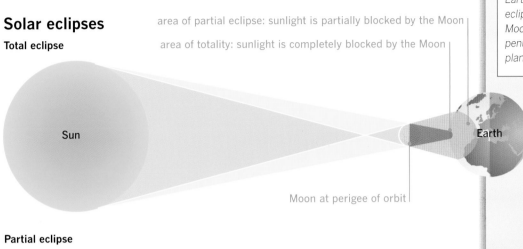

Sun

Earth

Moon at perigee of orbit

**Partial eclipse**

Sun

area of partial eclipse

total eclipse shadow misses Earth

Earth

Moon

## Lunar eclipses

**Total eclipse**

Moon enters Earth's total shadow

total shadow cast by Earth

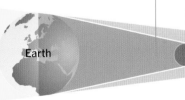

Sun

Earth

**Partial eclipse**

partial shadow cast by Earth

total shadow cast by Earth

Sun

Earth

Moon enters Earth's partial shadow

### Eclipse

- An *eclipse* occurs when one heavenly body blocks the light shining from a second onto a third.

### Solar eclipse

- A solar eclipse happens when the Moon comes between the Sun and Earth. This kind of eclipse occurs on Earth at places crossed by the Moon's shadow.
- Where the Moon completely blots out the Sun, the *umbra*, the darkest part of the Moon's shadow, produces a total eclipse. Here the sky becomes dark as if it were night.
- Where the Moon conceals only part of the Sun, its partial shadow or *penumbra* produces a partial eclipse.

### Lunar eclipse

- A lunar eclipse happens when Earth passes between the Sun and the Moon.
- If Earth completely blots out the Sun, Earth's umbra produces a total eclipse of the Moon.
- If only Earth's penumbra falls on the Moon, the latter is partially eclipsed from the position of an observer on Earth.
- During most lunar eclipses, the Moon remains visible from Earth as it receives some sunlight bent by Earth's atmosphere.

**Key words**

| | |
|---|---|
| core | rock |
| crust | |
| Earth | |
| element | |
| mantle | |

# Structure of Earth

## Structure of Earth

- During Earth's formation, heavy elements moved toward the center, while light ones gathered at the surface.
- The hot, high-pressure core is mainly solid iron and nickel.
- Earth's outer core may be mainly iron and nickel with some silicon.
- Part of the mantle is semimolten and flows in sluggish currents.
- A crust of relatively light rocks rests on the mantle.

### Composition

solid metal inner core with a radius of 1,000 miles (1,600 km)

molten outer core 1,140 miles (1,820 km) thick

semimolten rocky lower mantle 1,430 miles (2,290 km) thick

upper mantle 390 miles (640 km) thick

crust 6.25–25 miles (10–40 km) thick

## Earth facts

- Earth is the only planet in the solar system known to support life.
- Earth takes 365.25 days to orbit the Sun (that is, one year).
- It spins on its own axis every 23 hours 56 minutes (one day).
- The average temperature on the surface is about 59°F (15°C).
- Earth is the only planet to have liquid water on its surface.
- Earth has one natural satellite, the Moon.

## Earth's crust

Earth's crust is a shell of solid rock that floats on a sea of molten magma.

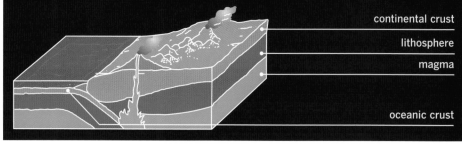

continental crust

lithosphere

magma

oceanic crust

# Earth's magnetic field

**Key words**

*core*
*Earth*
*geomagnetism*

## Earth's magnetic field

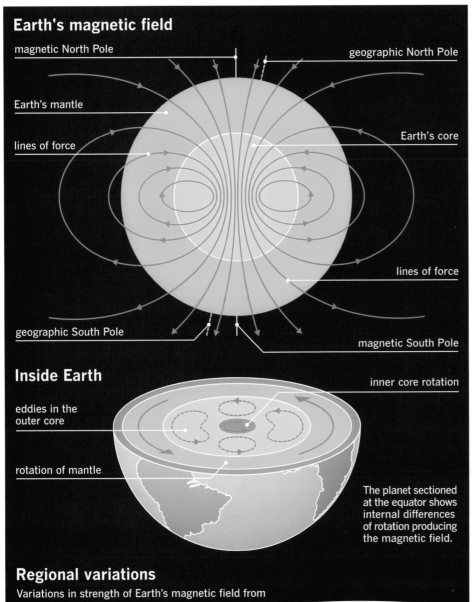

magnetic North Pole

geographic North Pole

Earth's mantle

lines of force

Earth's core

lines of force

geographic South Pole

magnetic South Pole

## Inside Earth

inner core rotation

eddies in the outer core

rotation of mantle

The planet sectioned at the equator shows internal differences of rotation producing the magnetic field.

## Regional variations

Variations in strength of Earth's magnetic field from
**1** (high) to **11** (low)

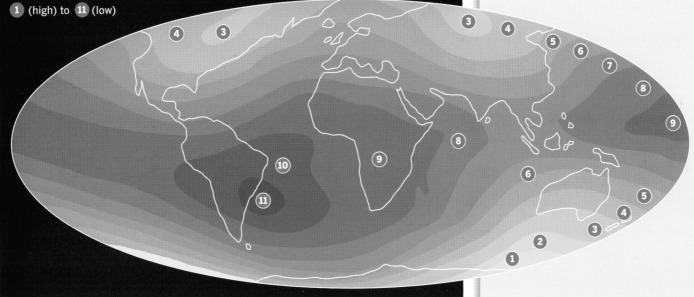

## Earth as a magnet

- Earth's crust and mantle rotate rather faster than its metallic core. This difference in speed produces a dynamo effect creating an immense magnetic field.
- This *geomagnetic* field consists of imaginary flux lines (lines of magnetic force) that curve around Earth between its north and south magnetic poles.
- Compass needles point to the magnetic poles.
- The magnetic poles do not coincide with the geographic poles, and their positions shift through time.

## Regional variations

- Earth's magnetic field varies in intensity from place to place across the planet's surface. Its intensity is greatest near the magnetic poles.
- Local variations indicate differences in subsurface rocks.

# Earth's magnetosphere

## Key words

aurora                    solar wind
cosmic ray
electromagnetic
  radiation
magnetosphere

## Van Allen belts

- The inner Van Allen belt has highly energetic protons produced by cosmic rays hitting atoms in the atmosphere. The satellite *Explorer 1*, designed by James Van Allen (b. 1914), discovered this belt in 1958.

- The outer radiation belt has electrons and various ions, but fewer high-energy particles than the inner belt. Like the inner belt, it was found by observations made by artificial satellites.

## Hypothetical undisturbed field

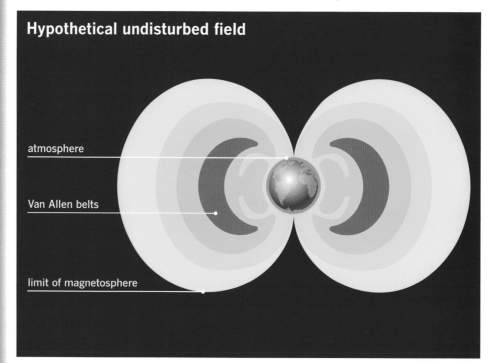

atmosphere

Van Allen belts

limit of magnetosphere

## Effect of the solar wind

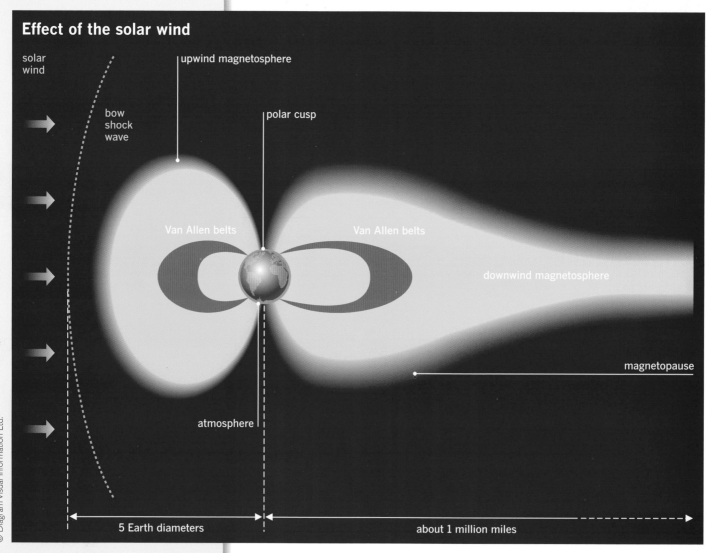

solar wind

upwind magnetosphere

bow shock wave

polar cusp

Van Allen belts

Van Allen belts

downwind magnetosphere

magnetopause

atmosphere

5 Earth diameters

about 1 million miles

# Meteors

## Meteors

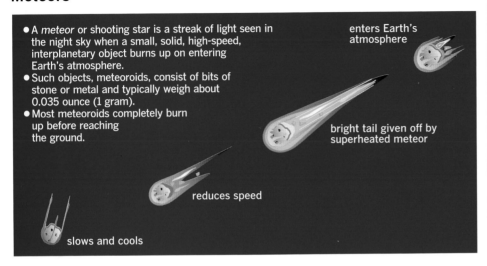

- A *meteor* or shooting star is a streak of light seen in the night sky when a small, solid, high-speed, interplanetary object burns up on entering Earth's atmosphere.
- Such objects, meteoroids, consist of bits of stone or metal and typically weigh about 0.035 ounce (1 gram).
- Most meteoroids completely burn up before reaching the ground.

enters Earth's atmosphere

bright tail given off by superheated meteor

reduces speed

slows and cools

## Orbits of major debris trails

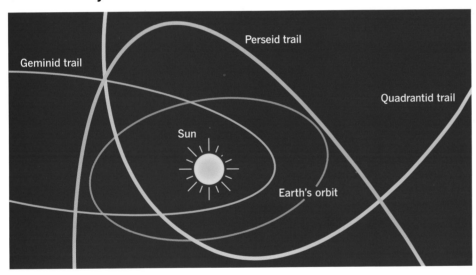

Perseid trail

Geminid trail

Quadrantid trail

Sun

Earth's orbit

## Major meteor showers

| Shower | Date | Parent comet | Meteor frequency (maximum number visible per hour) |
|---|---|---|---|
| Quadrantids | January 4 | unknown | 110 |
| Lyrids | April 22 | Thatcher | 8 |
| Eta Aquarids | May 5 | Halley | 18 |
| Delta Aquarids | July 3 | unknown | 30 |
| Perseids | August 12 | Swift-Tuttle | 65 |
| Orionids | October 21 | Halley | 25 |
| Taurids | November 8 | Encke | 10 |
| Leonids | November 17 | Temple-Tuttle | 15 |
| Geminids | December 14 | Asteroid 3200 | 55 |
| Ursids | December 23 | Tuttle | 20 |

Note: Dates given are for peak activity and meteor frequencies apply to those dates.

### Key words

*atmosphere*
*comet*
*Earth*
*meteor*
*meteoroid*

## Classification

- Occasionally a meteor shower may be very intense with frequencies of up to 1,000 meteors per minute. These are known as meteor storms.
- Meteor storms occur when the parent comet or body has recently passed close to Earth, when its debris trail is particularly dense.
- Leonid meteor storms were observed in 1799, 1833, 1866, and 1966. Others have also been observed.

## Sporadic and regular showers

- Meteors enter the atmosphere at a constant rate of about six per hour. These are known as sporadic showers.
- At certain regular times of the year large numbers of meteors enter the atmosphere. To an observer on the ground each of these showers seems to emanate from a particular area of the sky. These are called regular showers.

## Regular showers

- Comets or asteroids in orbits around the Sun may leave a trail of debris.
- Some of these trails cross Earth's orbital path.
- When Earth passes through a debris trail some of that debris enters the atmosphere as meteors.
- Every year Earth passes through the same debris trails, giving rise to regular annual showers of meteors.
- These regular showers are named for the constellations they appear to emanate from.

**Key words**

atmosphere
bolide
impact crater
meteorite

## Meteorites

- *Meteorites* are lumps of stone or metal that have fallen onto Earth from space. Meteorites are classified as stony (the majority), stony irons, or irons.
- The largest meteorites originated as asteroids. Such objects produce brilliant fireballs known as *bolides* because they glow on entering the atmosphere.
- Meteorites several miles (km) across have gouged huge impact craters on Earth's surface. Through time large meteorites may have caused several mass extinctions.
- Meteorites, impact craters, or debris ejected from such craters occur on every continent.

## Types of meteorite

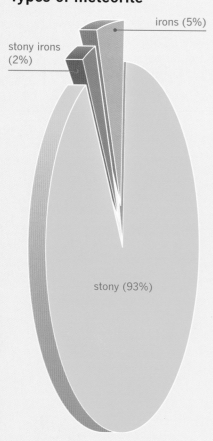

irons (5%)

stony irons (2%)

stony (93%)

# Meteorites

## Bombs from space: major impact craters

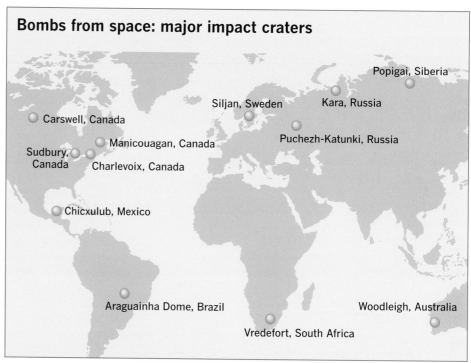

Popigai, Siberia

Siljan, Sweden    Kara, Russia

Carswell, Canada

Puchezh-Katunki, Russia

Manicouagan, Canada

Sudbury, Canada    Charlevoix, Canada

Chicxulub, Mexico

Araguainha Dome, Brazil    Woodleigh, Australia

Vredefort, South Africa

## Formation of a meteorite crater

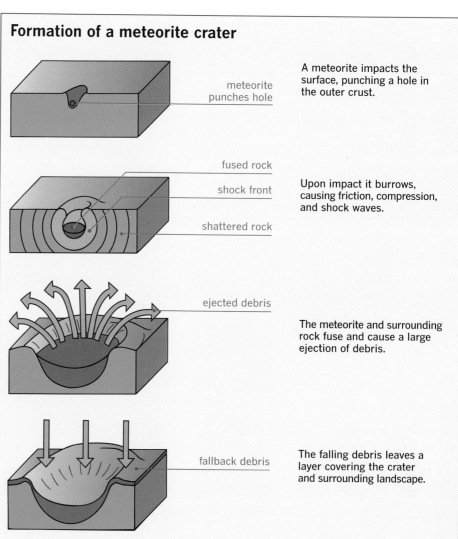

meteorite punches hole

A meteorite impacts the surface, punching a hole in the outer crust.

fused rock

shock front

shattered rock

Upon impact it burrows, causing friction, compression, and shock waves.

ejected debris

The meteorite and surrounding rock fuse and cause a large ejection of debris.

fallback debris

The falling debris leaves a layer covering the crater and surrounding landscape.

# Elements: universal abundance

**Key words**

electron            star
element
neutron
nucleosynthesis
proton

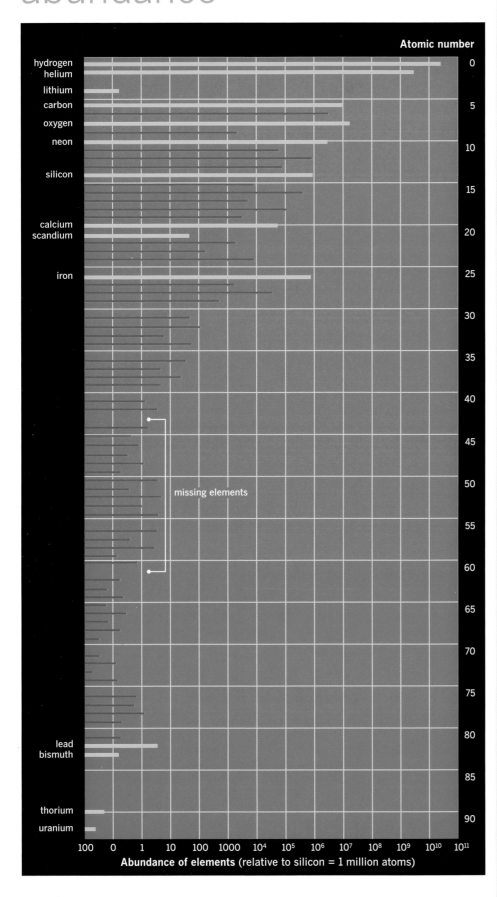

Atomic number

hydrogen — 0
helium
lithium
carbon — 5
oxygen
neon — 10
silicon — 15
calcium — 20
scandium
iron — 25
— 30
— 35
— 40
— 45
— 50
missing elements
— 55
— 60
— 65
— 70
— 75
— 80
lead
bismuth
— 85
thorium — 90
uranium

100  0  1  10  100  1000  $10^4$  $10^5$  $10^6$  $10^7$  $10^8$  $10^9$  $10^{10}$  $10^{11}$
**Abundance of elements (relative to silicon = 1 million atoms)**

## Varying abundance

- There are about ten hydrogen atoms for each helium atom. These two lightest *elements* comprise about 99 percent of all known matter.
- The remaining one percent consists of progressively heavier elements: the lithium group, of low abundance; the more plentiful carbon, silicon, and iron groups; then the successively scarcer middleweight and heaviest groups.

## Evolving elements

- The early universe teemed with elementary particles. *Neutrons* decaying into *electrons* and *protons* formed hydrogen nuclei, each with one electron and one proton.
- Proton and neutron capture converted some hydrogen nuclei into helium nuclei.
- Hydrogen and helium formed the earliest stars.
- Stars passed through cycles of heating, expansion, cooling, and contraction, generating ever heavier elements in their cores by processes of stellar nucleosynthesis.

## How we know

- Knowledge of the universal abundance of elements largely comes from spectroscopy.
- Every element emits light at particular wavelengths, appearing in its spectrum as bright emission lines. Their relative intensities reveal the relative abundances of elements in stars and planets.
- Dark absorption lines reveal the make-up of light-absorbing interstellar gas clouds.
- The knowledge that light elements gave rise to heavy elements derives from experiments in nuclear laboratories.

© Diagram Visual Information Ltd.

**Key words**

| erosion | tilting |
|---|---|
| folding | uplift |
| layer | |
| stratum | |
| superposition | |

## Superposition

- The principle of *superposition* states that in an undisturbed sequence of strata the lowest stratum is the oldest and the highest is youngest.
- A rock layer is laid down under water on the floor of a sea, lake, or river (**a**).
- A second layer of sedimentary rock is laid down on top of the first (**b**).
- A third layer is laid down on the second. In this undisturbed sequence, three horizontal sedimentary rock layers lie stacked on top of each other in the order in which they formed (**c**).

## Tilting, uplift, and erosion

- Strata are affected by *tilting* and *erosion*:
- Different layers of rock are laid down over millions of years (**a**).
- Pressure from within Earth causes movement of these layers (**b**).
- The upper surface may subsequently be eroded, leaving different layers of rock exposed (**c**).

## Folding, uplift, and erosion

- Strata can be affected by *folding* and erosion:
- Horizontal layers (**a**) are sometimes disturbed by Earth's internal pressures (**b**).
- The layers are folded and creased, resulting in uplifts of some areas.
- Subsequent erosion reveals different types of rock on Earth's surface (**c**).

# Superposition

## Sequence of formation of sedimentary rocks

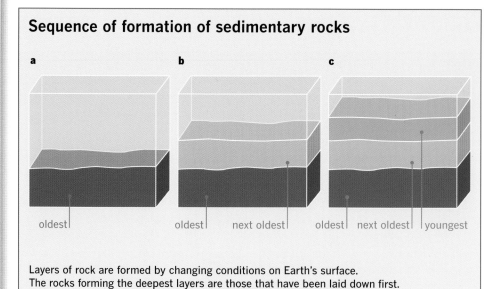

a     b     c

oldest    oldest   next oldest    oldest   next oldest   youngest

Layers of rock are formed by changing conditions on Earth's surface.
The rocks forming the deepest layers are those that have been laid down first.

## How tilting, uplift, and erosion affect superposition

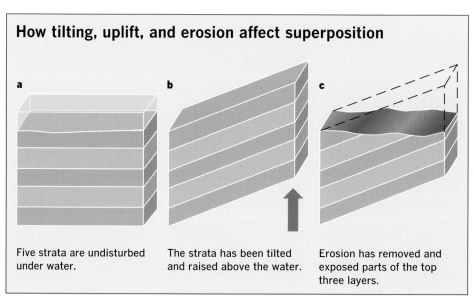

a     b     c

Five strata are undisturbed under water.

The strata has been tilted and raised above the water.

Erosion has removed and exposed parts of the top three layers.

## Effects of folding, uplift, and erosion

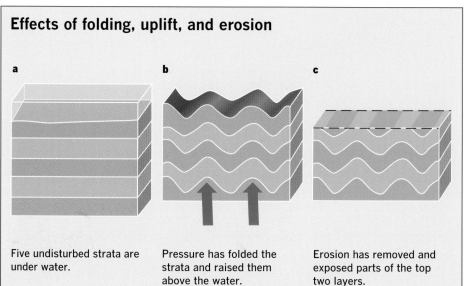

a     b     c

Five undisturbed strata are under water.

Pressure has folded the strata and raised them above the water.

Erosion has removed and exposed parts of the top two layers.

# Unconformities

## Angular unconformity and tilted rock layers

**a Tilting, uplift, and erosion**   **b Sinking**   **c Renewed deposition**

angular
unconformity

In a succession of rocks, an unconformity is a surface showing where a period of erosion or nondeposition marks a time gap in the formation of the whole sequence.

## Angular unconformity and folded rock layers

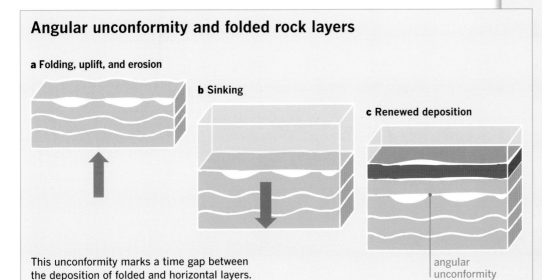

**a Folding, uplift, and erosion**

**b Sinking**

**c Renewed deposition**

This unconformity marks a time gap between the deposition of folded and horizontal layers.

angular
unconformity

## Disconformity

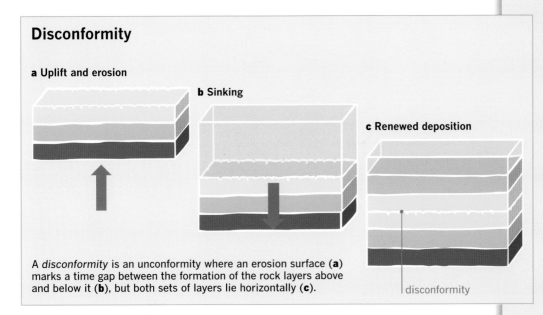

**a Uplift and erosion**

**b Sinking**

**c Renewed deposition**

A *disconformity* is an unconformity where an erosion surface (**a**) marks a time gap between the formation of the rock layers above and below it (**b**), but both sets of layers lie horizontally (**c**).

disconformity

**Key words**

| | |
|---|---|
| angular | stratum |
| unconformity | strike |
| dip | |
| disconformity | |
| erosion | |

## Angular unconformities and tilted rock layers

- Rock layers overlying an *angular unconformity* show different *dips* or *strikes* from those of the rocks below. In angular unconformity, horizontal strata overlie tilted *strata*:
- First, a horizontal sequence of sedimentary rocks laid down under water is tilted and uplifted (**a**). Erosion then exposes several layers.
- Next, Earth movements lower the eroded tilted rocks below sea level (**b**).
- Horizontal layers of sedimentary rocks form on top of the eroded tilted rocks (**c**).
- An angular unconformity marks the boundary between the tilted and horizontal sedimentary rock layers.

## Angular unconformities and folded rock layers

- Angular unconformities also often occur where horizontal strata overlie folded strata:
- First, a horizontal sequence of sedimentary rocks laid down under water is folded and uplifted (**a**). Erosion lays bare several layers.
- Next, Earth movements lower the eroded folded rocks until they lie below sea level (**b**).
- Horizontal layers of sedimentary rocks form on top of the eroded folded rocks.
- An angular unconformity marks the boundary between the tilted and horizontal sedimentary rock layers (**c**).

# Complex rock sequences

## Key words

| | |
|---|---|
| dike | nonconformity |
| faulting | sill |
| folding | tilting |
| igneous rock | |
| intrusion | |

## Igneous and sedimentary rocks

- A sequence of sedimentary rocks may be interrupted by molten igneous rock intruded as a *sill* or a *dike*.
- A sill is a horizontal sheet of igneous rock injected between layers of rock.
- A dike is a wall of igneous rock injected through a crack in rocks.

## Complex sequences

- A section through part of Earth's crust may reveal tilting, folding, faulting, igneous intrusions, and a *nonconformity*—an unconformity where sedimentary rock overlies granite or another igneous or metamorphic rock.

## Igneous and sedimentary rocks

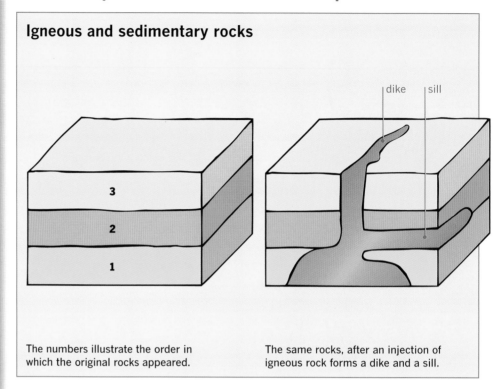

The numbers illustrate the order in which the original rocks appeared.

The same rocks, after an injection of igneous rock forms a dike and a sill.

## Complex rock sequence

Here, molten igneous rocks have inserted a sill and dike into horizontal rocks overlying older tilted rocks.

Key: (**a–k**) order in which rocks appeared

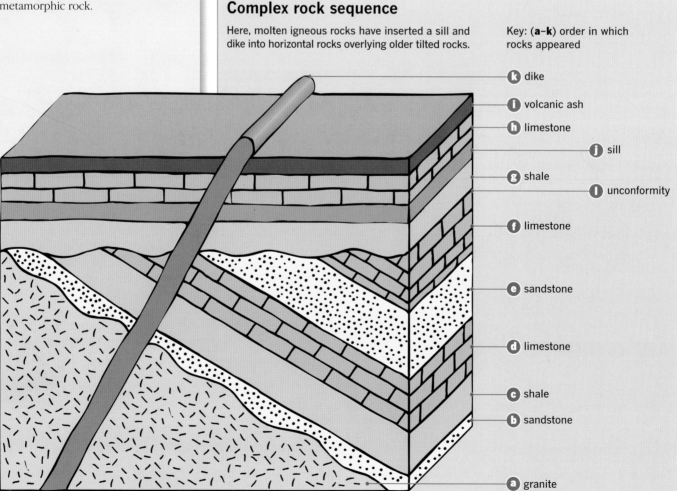

- **k** dike
- **i** volcanic ash
- **h** limestone
- **j** sill
- **g** shale
- **l** unconformity
- **f** limestone
- **e** sandstone
- **d** limestone
- **c** shale
- **b** sandstone
- **a** granite

# Paleomagnetic dating

### Key words

*geologic time*
*magnetic pole*

## Earth's magnetic poles

**Reversed polarity**

S

N

**Normal polarity**

N

S

**Pole reversals**
From time to time through geologic time, Earth's magnetic field has suddenly become reversed, switching its magnetic poles around. At each reversal, what had been the south magnetic pole becomes the north magnetic pole and vice versa.

## Paleomagnetic dating

● A known sequence of past changes in polarization recorded in rocks enables scientists to date rocks and fossils formed tens of millions of years ago.

**Phases of normal and reversed magnetism recorded in rocks formed in the last 70 million years**

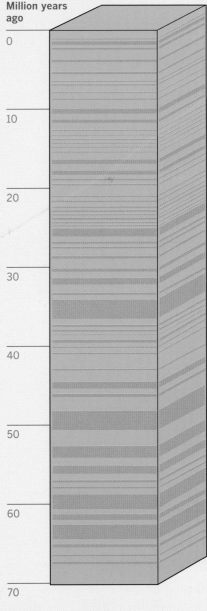

Million years ago

0

10

20

30

40

50

60

70

☐ normal  ☐ reversed

## Alignment of magnetized minerals

The alignment of magnetized minerals in successive lava flows records reversals in Earth's magnetic field.

→ normal
← reversed

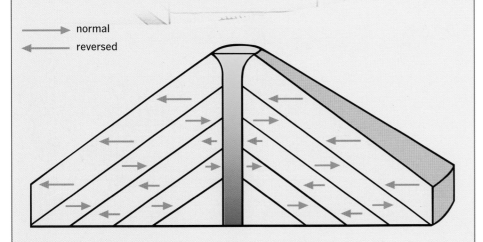

**The traces of geologic time**
Certain particles in volcanic and some other rocks remain aligned according to Earth's magnetic field at the time they were formed. This polarization of minerals such as magnetite and hematite helps geologists to determine their geologic ages.

**Key words**

cast
fossil
sediment

## Types of fossil

- Most fossils are the remains of the hard parts of ancient organisms that were preserved soon after death by sediments that later turned to rock.
- Dissolved minerals permeate dead organisms or completely replace them.
- Rarely, soft tissues are preserved—as carbonaceous films, or in fine-grained sediments, peat, or permafrost.
- Buried organisms that dissolve away completely may leave fossils in the form of molds or *casts*.
- Fossil traces left by living organisms also include footprints, burrows, and coprolites (fossil droppings).

## Shell mold and cast

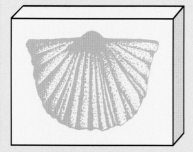

A shell in rock dissolves to leave a shell-shaped hollow called a mold.

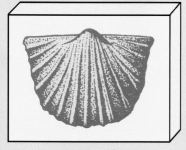

Minerals later filled the mold to form a cast.

# How fossils form

## Formation and exposure of fossil fish

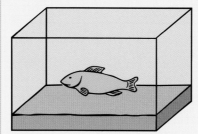

A fish lives in the sea.

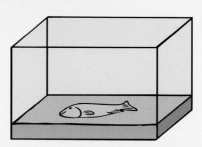

The fish dies and lies on the seabed.

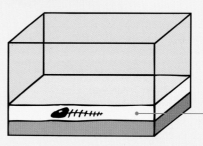

Flesh rots revealing bones that are soon covered by a layer of sediment.

sediment

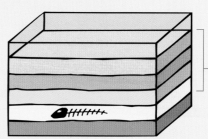

Layers of mud and sand cover the bones, preventing decay.

layers of sediment

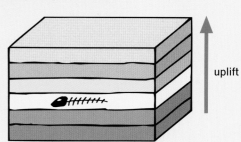

Layers of mud and sand harden into rocks, burying the bones, which are now reinforced and fossilized by minerals. Uplift from Earth's crust raises the rocks and fossil above sea level.

uplift

Weather exposes the fossil bones by eroding the layered rocks above.

# Fossil use in rock correlation

**Key words**

*fossil*

## Marine fossils

- Fossils of widespread but short-lived marine invertebrate species help geologists match sedimentary rocks' relative ages worldwide.

- Many such index fossils belong to groups whose timelines and relative abundances are indicated below.

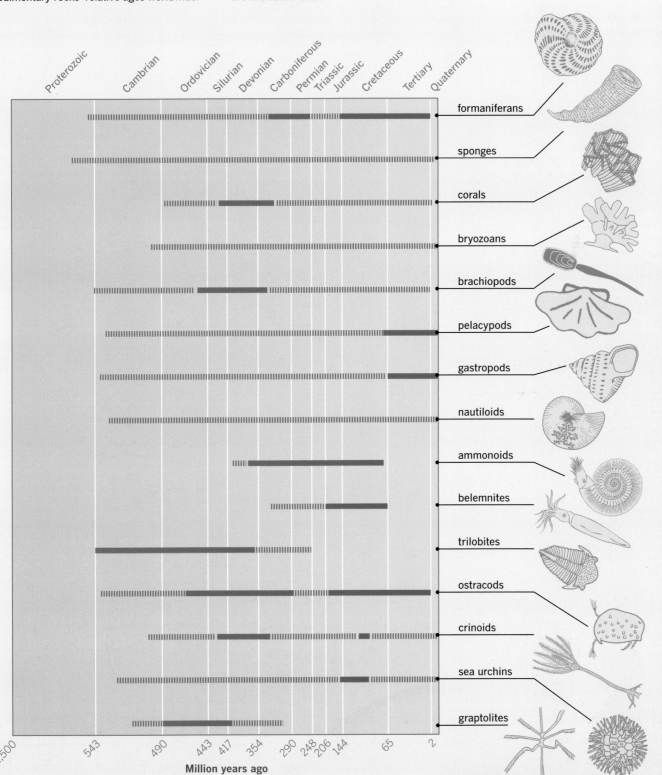

formaniferans

sponges

corals

bryozoans

brachiopods

pelacypods

gastropods

nautiloids

ammonoids

belemnites

trilobites

ostracods

crinoids

sea urchins

graptolites

**Million years ago**

**Key words**

*granite*
*igneous rock*
*sedimentary rock*

## Physical correlation

- The same sequence of layered rocks found in different places enables geologists to match their relative ages.
- This method of relative dating works best for sedimentary rocks in places where Earth movements have not disturbed or interrupted the sequence in which the rocks have been laid down.
- Complications can arise where a whole rock layer has been worn away, layers have been tilted or inverted, or granite or other igneous rocks have been injected between preexisting layers.

## Using index fossils

- Most index fossils used in the relative dating of sedimentary rocks are those of marine invertebrates, because most sedimentary rocks were laid down beneath the sea.
- However, land animals preserved in rocks occasionally provide valuable index fossils too.
- A famous example is that of the proto-horse between North America and Europe: foot bones of the same kind of proto-horse occur in Eocene epoch rocks laid down in both western North America and Europe. Known as *Eohippus* in North America and *Hyracotherium* in Europe, these fossils show a species that evolved while both continents were linked.

# Correlating rocks

## Physical correlation of rock sequences

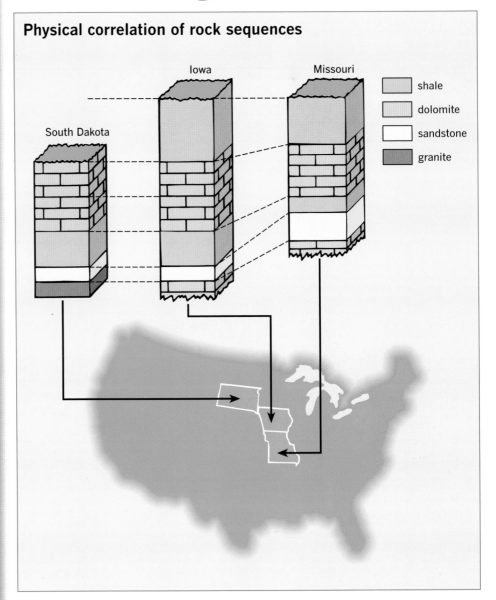

## Correlation of index fossils

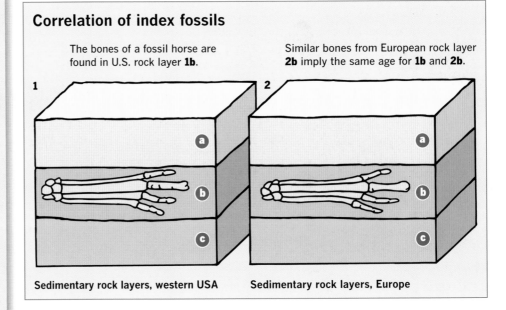

The bones of a fossil horse are found in U.S. rock layer **1b**.

Similar bones from European rock layer **2b** imply the same age for **1b** and **2b**.

Sedimentary rock layers, western USA     Sedimentary rock layers, Europe

# Tree of life

## Evolving organisms

This family tree shows broad evolutionary relationships between most major groups of living things.

━━━◆━━━ abundance of species

*Mississippian and Pennsylvanian equivalents in North America

**Key words**

*period*

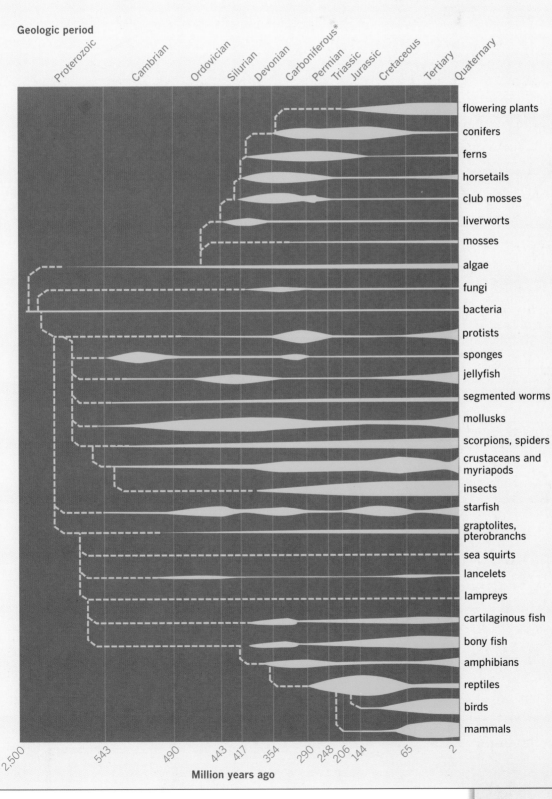

Geologic period

Proterozoic · Cambrian · Ordovician · Silurian · Devonian · Carboniferous* · Permian · Triassic · Jurassic · Cretaceous · Tertiary · Quaternary

flowering plants
conifers
ferns
horsetails
club mosses
liverworts
mosses
algae
fungi
bacteria
protists
sponges
jellyfish
segmented worms
mollusks
scorpions, spiders
crustaceans and myriapods
insects
starfish
graptolites, pterobranchs
sea squirts
lancelets
lampreys
cartilaginous fish
bony fish
amphibians
reptiles
birds
mammals

2,500 · 543 · 490 · 443 · 417 · 354 · 290 · 248 · 206 · 144 · 65 · 2

**Million years ago**

## Plants

● From green algae evolved liverworts, mosses, club mosses, and eventually flowering plants.

## Algae

● This diverse group includes the green, red, and brown seaweeds.

## Fungi

● Fungi are organisms perhaps more closely related to animals than plants.

## Bacteria

● Arguably divided into Eubacteria and Archaebacteria, these life forms are ancestral to all others.

## Protists

● Among these diverse groups of single-celled organisms were the ancestors of animals.

## Invertebrates

● This loose term embraces all animals from sponges through lancelets.

## Vertebrates

● These backboned animals range from lampreys through mammals.

# Evolutionary clocks

Key words

*geologic time*

## Time and the universe

- On a 12-hour clock representing time since the universe began, Earth's geologic time started less than four hours ago, life on Earth appeared about three hours ago and animals and plants emerged less than half an hour ago.

## Evolving life

- On a 12-hour clock representing time since animals emerged, our hominid ancestors only appeared about eight minutes ago.

## Events since the universe began

(12 hours = 15 billion years)

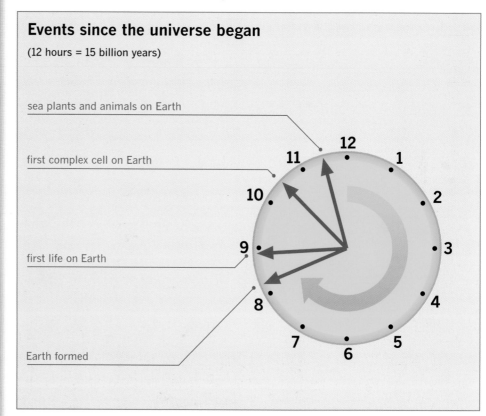

sea plants and animals on Earth

first complex cell on Earth

first life on Earth

Earth formed

## Events since sea plants and animals became plentiful

(12 hours = 600 million years)

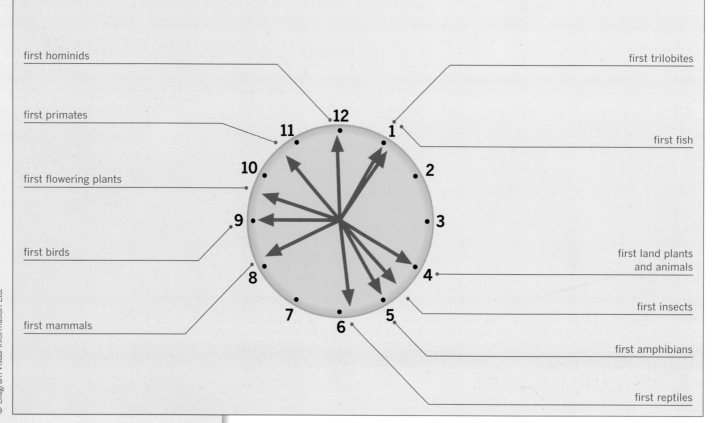

first hominids

first primates

first flowering plants

first birds

first mammals

first trilobites

first fish

first land plants and animals

first insects

first amphibians

first reptiles

# Mass extinctions

**Key words**

*period*

## Life lines

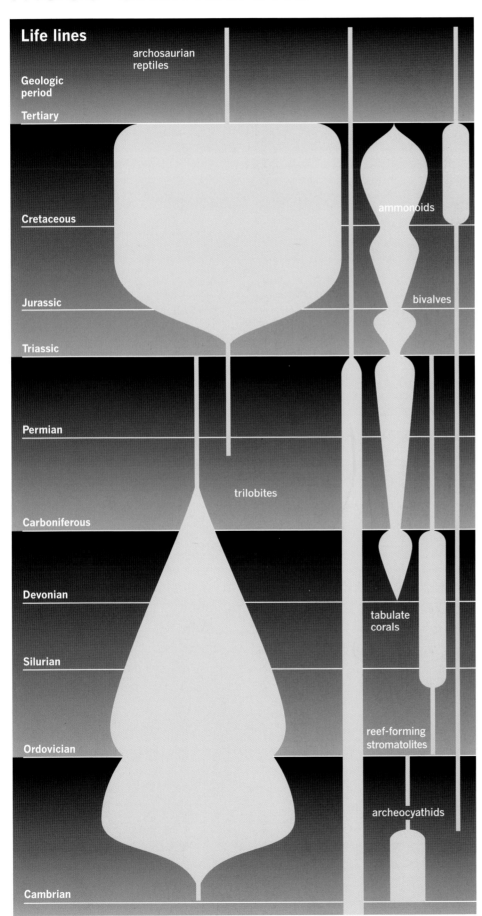

Geologic period

- Tertiary
- Cretaceous
- Jurassic
- Triassic
- Permian
- Carboniferous
- Devonian
- Silurian
- Ordovician
- Cambrian

archosaurian reptiles

ammonoids

bivalves

trilobites

tabulate corals

reef-forming stromatolites

archeocyathids

## Life lines

- Vertical lines of varying thickness indicate the expansion and collapse of certain groups of organisms through prehistoric time.
- Abrupt contractions and endings of vertical lines mark significant extinctions that changed the makeup of sea or land communities.

## Major extinctions

- Paleontologists disagree about the number of mass extinctions. At least ten have wiped out large numbers of animal species, leaving vacant ecological niches for other kinds to fill. The six greatest mass extinctions were:
- Late Cambrian
- End Ordovician
- Late Devonian
- End Permian (destroyed 95 percent of marine species)
- Late Triassic
- End Cretaceous (destroyed up to 75 percent of marine genera and large land animals including all non-bird dinosaurs).

## Causes of extinctions

- Various factors (and sometimes several combined) have probably contributed to different mass extinctions. Likely causes include an impact by asteroid or comet; massive volcanic eruptions; climatic change; and sea level change.

© Diagram Visual Information Ltd.

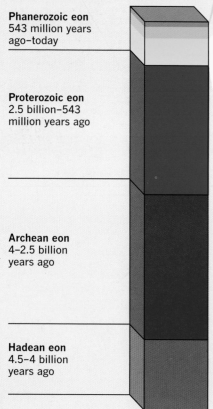

## Time units

● Earth history is divided into four major units of time known as *eons*.

● An eon is divided into *eras*.

● Each era consists of subdivisions called *periods*.

● Each period can be further split into *epochs*.

## The four eons

**Phanerozoic eon**
543 million years ago–today

**Proterozoic eon**
2.5 billion–543 million years ago

**Archean eon**
4–2.5 billion years ago

**Hadean eon**
4.5–4 billion years ago

# Geologic time

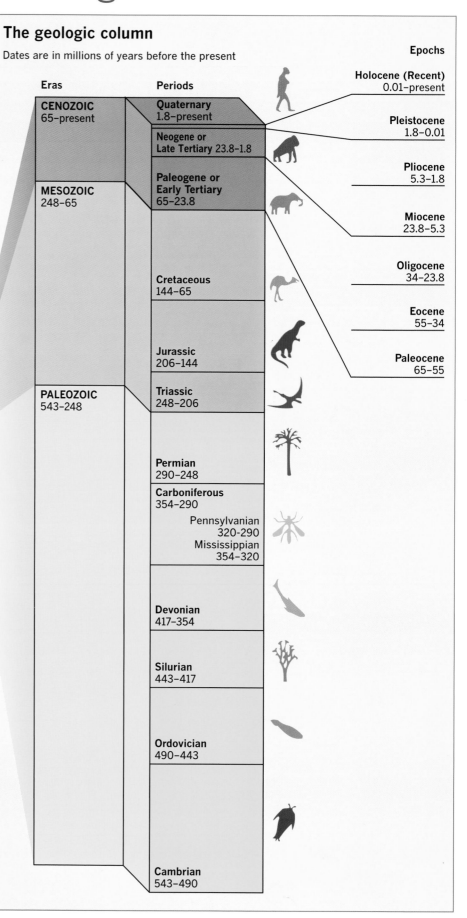

## The geologic column

Dates are in millions of years before the present

**Eras**

| CENOZOIC 65–present | MESOZOIC 248–65 | PALEOZOIC 543–248 |

**Periods**

Quaternary 1.8–present

Neogene or Late Tertiary 23.8–1.8

Paleogene or Early Tertiary 65–23.8

Cretaceous 144–65

Jurassic 206–144

Triassic 248–206

Permian 290–248

Carboniferous 354–290
　　Pennsylvanian 320–290
　　Mississippian 354–320

Devonian 417–354

Silurian 443–417

Ordovician 490–443

Cambrian 543–490

**Epochs**

Holocene (Recent) 0.01–present

Pleistocene 1.8–0.01

Pliocene 5.3–1.8

Miocene 23.8–5.3

Oligocene 34–23.8

Eocene 55–34

Paleocene 65–55

# Archean eon

## Duration

**Archean eon**
4–2.5 billion years ago

present day

## Archean rocks in modern continents

■ Archean rock

■ present-day continents

## Emerging microcontinents

Convection currents within the mantle may have separated and resorted different rocks in the primal crust, giving rise to the microcontinents of Archean rock around which the continents then formed.

bulge of light granitic rock

primal crust

mantle

bulge of greenstone

ocean

Mantle currents meeting and descending may have tugged at the primal crust, triggering a bulge of light granitic rock, the "craton" or core for a new continent.

A rising current within the mantle may have brought up material to form a greenstone island, many of which lie in belts around a continent's Archean core.

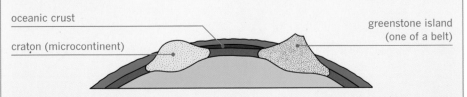

oceanic crust

craton (microcontinent)

greenstone island
(one of a belt)

Early oceanic crust of heavier rock can form between a craton and a greenstone island belt.

### Key words

| | |
|---|---|
| atmosphere | metamorphic |
| craton | rock |
| crust | microcontinent |
| igneous rock | ocean |
| | rock |

## Primeval times

- Few traces remain of rocks formed in the Hadean eon, when Earth's early crust was still molten.
- By Archean times there was some continental rock, an ocean, and an atmosphere, produced by resorting of Earth's less dense components.
- A light scum of igneous and metamorphic rocks created *microcontinents*—the cores of the present-day continents.
- Fossil cyanobacteria show life was already established in the sea at least 3.5 billion years ago

# Proterozoic eon

## Proterozoic rocks in modern continents

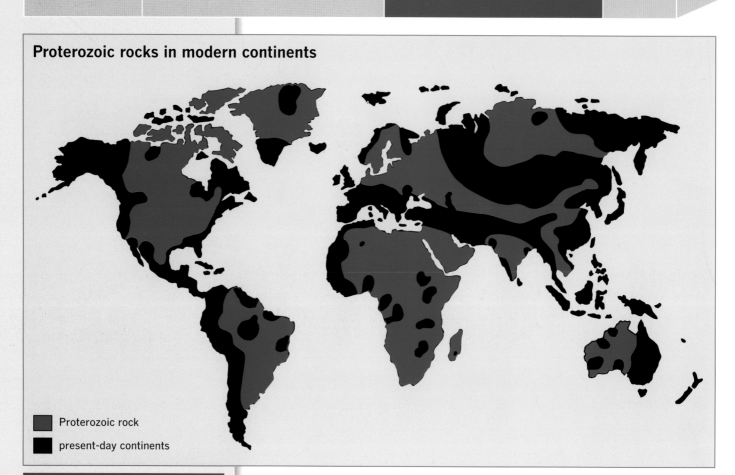

- ⬛ Proterozoic rock
- ⬛ present-day continents

### Key words

*atmosphere*
*plate*
*plate tectonics*
*subduction*

### The age of former life

- The first large continents had appeared by Proterozoic times. *Plate tectonics* were already operating: continents were drifting and the ocean floor was rifting and being subducted under continents. Major continents became stuck together for a time.
- Dissolved salts gave the sea its present saltiness and cyanobacteria released oxygen that began to accumulate in the sea and atmosphere.
- By 600 million years ago, complex multicellular organisms were evolving in shallow, offshore seas.

## Late Proterozoic marine organisms

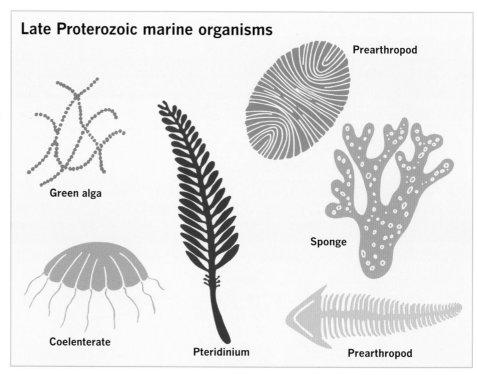

Green alga

Prearthropod

Sponge

Coelenterate

Pteridinium

Prearthropod

# Phanerozoic eon

## Duration

**Phanerozoic eon**
543 million years ago–present day

## Phanerozoic rocks in modern continents

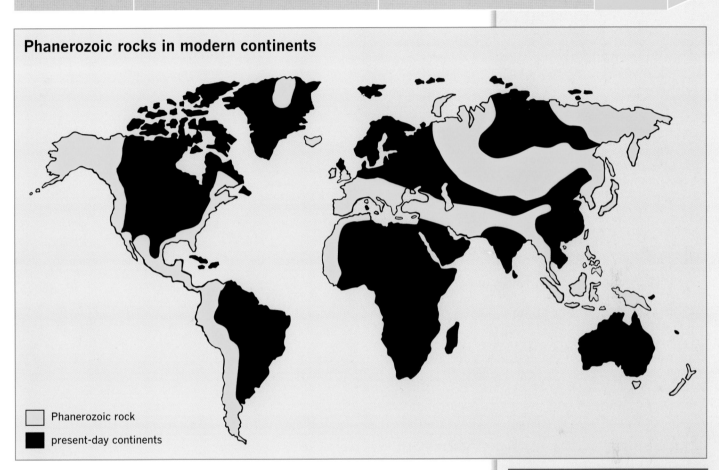

☐ Phanerozoic rock

■ present-day continents

## Phanerozoic organisms

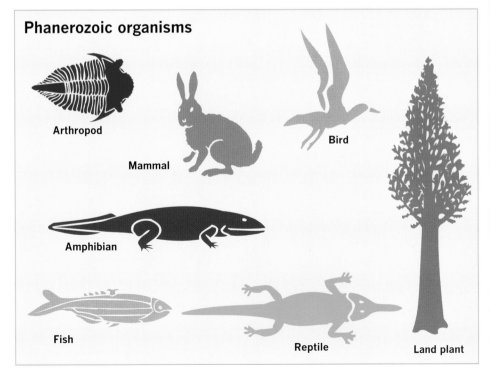

**Arthropod**

**Mammal**

**Bird**

**Amphibian**

**Fish**

**Reptile**

**Land plant**

### Key words

*continental drift*
*ice sheet*

### The world remade

● Through Phanerozoic time *continental drift* saw continents coalesce and break up. Uplift and erosion raised and wore down chains of mountains. Seas and oceans spread and shrank. *Ice sheets* waxed and waned.

● All of the major groups of living things became established early on. In time fish gave rise to amphibians, reptiles, birds, and mammals. From the first lowly land plants came trees and later flowers.

© Diagram Visual Information Ltd.

### Key words

*Burgess shale*
*Gondwana*
*orogeny*
*period*

## Land, sea, and the United States

- In Cambrian times (543–490 million years ago), the equator probably crossed what is now the United States, but present west faced north. Little land stood above the sea but, below this, sedimentary rocks accumulated.
- Today's southern continents formed the supercontinent *Gondwana*. Lesser chunks of continental crust formed the cores of North America, Greenland, Europe, and Northwest Africa. The pre-Atlantic Iapetus Ocean had opened between these once-fused lands. Within it lay Avalonia, an archipelago the rocks of which today lie scattered from the Carolinas north through Newfoundland to parts of Ireland and Wales.
- Mountains had sprouted in the Avalonian *orogeny* when a slab of land struck North America to form New England.

## Cambrian life

- Fossils suddenly appear more numerous and varied in Cambrian times. The fine-grained *Burgess shale* of southwest Canada preserves a rich sample of life below the waves more than 500 million years ago.
- Down here lived soft-bodied animals, including members of most major groups alive today. Some Cambrian invertebrates, notably the trilobites, evolved the ability to use chemicals dissolved in water to build hard protective outer shells.
- From this period also date early fishlike lancelets and the first vertebrates—small jawless fish.

# Cambrian period

## Alignment of the land of the USA in Cambrian times

The maps show the present shape but a past alignment of the United States. In fact what is now its western rim once stopped far short of that position. New land was gradually added as the continental North American Plate overrode the oceanic Farallon and Pacific plates. Sediments and igneous rocks scraped from these subducting plates continually extended the west.

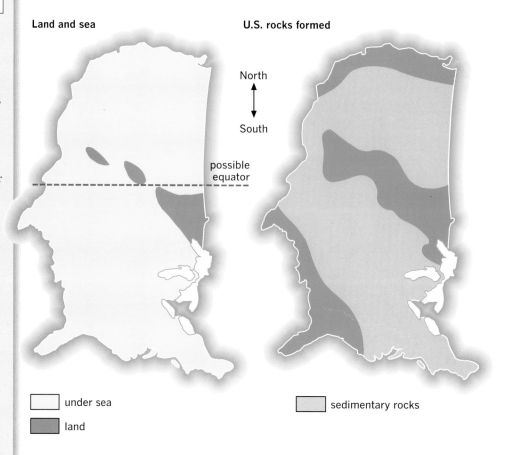

Land and sea

U.S. rocks formed

North

South

possible equator

☐ under sea
■ land

☐ sedimentary rocks

## Cambrian life-forms

These fossil organisms lived in Cambrian times (not shown to scale).

**Annelid worm**

**Coelenterate**

**Trilobite**

**Mollusk**

**Lancelet**

**Onychophoran**

# Ordovician period

## Alignment of the land of the USA in Ordovician times

**Key words**

*period*

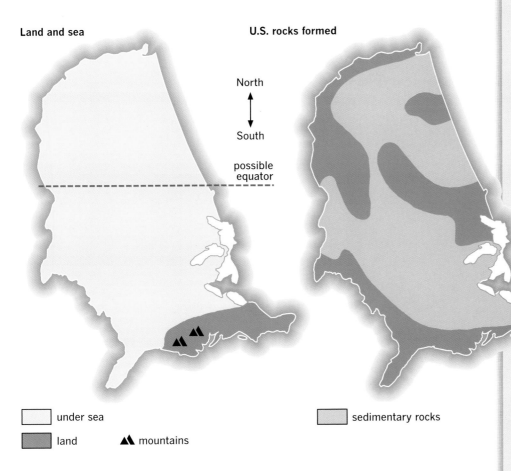

**Land and sea**

North

South

possible equator

**U.S. rocks formed**

☐ under sea
☐ land   ▲▲ mountains

☐ sedimentary rocks

### Land, sea, and the United States

- In Ordovician times (490–443 million years ago) the future northeast stood above the sea. Elsewhere, sedimentary rocks were being formed.
- Closure of the Iapetus Ocean brought Laurentia (proto-North America and Greenland) close to Baltica (proto-Europe) and the Taconic orogeny thrust up mountains in the Appalachian region.

### Ordovician life

- Life was still concentrated in the sea. The arthropods called trilobites were numerous. Graptolites and brachiopods teemed below the waves.
- Coelenterates related to today's jellyfish and coral polyps flourished.
- Mollusks evolved apace: bivalves resembling modern clams and oysters; gastropods (relatives of whelks and limpets); and cephalopods including straight-shelled nautiloids, which are related to modern octopus and squid.
- The seas were also home to various echinoderms: the group that includes sea urchins and starfish.
- Early vertebrates—the jawless fish—were also diversifying at this time.

## Ordovician life-forms

These fossil organisms lived in Ordovician times (not shown to scale).

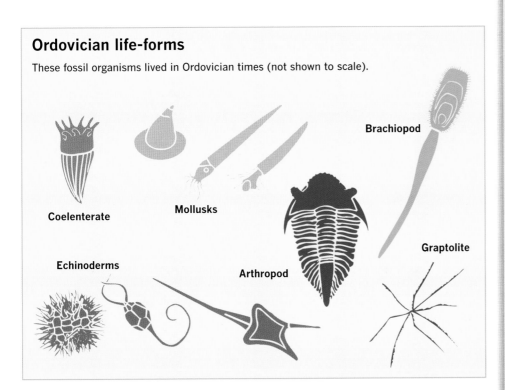

**Coelenterate**

**Mollusks**

**Brachiopod**

**Echinoderms**

**Arthropod**

**Graptolite**

## Key words

*coral*
*orogeny*
*period*
*reef*

# Silurian period

## Alignment of the land of the USA in Silurian times

**Land and sea**

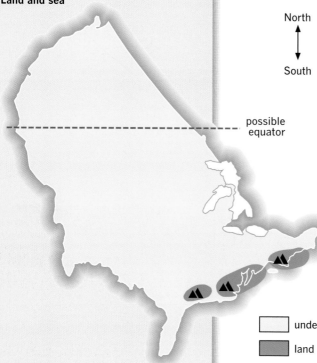

North

South

possible equator

**U.S. rocks formed**

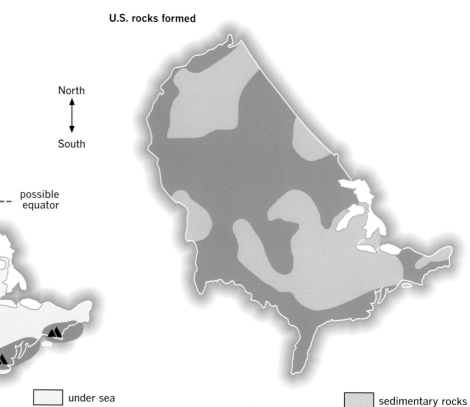

☐ under sea

▨ land

▲▲ mountains

▨ sedimentary rocks

## Land, sea, and the United States

● In Silurian times (443–417 million years ago), the equator still crossed the United States, and modern "west" faced northwest.

● North America began colliding with proto-Europe, pushing up the forerunners of the Appalachian Mountains. Little else of North America stood above the sea yet.

## Silurian life

● Marine life included reef-building solitary corals, sea scorpions, jawless fish, and acanthodians and placoderms (fish with jaws).

● Plants, millipedes, and scorpions appeared on land.

## Silurian life-forms

These fossil organisms lived in Silurian times (not shown to scale).

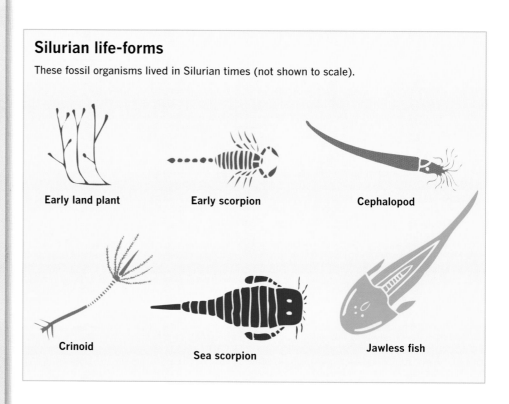

**Early land plant**

**Early scorpion**

**Cephalopod**

**Crinoid**

**Sea scorpion**

**Jawless fish**

# Devonian period

## Alignment of the land of the USA in Devonian times

**Key words**

*orogeny*
*period*

**Land and sea**

North

South

possible equator

**U.S. rocks formed**

☐ under sea

■ land

☐ sedimentary rocks

▲▲ mountains

## Devonian life-forms

These fossil organisms lived in Devonian times (not shown to scale).

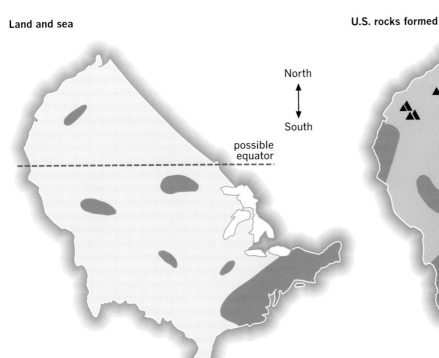

**Early insect**

**Fern ancestor**

**Cephalopod**

**Early amphibian**

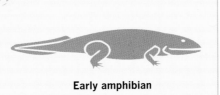

**Shark**

**Bony fish**

## Land, sea, and the United States

● In Devonian times (417–354 million years ago) North America still straddled the equator and the Acadian orogeny uplifted much of what is now the northeast.

● Elsewhere sedimentary rocks were being laid down and locally there was some volcanic activity.

## Devonian life

● Evolving land plants produced early seed plants and the first trees and forests.

● Evolving osteichthyan (bony) fish produced amphibians, the first vertebrates to walk on land.

● On land, wingless insects and spiderlike arachnids flourished.

**Key words**

*limestone*
*Pangaea*
*period*
*tropic*

# Mississippian period

## Alignment of the land of the USA in Mississippian times

**Land and sea**

North

South

possible equator

U.S. rocks formed

☐ under sea
■ land

☐ sedimentary rocks

## Land, sea, and the United States

- In Mississippian times (354–320 million years ago), the United States still lay inside the tropics.
- At this time limestones were laid down beneath a shallow sea covering much of the future Mississippi region.
- In the wider world, northern and southern continents began colliding in a process that would form a single landmass, *Pangaea*.

## Mississippian life

- Giant club mosses and amphibians flourished on low swampy land.
- Bryozoans, crinoids, brachiopods, and lobe-finned bony fish called coelacanths were among creatures living in the sea at this time.

## Mississippian life-forms

These fossil organisms lived in Mississippian times (not shown to scale).

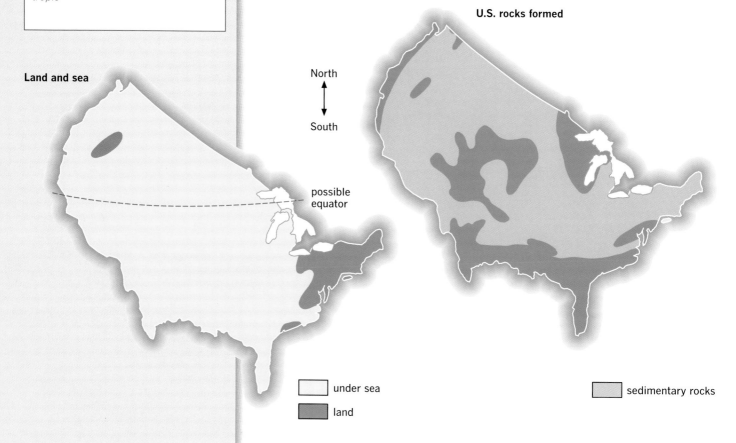

Giant club moss

Lobe-finned bony fish

Amphibian

Crinoid

Brachiopod

Bryozoan

# Pennsylvanian period

## Alignment of the land of the USA in Pennsylvanian times

**Key words**

*coal forest*
*coal measure*
*period*

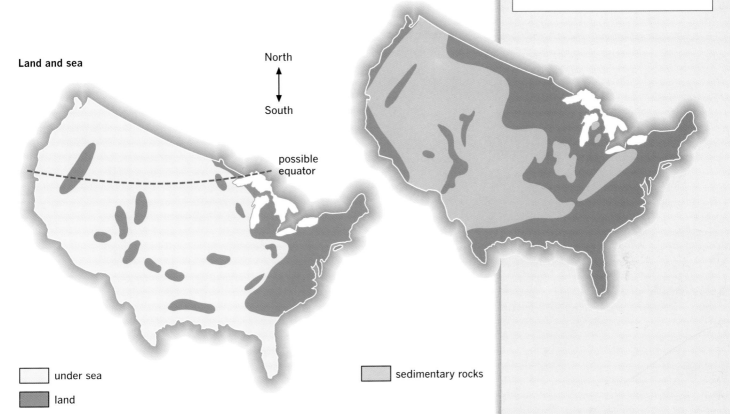

**Land and sea**

North ↕ South

possible equator

**U.S. rocks formed**

☐ under sea

☐ land

☐ sedimentary rocks

## Pennsylvanian life-forms

These fossil organisms lived in Pennsylvanian times (not shown to scale).

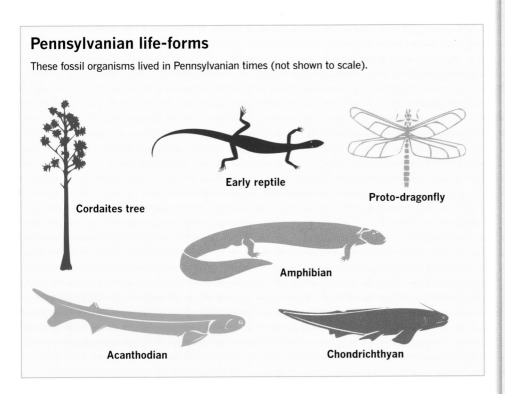

**Cordaites tree**

**Early reptile**

**Proto-dragonfly**

**Amphibian**

**Acanthodian**

**Chondrichthyan**

## Land, sea, and the United States

● Pennsylvanian time (320–290 million years ago) is named for *coal measures* formed in Pennsylvania from the compressed remains of tropical swamp forests that flourished at this time.

● North America's Mississippian and Pennsylvanian periods are considered together as the Carboniferous period elsewhere in the world.

## Pennsylvanian life

● *Coal forests* included giant club mosses, horsetails, and Cordaites.

● Land animals featured the first small lizardlike reptiles, amphibians the size of crocodiles, and huge proto-dragonflies.

● Fish included acanthodians, and chondrichthyans—sharks and relatives—with a skeleton composed of cartilage, not bone.

© Diagram Visual Information Ltd.

**Key words**

Pangaea
period

# Permian period

## Alignment of the land of the USA in Permian times

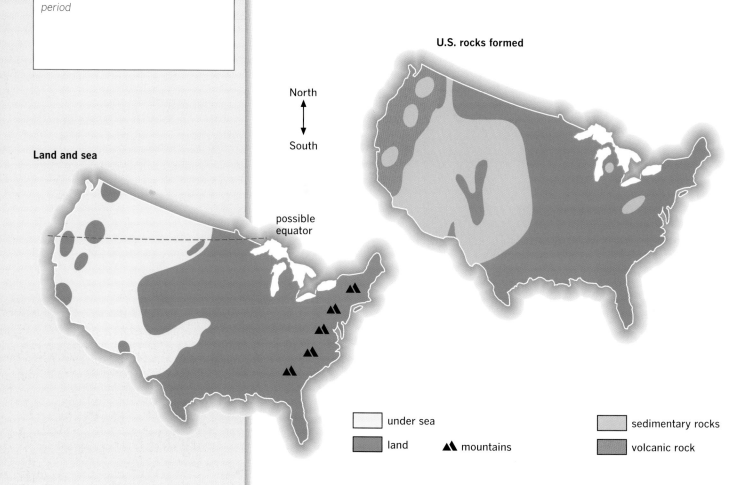

**U.S. rocks formed**

North

South

**Land and sea**

possible
equator

| | under sea | | sedimentary rocks |
| | land | ▲▲ mountains | volcanic rock |

## Land, sea, and the United States

- By the Permian period (290–248 million years ago), in what is now the United States a great extent of land stood above the sea.
- Southeast North America's collision with Africa or South America thrust up the southern Appalachians.
- All continents lay jammed together as the supercontinent Pangaea.

## Permian life

- Much of what we know about Permian life on land comes from fossil reptiles and synapsids that have been found in Texas.
- Permian synapsids included the early ancestors of mammals.
- Conifers now figured strongly among seed plants.

## Permian life-forms

These fossil organisms lived in Permian times (not shown to scale).

Cockroach

Amphibian

Conifer

Bony fish

Carnivorous synapsid

Herbivorous synapsid

# Triassic period

## Alignment of the land of the USA in Triassic times

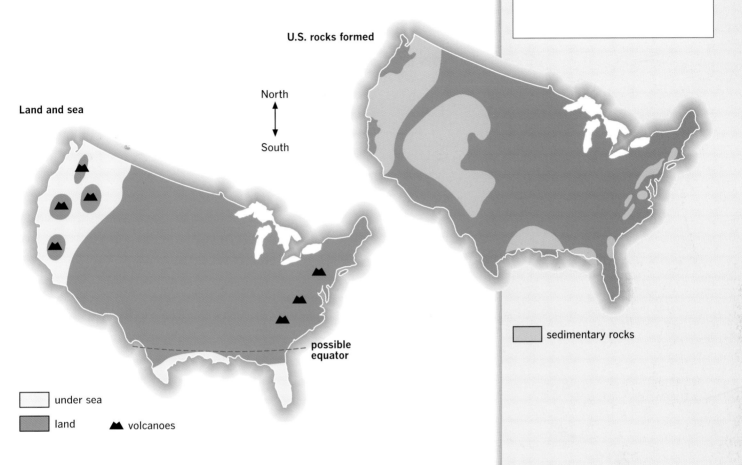

**U.S. rocks formed**

North ↕ South

**Land and sea**

possible equator

sedimentary rocks

under sea

land ▲▲ volcanoes

## Triassic life-forms

These fossil organisms lived in Triassic times (not shown to scale).

**Lycopsid**

**Cycad**

**Early mammal**

**Theropod dinosaur**

**Turtle**

**Crocidilian**

**Prosauropod dinosaur**

**Ichthyosaur**

## Land, sea, and the United States

- In Triassic times (248–206 million years ago), what is now the United States was moving north of the equator and oriented nearly as it is today.
- The area that stood above the sea extended farther west than ever.
- The interior was largely desert.

## Triassic life

- North American life-forms now included early dinosaurs and crocodilians, relatives within a major group of reptiles known as archosaurs.
- Aquatic reptiles now included ichthyosaurs and turtles.
- Therapsid synapsids gave rise to shrewlike proto-mammals.

© Diagram Visual Information Ltd.

**Key words**

*Pangaea*
*period*

# Jurassic period

## Alignment of the land of the USA in Jurassic times

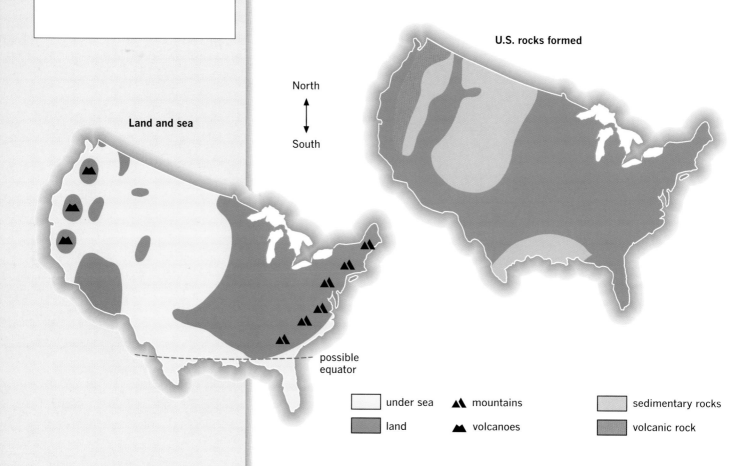

U.S. rocks formed

North

South

Land and sea

possible equator

| | | |
|---|---|---|
| ▢ under sea | ▲▲ mountains | ▨ sedimentary rocks |
| ▨ land | ▲ volcanoes | ▨ volcanic rock |

## Land, sea, and the United States

- In Jurassic times (206–144 million years ago), shallow seas invaded much of what is now the United States, but—forced against westward moving North America—Pacific sediments became tacked onto the west, and mountains rose.
- The Atlantic Ocean filled a rift now opening between North America and Africa as Pangaea began to break up.

## Jurassic life

- Huge sauropod and ornithischian dinosaurs flourished in what are now Colorado and Wyoming.
- Flying animals now included pterosaurs, and early birds derived from theropod dinosaurs.
- Plesiosaurs and ammonite cephalopods swam in shallow seas.

## Jurassic life-forms

These fossil organisms lived in Jurassic times (not shown to scale).

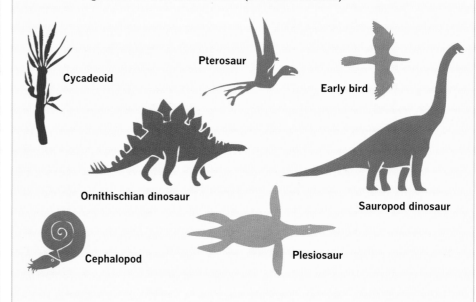

Cycadeoid

Pterosaur

Early bird

Ornithischian dinosaur

Sauropod dinosaur

Cephalopod

Plesiosaur

# Cretaceous period

## Alignment of the land of the USA in Cretaceous times

### Key words

continental drift    subduction
Laurasia             volcano
oceanic crust
Pangaea
period

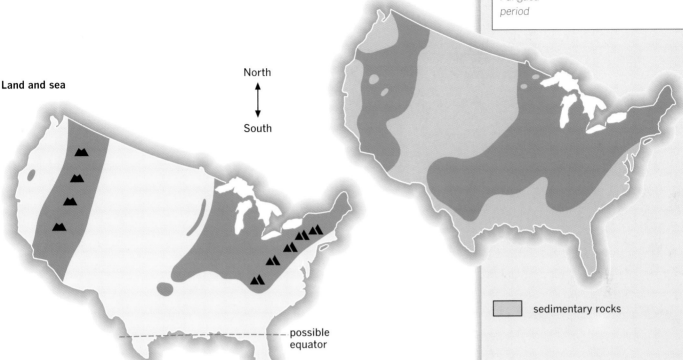

U.S. rocks formed

North

South

Land and sea

possible equator

sedimentary rocks

under sea    ▲▲ mountains

land         ▲▲ volcanoes

## Cretaceous life-forms

These fossil organisms lived in Cretaceous times (not shown to scale).

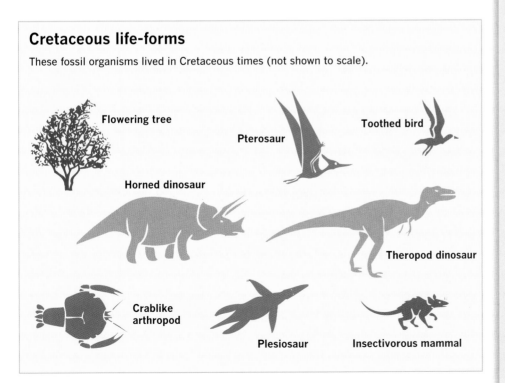

Flowering tree

Pterosaur

Toothed bird

Horned dinosaur

Theropod dinosaur

Crablike arthropod

Plesiosaur

Insectivorous mammal

## Land, sea, and the United States

● In Cretaceous times (144–65 million years ago) a shallow sea bisected the United States.
● Westward continental drift subducted oceanic crust, throwing up volcanoes and the Brooks Range in Alaska.
● Pangaea's break-up left North America as part of the northern supercontinent, Laurasia.

## Cretaceous life

● Huge horned and theropod dinosaurs appeared.
● Large swimming reptiles and flying reptiles (pterosaurs) persisted.
● Mammals and birds diversified.
● Flowering plants spread.
● The Cretaceous period ended with the extinction of most large animals, including dinosaurs.

© Diagram Visual Information Ltd.

**Key words**

epoch
equator
period
volcanic

# Paleocene epoch

## Alignment of the land of the USA in Paleocene times

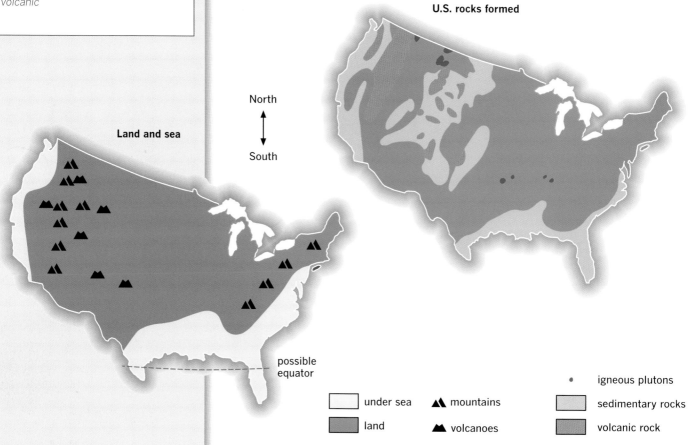

U.S. rocks formed

North
↕
South

Land and sea

possible equator

under sea

land

▲▲ mountains

▲▲ volcanoes

• igneous plutons

sedimentary rocks

volcanic rock

## Land, sea, and the United States

- By the start of the Paleogene period—the Paleocene epoch (65–55 million years ago)—rotation had aligned North America almost as it is today and it had drifted well to the north of the equator.
- Mountain building, much of it volcanic, continued in the west.
- The shallow sea bisecting North America had drained away.

## Paleocene life

- Primitive kinds of mammal waned as the more advanced placentals took their place.
- Early hoofed mammals such as condylarths and pantodonts shared lands with early odd-toed ungulates related to the modern horse and hippopotamus; flesh-eating creodonts; rodents; and squirrel-like primates.

## Paleocene life-forms

These fossil organisms lived in Paleocene times (not shown to scale).

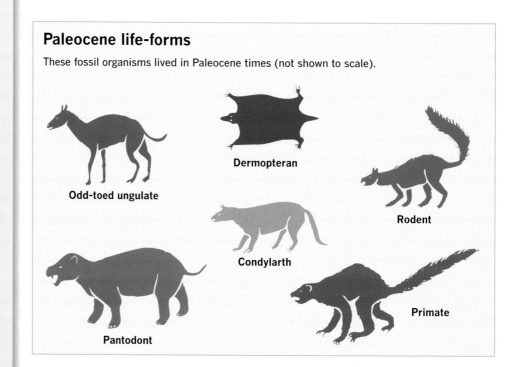

Odd-toed ungulate

Dermopteran

Rodent

Condylarth

Pantodont

Primate

# Eocene epoch

## Alignment of the land of the USA in Eocene times

**Key words**

*basin*
*epoch*
*volcano*

**U.S. rocks formed**

North ↕ South

**Land and sea**

possible equator

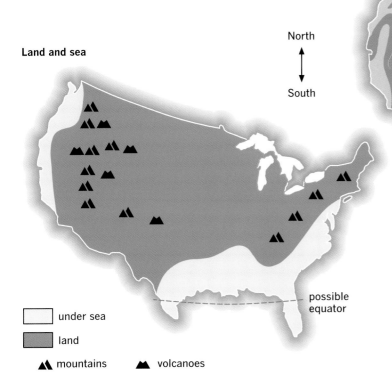

- under sea
- land
- ▲▲ mountains    ▲ volcanoes

- • igneous plutons
- sedimentary rocks
- volcanic rock

## Eocene life-forms

These fossil organisms lived in Eocene times (not shown to scale).

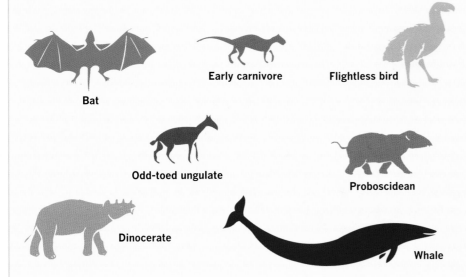

**Bat**

**Early carnivore**

**Flightless bird**

**Odd-toed ungulate**

**Proboscidean**

**Dinocerate**

**Whale**

## Land, sea, and the United States

- In the Eocene epoch (55–34 million years ago), volcanoes and other mountains were rising in the west.
- Eroding uplands shed debris, filling intermontane basins.
- Accumulating sediments pushed out the Mississippi shoreline.
- The widening North Atlantic cut off North America from Europe.

## Eocene life

- Insectivores gave rise to bats.
- The Carnivora diversified.
- Primates included ancestors of tarsiers and lemurs.
- Hoofed mammals included ungainly dinocerates but also early horses, tapirs, and rhinoceroses.
- Whales and sea cows appeared.

© Diagram Visual Information Ltd.

**Key words**

epoch
sediment
temperate
tropical

# Oligocene epoch

## Alignment of the land of the USA in Oligocene times

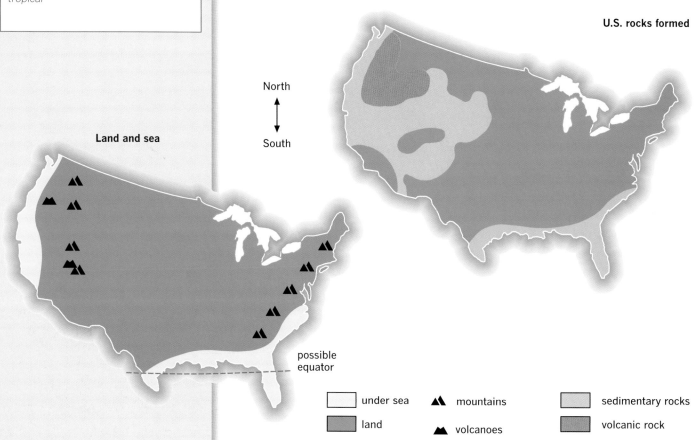

Land and sea

U.S. rocks formed

North

South

possible equator

| | under sea | ▲▲ mountains | | sedimentary rocks |
| | land | ▲ volcanoes | | volcanic rock |

## Land, sea, and the United States

- In the Oligocene epoch (34–23.8 million years ago) the present-day western United States became uplifted.
- Eroding western mountains dumped sediments east to South Dakota.
- Mississippi sediments helped push the Gulf Coast further south.

## Oligocene life

- Where climates cooled, grasses and temperate trees began replacing tropical vegetation.
- Grazing and browsing even-toed ungulates multiplied, and brontotheres (odd-toed ungulates) roamed North America.
- Pyrotheres were among hoofed mammals unique to what was then the island continent of South America.

## Oligocene life-forms

These fossil organisms lived in Oligocene times (not shown to scale).

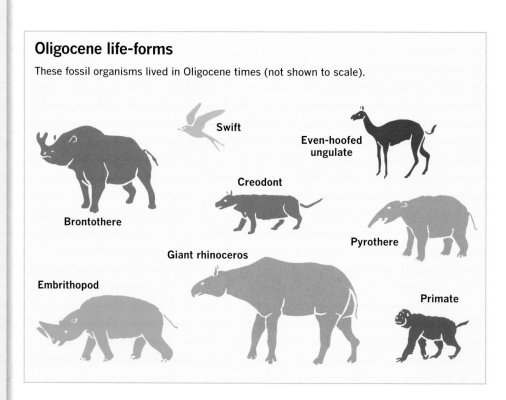

Swift

Even-hoofed ungulate

Creodont

Brontothere

Pyrothere

Giant rhinoceros

Embrithopod

Primate

# Miocene epoch

## Alignment of the land of the USA in Miocene times

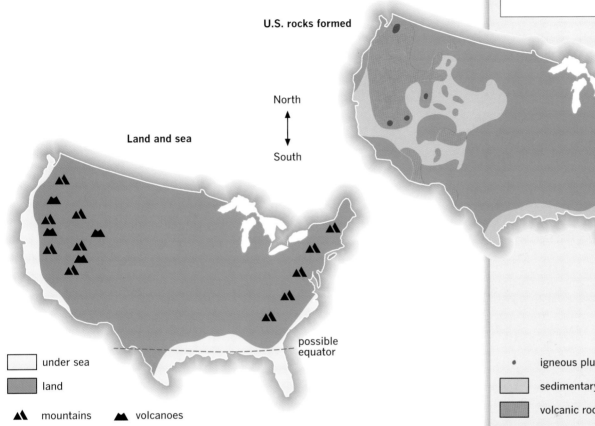

U.S. rocks formed

North

South

Land and sea

possible equator

under sea

land

▲▲ mountains    ▲ volcanoes

• igneous plutons

sedimentary rocks

volcanic rock

## Miocene life-forms

These fossil organisms lived in Miocene times (not shown to scale).

Seal

Hippopotamus

Flightless bird

Primate

Hyena

Chalicothere

Platypus

Deinothere

## Land, sea, and the United States

- In the Miocene epoch (23.8–5.3 million years ago) uplift and volcanic action produced fresh mountain building in the west.
- The Colorado Plateau, Rocky Mountains, and Cascade Range rose, and the coast of California extended further west.

## Miocene life

- Grasslands spread extensively.
- North American mammals included horses, oreodonts, rhinoceroses, pronghorns, camels, protoceratids, chalicotheres, bear dogs, and saber-toothed cats.
- Worldwide, mammals reached their richest ever variety.

© Diagram Visual Information Ltd.

**Key words**

*epoch*
*equator*
*lava*
*uplift*
*volcanic*

# Pliocene epoch

## Alignment of the land of the USA in Pliocene times

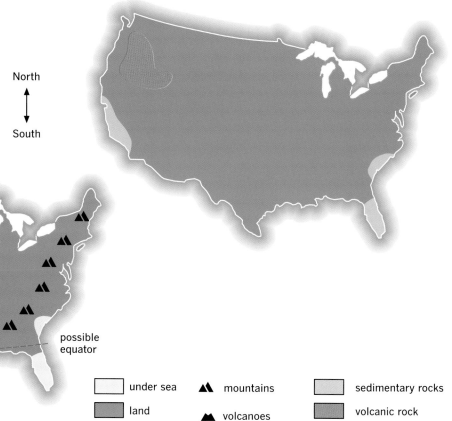

**U.S. rocks formed**

North ↕ South

**Land and sea**

possible equator

| | | |
|---|---|---|
| ☐ under sea | ▲▲ mountains | ☐ sedimentary rocks |
| ☐ land | ▲▲ volcanoes | ☐ volcanic rock |

## Land, sea, and the United States

- In the Pliocene epoch (5.3–1.8 million years ago) the west experienced renewed uplift, and volcanic activity with lava flows.
- California's Great Valley emerged above the sea, and a Californian coastal strip was moving north.
- By now the United States lay far to the north of the equator and land linked North and South America.

## Pliocene life

- Mammals moved from North to South America and vice versa.
- Grazing mammals replaced browsers as North America grew cooler and drier.
- Hominids evolved in Africa.

## Pliocene life-forms

These fossil organisms lived in Pliocene times (not shown to scale).

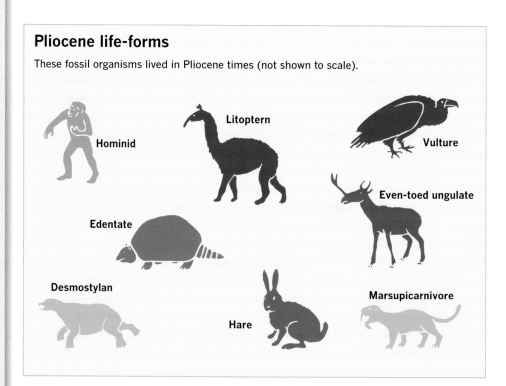

**Hominid**

**Litoptern**

**Vulture**

**Even-toed ungulate**

**Edentate**

**Desmostylan**

**Hare**

**Marsupicarnivore**

# Pleistocene epoch

## Land of the USA in Pleistocene times

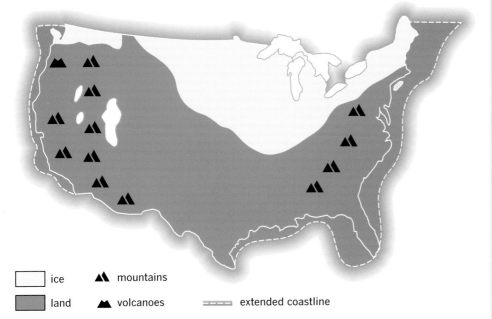

- ☐ ice
- ☐ land
- ▲▲ mountains
- ▲ volcanoes
- ▦▦▦ extended coastline

**Key words**

epoch
erosion
ice sheet
ocean

## Land, sea, and the United States

- In the Pleistocene epoch (1.8–0.1 million years ago) advancing ice sheets eroded northern uplands.
- So much water was locked up in ice sheets that ocean levels fell. Land now extended out into the sea, especially along the Atlantic and Gulf coasts.

## Major temperature phases in the Pleistocene epoch

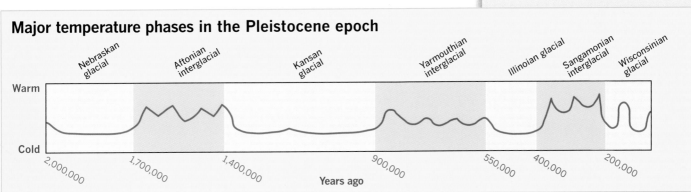

Nebraskan glacial • Aftonian interglacial • Kansan glacial • Yarmouthian interglacial • Illinoian glacial • Sangamonian interglacial • Wisconsinian glacial

Warm
Cold

2,000,000 — 1,700,000 — 1,400,000 — 900,000 — 550,000 — 400,000 — 200,000

**Years ago**

## Pleistocene life-forms

These fossil organisms lived in Pleistocene times (not shown to scale).

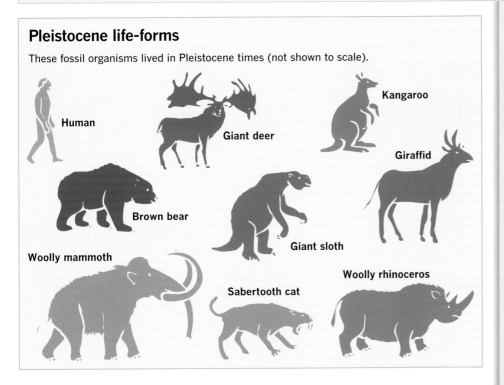

- Human
- Giant deer
- Kangaroo
- Giraffid
- Brown bear
- Giant sloth
- Woolly mammoth
- Sabertooth cat
- Woolly rhinoceros

## Ice advance and retreat

- There were major temperature fluctuations in the Pleistocene epoch:
- Cold phases—glacials—saw ice sheets advancing south through North America.
- During warm phases—interglacials— ice sheets retreated north.

## Pleistocene life

- Horses, camels, deer, tapirs, mastodonts, mammoths, bears, dogs, and saber-toothed cats, and also giant sloths from South America lived in North America, but most of these eventually died out there.
- By early in the Pleistocene, evolving hominids had given rise to our own species, Homo sapiens.

**Key words**

| | |
|---|---|
| coast | sea level |
| epoch | |
| ice sheet | |
| earthquake | |
| eruption | |

## Some changes affecting the United States

● In recent times (the last 10,000 years), earthquakes and volcanic eruptions have featured in the west. Melted ice sheets filled the Great Lakes, dumped rocky debris, and raised sea level, drowning the Atlantic and Gulf of Mexico coasts.

## Worldwide sea level changes

● This graph shows how global sea level has risen from a low point more than 15,000 years ago, when vast quantities of water lay locked up in ice sheets. Melting ice raised sea level 300 feet (90 m) or more, and drowned low coasts that had formerly been exposed. This caused the Atlantic and Gulf shorelines to retreat inland.

## Evolution of the Great Lakes

● The Great Lakes grew as a nearby ice sheet shrank. At first they drained south to the Gulf, later east to the Atlantic.

# Holocene (recent) epoch

## Some changes affecting the United States

## Worldwide sea level changes

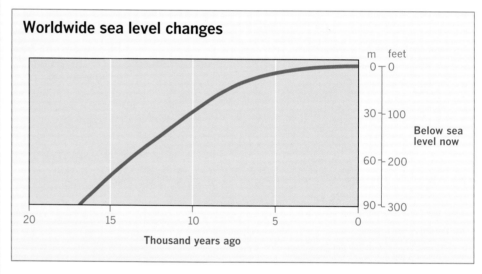

## Evolution of the Great Lakes

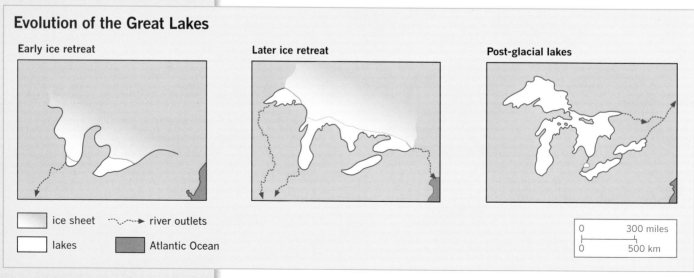

# Origins

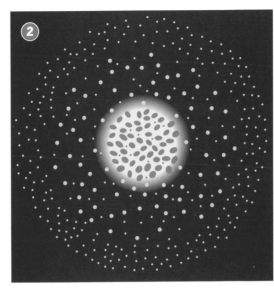

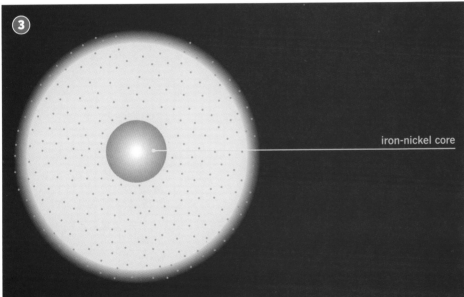

iron-nickel core

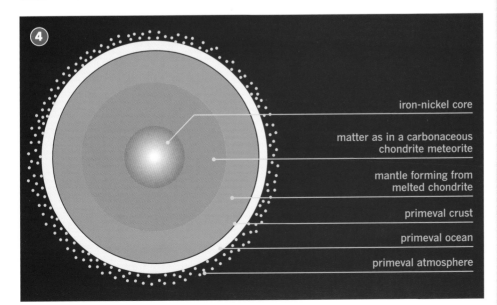

iron-nickel core

matter as in a carbonaceous chondrite meteorite

mantle forming from melted chondrite

primeval crust

primeval ocean

primeval atmosphere

## Key words

*atmosphere*
*element*
*meteorite*
*planetesimal*

## The origins of planet Earth

- Earth may have formed in four stages:

1. Clouds of particles revolved around the Sun.
2. Where there were areas of extra-dense particles, they gravitated toward each other, forming a closer group of spherical massed particles.
3. These in turn ultimately formed into a dense iron and nickel core. Less dense matter similar to that of the meteorites called carbonaceous chondrites formed around the core.
4. Ultimately this spinning ball gained a solid crust supporting oceans and a primeval atmosphere.

## Planetesimals

- Earth and other rocky planets arguably formed from coalescing particles orbiting the Sun.
- Aggregating particles in time formed large asteroids or miniature planets known as *planetesimals*.
- Collisions smashed planetesimals but their coalescing debris then formed larger planetary bodies.
- The early Earth grew bigger as its gravitational attraction pulled in lesser bodies including asteroids and comets.

## Heating up

- Heat helped the early Earth evolve.
- Its spinning dust cloud generated heat by the energy of motion.
- Asteroids and comets produced heat as they bombarded Earth.
- Heavy elements gave off heat by radioactive decay.
- Heat melting Earth's early crust helped to redistribute its elements. The heaviest became concentrated in Earth's core. The lightest formed the type of crust it has today.
- Volcanic gases including water vapor and possibly ice from comets between them fed the oceans and primeval atmosphere.

# Elements

**Key words**

*degassing*
*element*

## Abundances compared

● Three diagrams contrast the relative abundances by weight of elements in the universe, Earth's crust, and Earth as a whole:

## Universe

● The two lightest elements, hydrogen and helium, are by far the most abundant elements in the universe.

## Earth's crust

● Oxygen and silicon are the most abundant elements in Earth's crust.

● Early on, free hydrogen and most helium, the lightest elements, escaped into space, a process that is called *degassing*.

## Whole Earth

● Iron is the most abundant element in Earth as a whole.

● During Earth's formation, this heavy element became largely concentrated in Earth's core.

### The universe

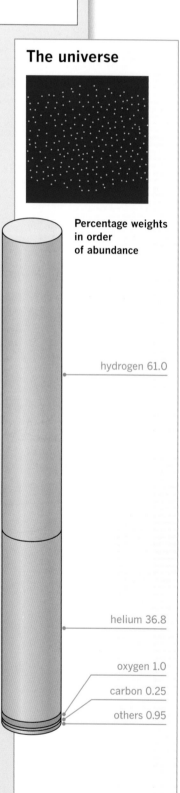

Percentage weights in order of abundance

hydrogen 61.0

helium 36.8

oxygen 1.0

carbon 0.25

others 0.95

### Earth's crust

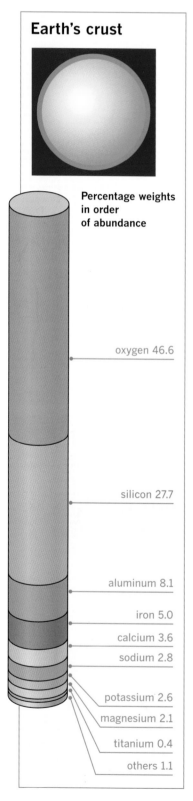

Percentage weights in order of abundance

oxygen 46.6

silicon 27.7

aluminum 8.1

iron 5.0

calcium 3.6

sodium 2.8

potassium 2.6

magnesium 2.1

titanium 0.4

others 1.1

### Whole Earth

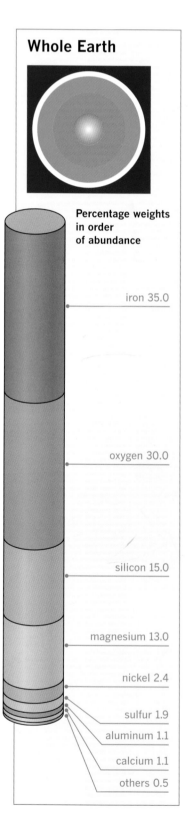

Percentage weights in order of abundance

iron 35.0

oxygen 30.0

silicon 15.0

magnesium 13.0

nickel 2.4

sulfur 1.9

aluminum 1.1

calcium 1.1

others 0.5

# Internal heat

**Key words**

| | |
|---|---|
| convection | spreading ridge |
| crust | trench |
| isotope | |
| mantle | |
| plate | |

## Temperature and depth

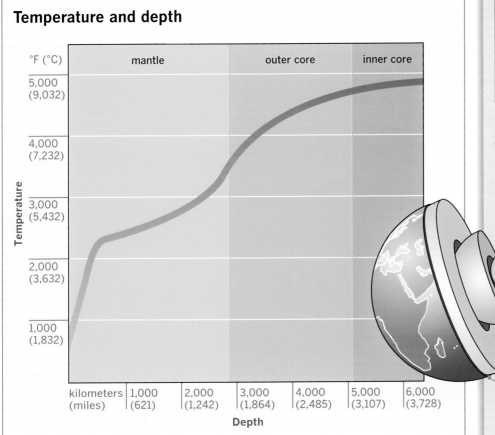

## Temperature and depth

- Below Earth's crust of oceanic plates and continental plates is the mantle, which has a temperature of at least 1,600°F (870°C). At the center the temperature is 9,000°F (5,000°C).

933 miles (1,400 km)

1,333 miles (2,000 km)

2,000 miles (3,000 km)

6.6 miles (10 km)

## Areas of high and low heat flow

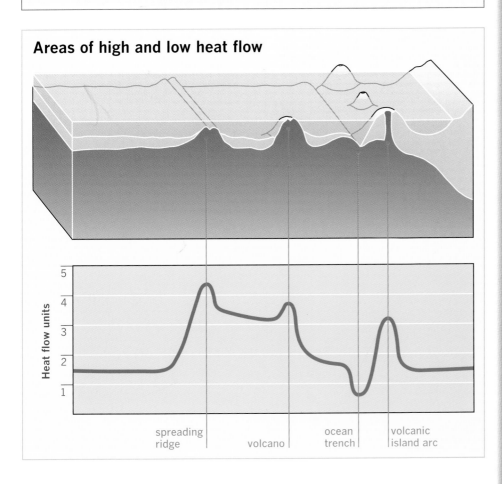

## Areas of high and low heat flow

- Oceanic *spreading ridges* (where coastal plates diverge), volcanic island arcs, and other volcanoes, are areas of high heat flow, where much heat from Earth's interior escapes up through the crust. Oceanic trenches, where crust descends into the mantle, are low heat flow areas, and cool.

## Heat sources

- The chief source of heat escaping from Earth's interior is the radioactive decay of isotopes of the heavy elements potassium, uranium, and thorium.
- Some 40 percent of continental heat flow comes from these elements located within the upper continental crust.
- Below the oceans, heat flow stems largely from the mantle.
- Heat escapes from Earth's interior mainly by convection.

# Periodic table

**Key words**

*element*

## Elements

- Calcium (Ca), gold (Au), and hydrogen (H) are chemical *elements* that are examples of basic chemical substances: they cannot be broken down into simpler forms.
- The periodic table gives information about all of the 116 known elements arranged in order of their atomic number: the number of protons in each element's atomic nucleus.
- Elements 110 through 116 have been produced artificially.
- It was devised in 1869 by the Russian chemist Dmitri Mendeleyev (1834–1907). The table groups elements into seven horizontal lines or periods. As we read from left to right the elements become less metallic. The elements in each vertical group have similar chemical properties.

## Hydrogen

| 1 |
|---|
| **H** |
| Hydrogen |

## Inert gases

| 2 |
|---|
| **He** |
| Helium |

## Light metals

| 3 | 4 |
|---|---|
| **Li** | **Be** |
| Lithium | Beryllium |
| 11 | 12 |
| **Na** | **Mg** |
| Sodium | Magnesium |

## Nonmetals

| 5 | 6 | 7 | 8 | 9 |
|---|---|---|---|---|
| **B** | **C** | **N** | **O** | **F** |
| Boron | Carbon | Nitrogen | Oxygen | Fluorine |
| 13 **Al** Aluminum | 14 **Si** Silicon | 15 **P** Phosphorus | 16 **S** Sulfur | 17 **Cl** Chlorine |

| 10 |
|---|
| **Ne** |
| Neon |
| 18 |
| **Ar** |
| Argon |

## Heavy metals

| 19 | 20 | 21 | 22 | 23 | 24 | 25 | 26 | 27 | 28 | 29 | 30 | 31 | 32 | 33 | 34 | 35 | 36 |
|---|---|---|---|---|---|---|---|---|---|---|---|---|---|---|---|---|---|
| **K** | **Ca** | **Sc** | **Ti** | **V** | **Cr** | **Mn** | **Fe** | **Co** | **Ni** | **Cu** | **Zn** | **Ga** | **Ge** | **As** | **Se** | **Br** | **Kr** |
| Potassium | Calcium | Scandium | Titanium | Vanadium | Chromium | Manganese | Iron | Cobalt | Nickel | Copper | Zinc | Gallium | Germanium | Arsenic | Selenium | Bromine | Krypton |
| 37 | 38 | 39 | 40 | 41 | 42 | 43 | 44 | 45 | 46 | 47 | 48 | 49 | 50 | 51 | 52 | 53 | 54 |
| **Rb** | **Sr** | **Y** | **Zr** | **Nb** | **Mo** | **Tc** | **Ru** | **Rh** | **Pd** | **Ag** | **Cd** | **In** | **Sn** | **Sb** | **Te** | **I** | **Xe** |
| Rubidium | Strontium | Yttrium | Zirconium | Niobium | Molybdenum | Technetium | Ruthenium | Rhodium | Palladium | Silver | Cadmium | Indium | Tin | Antimony | Tellurium | Iodine | Xenon |
| 55 | 56 | 57–71 | 72 | 73 | 74 | 75 | 76 | 77 | 78 | 79 | 80 | 81 | 82 | 83 | 84 | 85 | 86 |
| **Cs** | **Ba** | – | **Hf** | **Ta** | **W** | **Re** | **Os** | **Ir** | **Pt** | **Au** | **Hg** | **Tl** | **Pb** | **Bi** | **Po** | **At** | **Rn** |
| Caesium | Barium | | Hafnium | Tantalum | Tungsten | Rhenium | Osmium | Iridium | Platinum | Gold | Mercury | Thallium | Lead | Bismuth | Polonium | Astatine | Radon |
| 87 | 88 | 89–103 | 104 | 105 | 106 | 107 | 108 | 109 | 110 | 111 | 112 | 113 | 114 | 115 | 116 | | |
| **Fr** | **Ra** | – | **Rf** | **Db** | **Sg** | **Bh** | **Hs** | **Mt** | **Ds** | **Uuu** | **Uub** | **Uut** | **Uuq** | **Uup** | **Uuh** | | |
| Francium | Radium | | Rutherfordium | Dubnium | Seaborgium | Bohrium | Hassium | Meitnerium | Darmstadtium | Unununium | Ununbium | Ununtrium | Ununquadium | Ununpentium | Ununhexium | | |

## Rare earths

| 57 | 58 | 59 | 60 | 61 | 62 | 63 | 64 | 65 | 66 | 67 | 68 | 69 | 70 | 71 |
|---|---|---|---|---|---|---|---|---|---|---|---|---|---|---|
| **La** | **Ce** | **Pr** | **Nd** | **Pm** | **Sm** | **Eu** | **Gd** | **Tb** | **Dy** | **Ho** | **Er** | **Tm** | **Yb** | **Lu** |
| Lanthanum | Cerium | Praseodymium | Neodymium | Promethium | Samarium | Europium | Gadolinium | Terbium | Dysprosium | Holmium | Erbium | Thulium | Ytterbium | Lutetium |
| 89 | 90 | 91 | 92 | 93 | 94 | 95 | 96 | 97 | 98 | 99 | 100 | 101 | 102 | 103 |
| **Ac** | **Th** | **Pa** | **U** | **Np** | **Pu** | **Am** | **Cm** | **Bk** | **Cf** | **Es** | **Fm** | **Md** | **No** | **Lr** |
| Actinium | Thorium | Protactinium | Uranium | Neptunium | Plutonium | Americium | Curium | Berkelium | Californium | Einsteinium | Fermium | Mendelevium | Nobelium | Lawrencium |

# Atoms

### Key words

*atom*
*electron*
*element*
*neutron*
*proton*

## Major subatomic particles

**Protons**
(electrically positive)

**Electrons**
(electrically negative)

**Proton and electron**

**Neutrons**
(electrically neutral)

## Subatomic particles

● Atoms are an element's indivisibly smallest constituents, but each atom comprises subatomic particles. The chief subatomic particles are *protons*, *electrons*, and *neutrons*.

## Different atoms

● In an atom, electromagnetic force attracts negatively charged electrons to an equal number of positively charged protons in the atomic nucleus. In every element except the common form of hydrogen, the nucleus also contains electrically neutral neutrons, held there by powerful nuclear force.

● Each kind of atom has a specific number of protons: for instance, two in helium, a light element; six in carbon, a heavier element.

## Electron shells

● Electrons are traditionally shown in one or more energy levels called shells, orbiting a nucleus. The heavier an element is, the more electrons its atoms contain and the more shells these tend to occupy.

## Examples of atoms

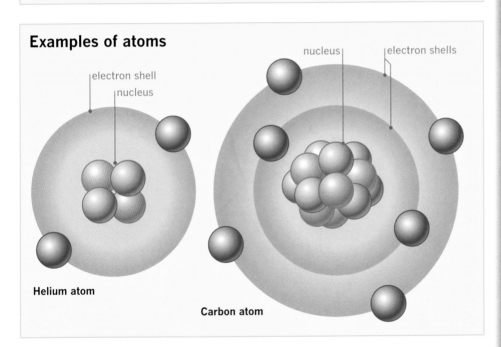

electron shell
nucleus
nucleus
electron shells

**Helium atom**

**Carbon atom**

## Electron shells

Energy levels each hold a definite number of electrons orbiting the nucleus. For clarity only one orbit per shell is shown here. Some atoms have as many as seven shells.

 nucleus        - - - - - - - electron orbit

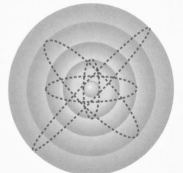

**One shell**
e.g., helium

**Two shells**
e.g., carbon

**Three shells**
e.g., aluminum

**Four shells**
e.g., calcium

# Compounds

## Key words

*compound*

## Compounds

● *Compounds* are chemically combined elements. Covalent or ionic bonds unite their atoms in fixed proportions, forming molecules of substances with their own special properties.

 electron in outer shell of atom

 protons in atomic nucleus

 lost electron shell

← → electrical attraction

## Outer-shell electrons in stable elements

The numbers of outer-shell electrons in common reactive elements are shown (e.g. argon has eight). Elements combine as compounds to gain a full complement of electrons.

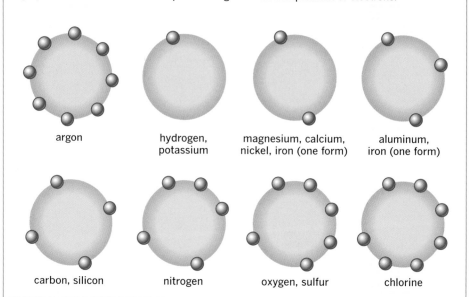

argon

hydrogen, potassium

magnesium, calcium, nickel, iron (one form)

aluminum, iron (one form)

carbon, silicon

nitrogen

oxygen, sulfur

chlorine

## Separate atoms

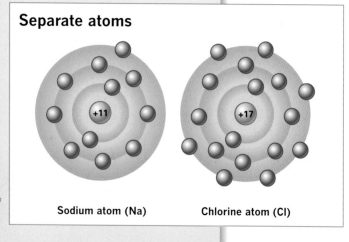

hydrogen atom (H)

carbon atom (C)

## Covalent bonding

The bonding of four hydrogen atoms and one carbon atom forms one methane molecule ($CH_4$).

## Separate atoms

Sodium atom (Na)          Chlorine atom (Cl)

## Ionic bonding

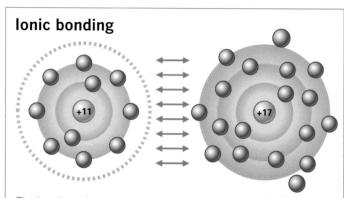

The bonding of one sodium atom and one chloride atom forms one sodium chloride molecule (NaCl).

# Isotopes and ions

## Ions and isotopes

- An ion is an electrically charged atom or group of atoms.
- Positive ions are atoms that have lost one or more electrons. Such ions are called cations.
- Negative ions are atoms that have gained one or more electrons. Such ions are called anions.
- Ions help living cells to function.

- *Isotopes* are atoms of an element with the same atomic number (number of protons in the nucleus) but different atomic mass (number of neutrons in the nucleus).
- Some elements occur in nature as a mixture of different isotopes.
- All elements have artificially produced *radioisotopes*.

### Key words

*isotope*
*radioisotope*

## Ions

Ions are atoms that have lost or gained electrons.

**Positively charged sodium ion**

**Negatively charged chlorine ion**

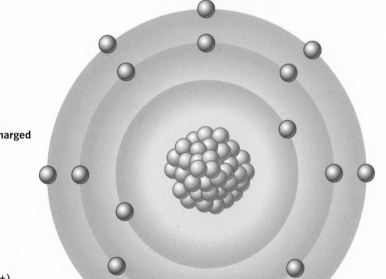

 proton (+)

 electron (-)

 neutron

## Hydrogen isotopes

Hydrogen isotopes are hydrogen atoms with the same atomic number (the number of protons in the nucleus) but different atomic mass numbers (the number of protons plus neutrons).

**Mass number: 1**

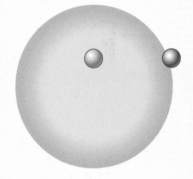

**Mass number: 2**

**Mass number: 3**

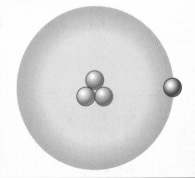

# Crystals and minerals

**Key words**

*crystal*
*igneous rock*
*magma*
*mineral*

## Crystals in rock

● As *magma* (molten rock) cools, *minerals* are precipitated out of solution as *crystals*.

● First crystals of one mineral are formed, then another, then a third, and so on, until interlocking crystals form a solid igneous rock.

## Sequence of minerals

● Crystallization follows a sequence in which each mineral "freezes out" at a particular temperature.

● A typical igneous rock contains a set of minerals that solidified at roughly the same temperature.

## Interlocking mineral crystals forming igneous rock

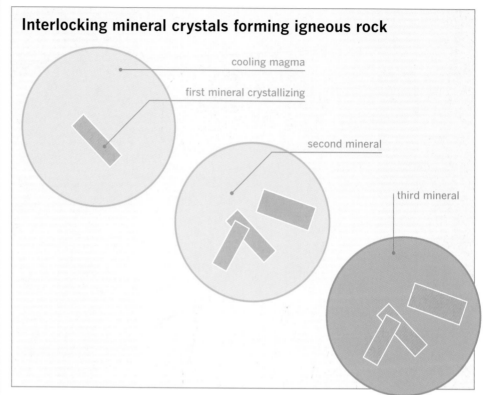

cooling magma

first mineral crystallizing

second mineral

third mineral

## Sequence of minerals formed in igneous rocks as magma cools

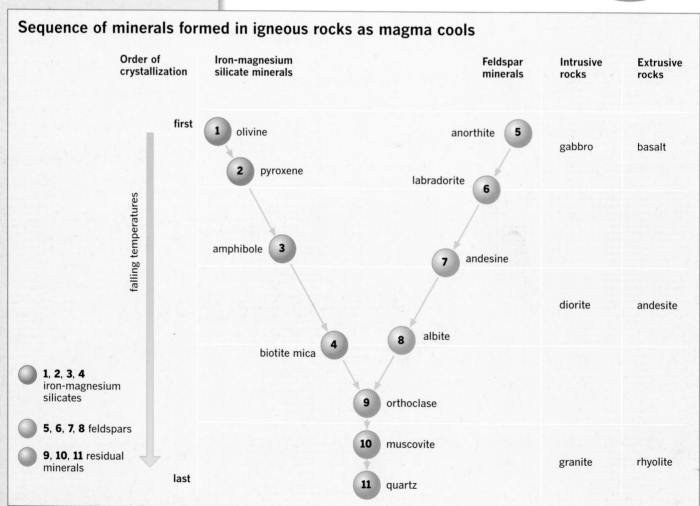

| Order of crystallization | Iron-magnesium silicate minerals | Feldspar minerals | Intrusive rocks | Extrusive rocks |
|---|---|---|---|---|
| first | 1 olivine | anorthite 5 | gabbro | basalt |
| | 2 pyroxene | labradorite 6 | | |
| | amphibole 3 | 7 andesine | diorite | andesite |
| | biotite mica 4 | 8 albite | | |
| | 9 orthoclase | | | |
| | 10 muscovite | | granite | rhyolite |
| last | 11 quartz | | | |

falling temperatures

**1, 2, 3, 4** iron-magnesium silicates

**5, 6, 7, 8** feldspars

**9, 10, 11** residual minerals

# Crystal systems

| System | Example | Ideal shape | Lengths of axis | Angles of axes' intersection |
|---|---|---|---|---|
| Cubic (isometric) | halite | | all equal | 90° |
| Tetragonal | zircon | | two horizontal equal; third different | 90° |
| Hexagonal | quartz | | three equal horizontal axes; fourth axis different | 60° 90° |
| Orthorhombic | sulfur | | three axes; unequal | 90° |
| Monoclinic | orthoclase | | three axes; unequal | only two 90° |
| Triclinic | albite | | three axes; unequal | none 90° |

© Diagram Visual Information Ltd.

## Key words

*axis*
*crystal*
*mineral*

## Crystals

- Within Earth's crust most elements occur as minerals—natural substances that differ chemically and have distinct atomic structures.
- Most minerals form from fluids that have solidified—a process that arranges their atoms geometrically, producing crystals.

## Crystal systems

- Scientists identify six crystal systems based on *axes* (singular: axis): imaginary lines passing through the middle of a crystal.
- Each system yields crystals with distinctive symmetry.
- Within each system, each mineral crystal grows in a special shape or habit, though this can be modified by temperature, pressure, and impurities.

## Six types of crystal

- Cubic, or isometric, crystals have three axes of equal length that intersect at right angles.
- Tetragonal crystals have three right-angled axes, one longer or shorter than the other two.
- Hexagonal crystals have four axes, three in the same plane.
- Orthorhombic crystals have three right-angled axes of different lengths.
- Monoclinic crystals have three axes of different lengths, two intersecting at an oblique angle.
- Triclinic crystals have three axes of different lengths intersecting at three different angles.

# Rock forming minerals

© Diagram Visual Information Ltd.

## Key words

*feldspar*
*silicate*

## Minerals in rocks

- Earth's rocks hold many minerals. Most are *silicates*—silicon and oxygen usually combined with a base or metal.
- The chief silicates are *feldspars* (silicates of aluminum combined with certain other elements), notably plagioclase and orthoclase.
- Other silicates include pyroxene, amphibole, quartz, mica, olivine.
- Silica-rich igneous rocks are termed "acid." Progressively less silica-rich rocks are termed intermediate, basic (mafic), and ultrabasic (ultramafic).

## Presence of minerals in Earth's crust

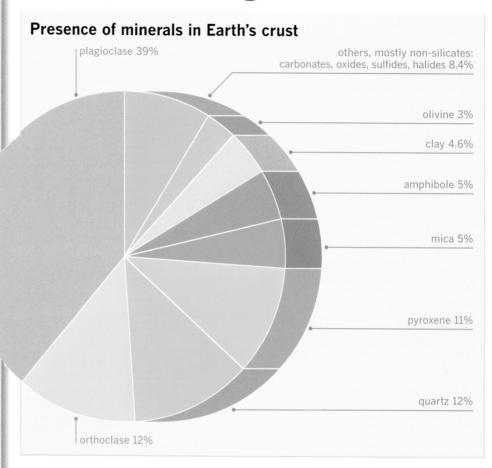

- plagioclase 39%
- others, mostly non-silicates: carbonates, oxides, sulfides, halides 8.4%
- olivine 3%
- clay 4.6%
- amphibole 5%
- mica 5%
- pyroxene 11%
- quartz 12%
- orthoclase 12%

## Silicate structures of common minerals

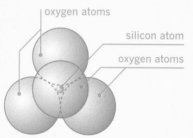

oxygen atoms
silicon atom
oxygen atoms

**Oxygen-silicon tetrahedron**

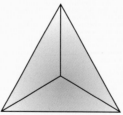

**Schematic representation of a tetrahedron**
e.g., olivine

**Double tetrahedron**
e.g., epidote

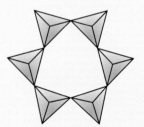

**Ring**
e.g., tourmaline

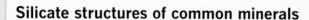

**Chain**
e.g., pyroxene

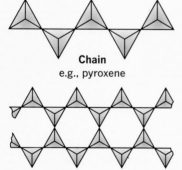

**Double chain**
e.g., amphibole

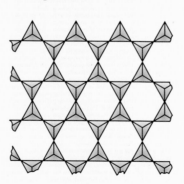

**Sheet**
e.g., mica

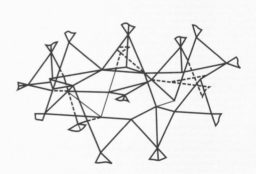

**Three-dimensional network**
e.g., quartz

# Hardness

**Key words**

*Mohs' scale*
*sclerometer*

## Mohs' scale

Each reference mineral scratches all with lower numbers.

diamond
**10**

corundum
**9**

topaz
**8**

quartz
**7**

orthoclase
**6**

apatite
**5**

fluorite
**4**

calcite
**3**

gypsum
**2**

talc
**1**

## Field scale of hardness

Used to determine the relative hardness of sample outside the laboratory.

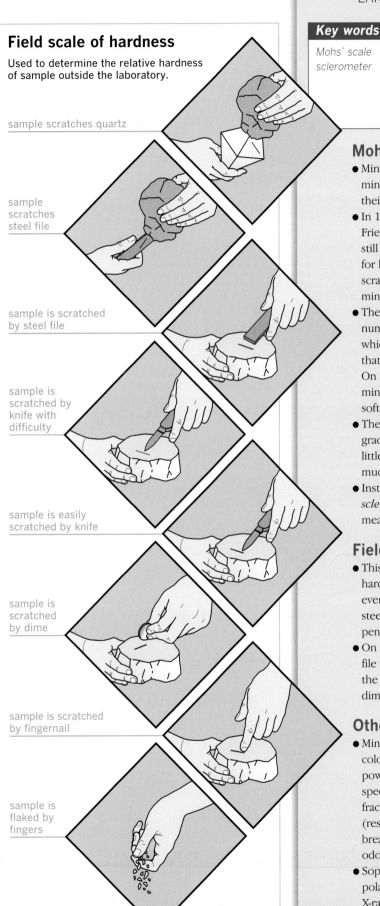

sample scratches quartz

sample scratches steel file

sample is scratched by steel file

sample is scratched by knife with difficulty

sample is easily scratched by knife

sample is scratched by dime

sample is scratched by fingernail

sample is flaked by fingers

## Mohs' scale

- Mineralogists often identify minerals by their hardness: their resistance to abrasion.
- In 1822 Austrian mineralogist Friedrich Mohs published the still widely used *Mohs' scale* for hardness, based on scratch tests developed by miners.
- The Mohs' scale features ten numbered minerals, each of which scratches all the others that have a lower number. On this scale the hardest mineral is diamond, the softest is talc.
- The Mohs' scale is not graduated in even steps: *4* is little harder than *3* but *10* is much harder than *9*.
- Instruments called *sclerometers* are used to measure absolute hardness.

## Field scale

- This scale determines relative hardness with the use of everyday objects including a steel file, pocketknife, copper penny, and fingernail.
- On the Mohs' scale the steel file would be numbered 7+; the pocketknife, 6+; the dime, 4; the fingernail 2+.

## Other tests

- Minerals are also identified by color, streak (color of the powdered mineral), luster, specific gravity, cleavage, fracture, form, tenacity (resistance to bending, breaking, and other forces), odor, taste, and feel.
- Sophisticated tests use polarizing microscopes, X-rays, and spectral analysis.

# Igneous rocks

**Key words**

*igneous rock*

## Igneous and other rocks

- *Igneous rocks* form from magma, either underground or on the surface.
- They comprise nearly two thirds of all rock in Earth's crust.
- Sedimentary and metamorphic rocks ultimately derive from igneous rocks.

## Kinds of igneous rock

- Igneous rocks can feature coarse-grained or fine-grained minerals.
- Many rocks hold the same minerals, but in different proportions.

## Rocks of Earth's crust

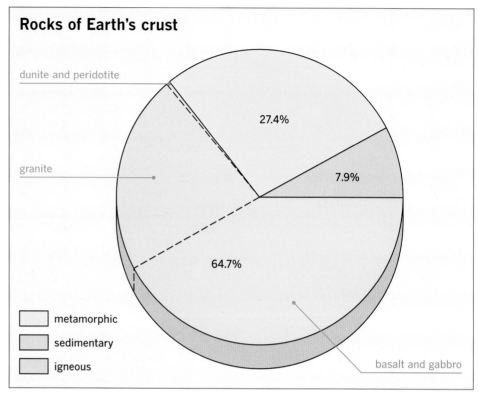

dunite and peridotite

granite

27.4%

7.9%

64.7%

□ metamorphic

□ sedimentary

□ igneous

basalt and gabbro

## Igneous rocks classified

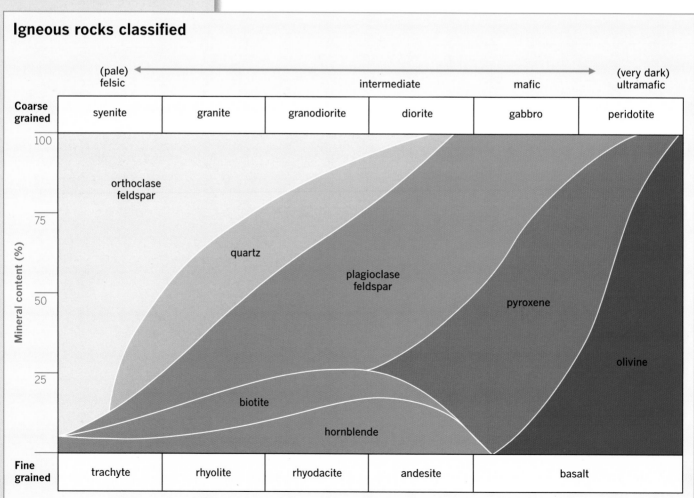

# Intrusive igneous rocks

## Fiery rocks formed underground

### How granite forms

- Granite forms when molten blobs called *plutons* rise, coalesce, and cool as masses known as *batholiths*—immense rock masses in the cores of mountain ranges such as the Sierra Nevada of California.
- Erosion of overlying rock exposes granite masses like the domes above California's Yosemite Valley and the tors of Dartmoor in southwest England.

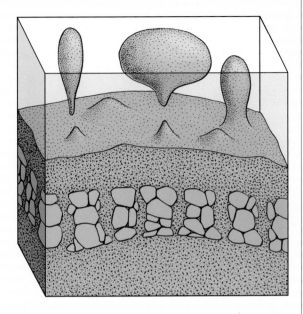

**Key words**

*batholith*
*hypabyssal*
*pluton*

### Intrusive rocks

- Intrusive igneous rocks are produced where magma cools and hardens underground. Geologists place intrusive rocks in two categories: *plutonic* and *hypabyssal*.

### Plutonic rocks

- Plutonic rocks include great masses formed deep in mountain-building zones: some develop from the partial fusion of lower continental crust; others come from magma rising from the mantle.
- Slow cooling produces big mineral crystals, forming coarse-textured rocks including (acid) granite and granodiorite; (intermediate) syenite and diorite; (basic) gabbro; and (ultrabasic) peridotite. Granite—mainly made of quartz, feldspar, and mica—is the chief igneous rock of continental crust.

### Hypabyssal rocks

- Hypabyssal rocks are relatively smaller masses, that are often strips or sheets. Such rocks cooled at a lesser depth and faster than plutonic rock, so they hold smaller crystals.
- Hypabyssal rocks include (acid) microgranite and microgranodiorite; (intermediate) microsyenite and microdiorite; and (basic) diabase (dolerite).

## Intrusive rocks produce these features

**Sill** A sheet of usually basic igneous rock intruded horizontally between rock layers.

**Dike** A wall of usually basic igneous rock, such as diabase (dolerite), injected up through a vertical crack in preexisting rock.

**Stock** Like a batholith but smaller, with an irregular surface area under 40 square miles (about 100 km²).

**Laccolith** A lens-shaped, usually acidic, igneous intrusion that domes overlying strata.

**Batholith** A huge, deep-seated, dome-shaped intrusion, usually of acid igneous rock.

**Lopolith** A saucer-shaped intrusion between rock strata; can be hundreds of miles across.

**Boss** A small circular-surfaced igneous intrusion less than 16 miles (26 km) across.

**Key words**

*igneous rock*
*magma*
*spreading ridge*

## Magma production

## Magma output

- Igneous, or "fiery," rocks floor the world's oceans and form rock masses that rise from the roots of continents. Such rocks arise directly from the molten underground rock material—magma—that occurs where heat melts parts of Earth's upper mantle and lower crust.

- Most magma that has cooled and solidified escaped up through the crust from oceanic spreading ridges. Smaller quantities came from destructive plate boundaries and colliding continents.

## Magma loss

- Old, solidified magma is lost from Earth's crust by subduction below oceanic trenches. Here, where tectonic plates meet, oceanic plates plunge beneath continental plates and their rock melts in Earth's mantle.

## Global balance

- The estimated amounts of global annual crustal output and loss shown here imply that Earth's crust is getting thicker. However, some studies suggest a balance between output and loss. If true, the thickness of Earth's crust remains about the same.

### Magma loss and production

**constructive plate boundaries (spreading ridges) 3.2 cubic miles (13.5 km³)**

**within oceanic plates 0.24 cubic miles (1 km³)**

**destructive plate boundaries (subduction zones) 0.7 cubic miles (2.7 km³)**

**within continental plates 0.17 cubic miles (0.7 km³)**

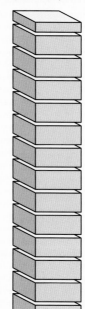

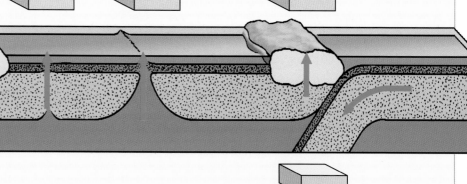

**plate material consumed at destructive plate boundaries 3.36 cubic miles (14 km³)**

# Volcanoes: active

### Key words

lithosphere
plate tectonics
volcano

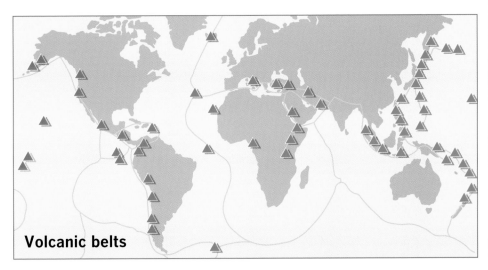

**Volcanic belts**

Laki, Iceland

Katmai, Alaska

Vesuvius, Italy

Mount Fuji, Japan

Mauna Loa, Hawaii

Faial Island, Azores

Paricutín, Mexico

Rakata (Krakatau)

**Famous volcanoes**

Villarrica, Chile

## Great eruptions

Volcanic eruptions release very large quantities of energy. This graph compares the energy released by three of the largest known volcanic events with the energy released by the most powerful nuclear explosion. Energy release is shown in Joules (J) and the approximate TNT equivalent in megatons (Mt) is also given.

### Volcanic eruptions

Tambora, Indonesia (1815)  $8 \times 10^{19}$ J (20,000 Mt)

Santorini, Greece (c. 1470 BCE)  $6 \times 10^{19}$ J (7,500 Mt)

Krakatau, Indonesia (August 1883)  $3 \times 10^{18}$ J (1,500 Mt)

### Nuclear explosions

Novaya Zemlya, USSR (October 1961)  $3 \times 10^{17}$ J (60 Mt)

## Volcanic belts

- Most volcanoes occur in belts along the edges of the lithospheric or tectonic plates that form Earth's crust. The most notable belt is the one around the Pacific Ocean rim.
- A less obvious one lies along the bottom of the Atlantic Ocean, visible on the surface only as a few volcanic islands.
- Rift valleys—cracks within a tectonic plate—are also key locations. However, some volcanoes occur away from lines of tectonic activity, notably the Hawaiian Islands.

## Some famous volcanoes

- Volcanoes generally achieve prominence because of the great violence of their past eruptions, or for their height, or for the beauty of their shape.
- Rakata (Krakatau), Indonesia, is famous for its huge eruption of 1883, and Vesuvius for its destruction of Pompeii and Herculaneum in 79 CE.
- Mauna Loa, Hawaii, is famous as a fine example of a shield volcano.
- Mount Fuji, Japan, is famous for the beauty of its classic conical shape.

## Great eruptions

- Volcanic eruptions release huge quantities of energy.
- The energy released by the eruptions of Tambora, Indonesia (1815), Santorini, Greece (c. 1470 BC), and Krakatau, Indonesia (1883) exceeded that released in hydrogen bombs exploded by the USA and USSR.
- Volcanic eruptions can also release vast quantities of rock.
- About 600,000 years ago, the last major eruption at Yellowstone, Wyoming, released some 240 cubic miles (1,000 km³) of rock, compared to 36 cubic miles (150 km³) from Tambora's eruption, the greatest in modern times.

**Key words**

*caldera*
*lava*
*volcano*

## Volcanic types

- The volcanic types below are discussed in order of increasing lava viscosity and violence of eruption.

## Gas eruption

- It is unusual for gas alone to be emitted during a volcanic eruption, but where this happens, the gas is usually carbon dioxide ($CO_2$).
- For example, Lake Nyos (Cameroon, West Africa) is a volcanic lake that in 1986 emitted a low-lying cloud of $CO_2$ that killed 1,700 people.

## Hawaiian eruption

- These commonly occur as lava rivers emerging from elongated fissures or tubular vents.
- They have a low gas content and are the least violent type of eruption that produces solid emissions.

## Strombolian eruption

- These eruptions are characterized by frequent but comparatively small emissions of glowing gas and ash that rise no more than 0.6 miles (1 km).
- They also produce viscous basaltic lava from the volcano's throat.

## Plinian (Vesuvian) eruption

- These are violent eruptions, characterized by the expulsion at high velocity of a vertical column of gas and rock, rising as high as 31 miles (50 km) into the atmosphere.
- Ash and pumice rain back down, often carried in the direction of the prevailing wind and thus forming asymmetric deposits.

# Volcanic types

⊢—⊣ = 1 mile (1.6 km)

## Flood or plateau basalt

The lava is very liquid. Lava flows are very widespread, and emitted from fractures.

## Shield volcano

Shield volcanoes (e.g., Mauna Loa, Hawaii) are built almost entirely from fluid lava flows. Successive eruptions produce lava that flows in all directions from a central vent. Over time a broad, gently sloping cone or dome is formed. Lava may also flow from fractures on the flanks of the cone. These volcanoes generally have diameters of 3 to 4 miles (5–6.5 km) and heights of 1,500 to 2,000 feet (457–610 m).

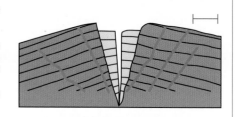

## Cinder cone volcano

Composed entirely of basaltic fragments, cinder cones are Earth's most common volcanic landform. Lava is thrown into the air during an eruption where it cools into small, solid lumps filled with gas bubbles. These "cinders" rain down and, over time, create a cone of material around the central vent. They commonly occur in clusters of a hundred or more in a region, but are rarely more than 1,000 feet (305 m) in altitude.

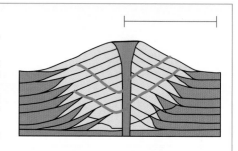

## Composite volcano or stratovolcano

Composite volcanoes consist of successive layers formed by lava flows, fragments, and ash. Lava erupts from a central vent, or cluster of vents. Lava flows also escape via fissures in the flanks of the volcano. Lava that solidifies within fissures forms dikes that strengthen the cone. The rigidity of the cone often leads to explosive eruptions as pressure builds up over long periods between eruptions. Mount St Helens, WA, is an example.

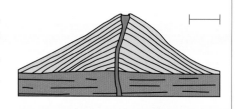

## Volcanic dome

Volcanic domes are formed as very viscous lava flows from a central vent to form a gradually expanding dome of material. They are often found on the outside slopes or within the craters of composite volcanoes. They can form a dense "plug" over the central vent of a volcano that can lead to pressure build-up and eventually an explosive eruption.

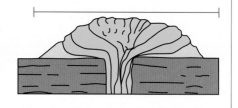

## Caldera

A *caldera* is a very large crater formed from the explosive eruption of a large composite volcano. An eruption that forms a caldera can eject hundreds of cubic miles ($km^3$) of material.

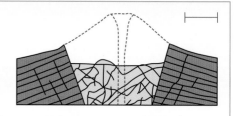

# Volcanoes: caldera

**Key words**

*caldera*
*magma*
*volcano*

## Lava plug blocks pipe

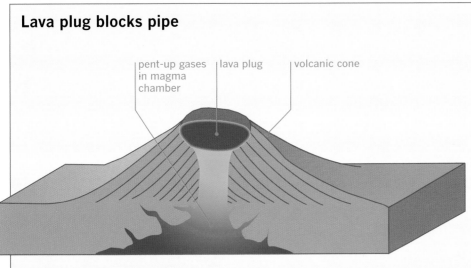

pent-up gases in magma chamber | lava plug | volcanic cone

A lava plug bottles up explosive gases below.

## Explosion blasts top of volcano

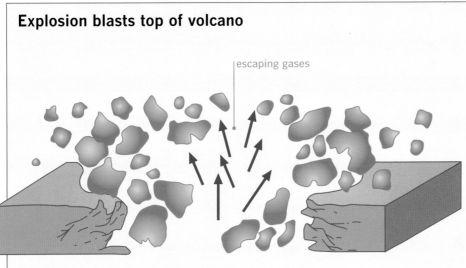

escaping gases

In time pent-up gas pressure blasts off the top of the volcano.

## Caldera (basal wreck)

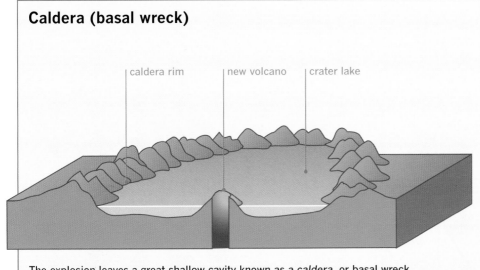

caldera rim | new volcano | crater lake

The explosion leaves a great shallow cavity known as a *caldera*, or basal wreck.

## Lava plug

- The first stage in caldera formation is magma rising in the magma chamber deep beneath a volcano.
- If a lava plug blocks the volcano's vent, the gas-rich magma gradually exerts increasing pressure on the magma chamber's walls.

## Explosion

- Over decades or centuries, the underground pressure becomes so great that gas-rich magma blasts a hole through the top of the volcano.
- Gas and magma escape up through the vent they have created, blasting off some of the top of the volcano.
- As the magma chamber empties, the rest of the volcano summit loses its support, cracks up, and falls—a process accompanied by more explosions, and lasting days.

## Caldera

- The resulting caldera is a great shallow cavity left by the collapse of all or part of a volcano summit.
- Calderas can occur where volcanoes are dormant, or (as at Kilauea in Hawaii), still active.
- Many calderas are circular in shape, though some are elongated.
- They can be hundreds of feet (m) to scores of miles (km) in diameter. The Yellowstone Caldera, the world's largest, measures 28 x 47 miles (45 x 76 km).
- Depth from crater rim to floor is often several hundred feet (m).
- Lakes occupy some calderas, for instance, Crater Lake in Oregon.

# Volcanoes: lava forms

**Key words**

| | |
|---|---|
| andesitic lava | rhyolitic lava |
| basalt | |
| basaltic lava | |
| lava | |
| pyroclast | |

## Basaltic lava

- *Basaltic lavas* are basic lavas low in silica. Oozing from shield and fissure volcanoes, they flow far before they harden. Varying conditions produce different forms:
- Aa has clinkery blocks shaped where gas spurted from sluggish molten rock capped by crust.
- Pahoehoe has skin wrinkled by molten lava flowing beneath it.
- Pillow lava forms mounds at undersea spreading ridges.
- Columnar *basalt* forms as lava cools evenly, contracts, and cracks.

## Andesitic lava

- *Andesitic lava* has a silica content intermediate between those of basaltic and rhyolitic lavas. It is rather viscous and flows a short way down composite volcanoes.

## Rhyolitic lava

- *Rhyolitic lava* is an acid lava with a high silica content. It is viscous and hardens before flowing far. It can produce explosive eruptions from composite volcanoes.
- Solid products of explosive eruptions are called *pyroclasts*. Pyroclasts include spindle bombs and pumice.

### Aa

These are used blocks of lava, common at Villarrica, Chile.

### Pahoehoe

"Ropy" lava, as seen in Iceland and Hawaii.

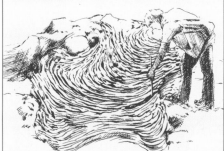

### Columnar basalt

The Giant's Causeway on the north coast of Ireland is a well-known example.

### Pillow lava

This is formed at underwater spreading ridges.

### Spindle bomb

A volcanic bomb shaped by a whizzing trajectory through the air.

### Pumice

Rafts of this light bubble-filled lava floated on the sea after Krakatoa (now Krakatau) exploded between Java and Sumatra in 1883.

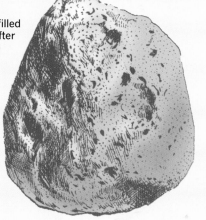

# Volcanoes: central

## Structure of a central volcano

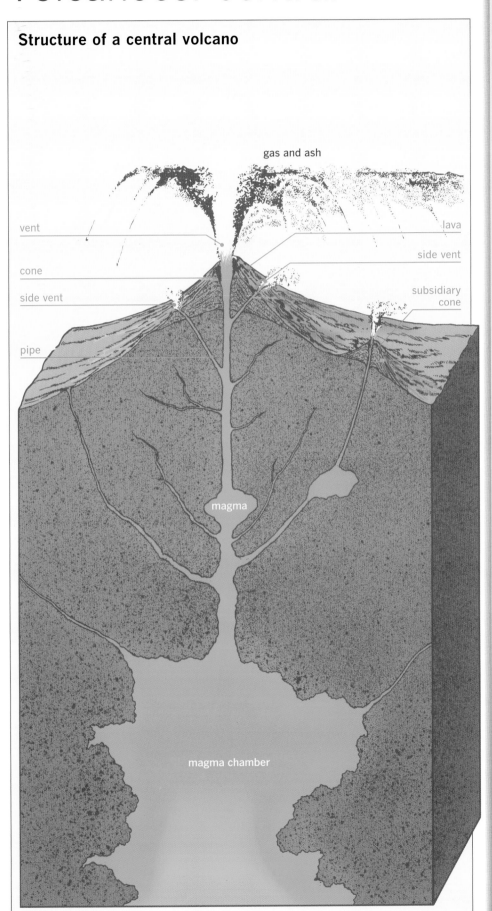

gas and ash

vent

cone

side vent

pipe

lava

side vent

subsidiary
cone

magma

magma chamber

**Key words**

*fissure*
*volcano*

## Two forms of volcano

● Volcanoes take two main forms: *fissure* volcanoes and central volcanoes.

● Central volcanoes yield lava, ash, and/or other products from a single hole, building a rounded or cone-shaped mound.

● In Mexico the cinder cone Paricutín grew 1,500 feet (450 m) in a year. In Argentina, the extinct composite volcano Aconcagua towers 22,834 feet (6,960 m) above sea level.

## Features of a central volcano

● A cross section through an active central volcano would reveal the following features as it develops:

● Deep below the surface lies the magma chamber, a reservoir of gas-rich molten rock under pressure. This pressurized magma may "balloon" outwards against the surrounding solid rock until it relieves the pressure by escaping through a weakness in the crust.

● From the chamber the magma then rises through a central conduit.

● As magma rises, the pressure on it is reduced, and its dissolved gases are freed as expanding bubbles.

● The force of gases blasts open a circular vent on Earth's surface.

● From this outlet ash, cinders, and/or lava build the main volcano.

● Vent explosions shape its top as an inverted cone or crater.

● From the central conduit, pipes to side vents release ash or lava, which then build subsidiary cones.

**Key words**

*basalt*
*fissure*
*plateau*

## Fissure volcanoes

- Most volcanic activity happens not at central volcanoes, but at long *fissures* in Earth's crust.
- The chief fissure systems occur along submarine spreading ridges. These yield the free-flowing basic lava that creates new ocean floor.
- Known also as Icelandic eruptions, fissure eruptions built Iceland, an island on the Mid-Atlantic Ridge.
- Fissure systems also occur on continents. Successive lava flows fed by plumes of molten rock risen from the mantle have covered vast tracts of land in basalt rock.
- Such flood basalts cover great areas of western North America, western India, and Siberia.

## Two basalt plateaus

- In the western United States, the Columbia River Flood Basalt province covers 63,300 square miles (164,000 km²) in basalt up to 1,150 feet (3,500 m) thick.
- In India the Deccan Plateau consists largely of basaltic lava about 6,500 feet (2,000 m) spread over some 200,000 square miles (518,000 km²).

# Volcanoes: fissure

## Fissure volcanoes

**Fissure leaks**
Lava flows from cracks (fissures) to form a long low layer of basalt covering the sedimentary layers below.

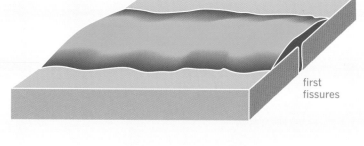

first fissures

**Basalt plateaus**
Later cracks occur alongside older extrusions to form a further covering of lava, which is called a basalt *plateau*.

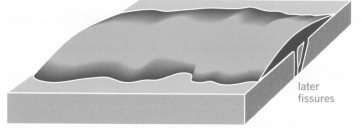

later fissures

## Basalt plateaus

**Columbia Plateau, USA**

Deccan Plateau, India

basalt

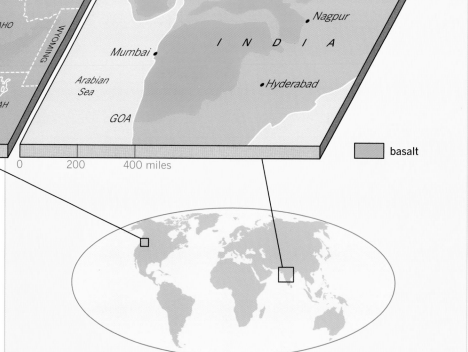

# Volcanoes: shield

## Shield volcanoes

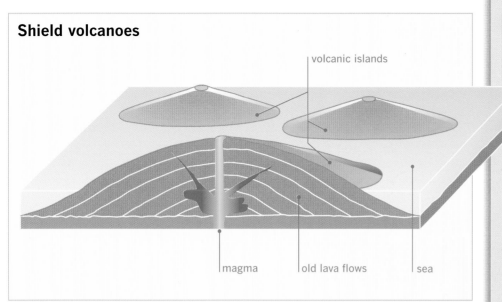

volcanic islands

magma    old lava flows    sea

**Key words**

*shield volcano*
*volcano*

### Shield volcanoes
- Repeated flows of fluid basaltic lava build the broad, gently sloping domes of *shield volcanoes*. Those of the Hawaiian Islands include the largest volcano on Earth, Mauna Loa.
- Mauna Loa on Hawaii has a volume of 10,200 cubic miles (42,500 km³); it rises 32,000 feet (9,750 m) above the ocean floor.

## Hawaii's shield volcanoes

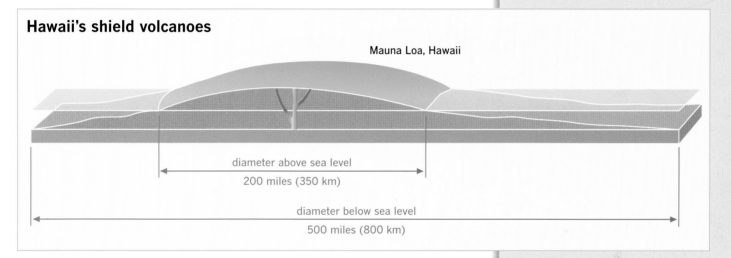

Mauna Loa, Hawaii

diameter above sea level
200 miles (350 km)

diameter below sea level
500 miles (800 km)

## Hawaiian Islands

### Hawaiian Islands
- In this volcanic island chain, the oldest and lowest islands lie in the north west, the youngest and highest in the south east.

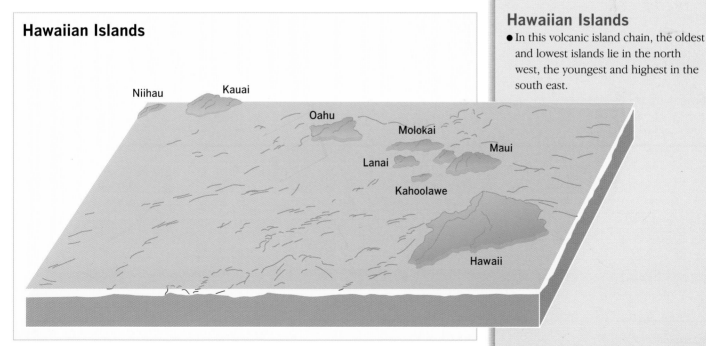

Niihau    Kauai
Oahu
Molokai
Maui
Lanai
Kahoolawe
Hawaii

**Key words**

| | |
|---|---|
| fissure | smoker |
| fumarole | solfatara |
| geyser | |
| mofette | |
| mud volcano | |

## Hot water underground

- Hot water, gas, and mud squirt or dribble from vents in the ground heated by volcanoes, often those nearing extinction.
- Such features abound in parts of Italy, Iceland, New Zealand, and the United States.

## Cavern geysers

- Water held in an underground cavity is heated by the hot rocks deep under the surface. Pressure builds up within the cavity until steam and hot water are ejected.

## Cavern and sump geysers

- *Fissures* in rocks allow water to sink deep underground. The water is converted into steam by steam below the sump and both are ejected from the mouth of the fissure.

## Fumarole

- *Fumaroles* are holes in volcanic areas that emit steam and other gases under pressure.

## Hot springs

- Trapped by impermeable rock, heated groundwater gushes from hillsides as hot springs.

## Related phenomena

- *Mud volcanoes* are low mud cones deposited by mud-rich water escaping from a vent.
- *Solfataras* are volcanic vents emitting steam and sulfurous gas.
- *Mofettes* are small vents emitting gases including carbon dioxide.
- *Smokers* are submarine hot springs at oceanic spreading ridges. Emitted sulfides build chimneys belching black smoky clouds.

# Geysers and hot springs

### Cavern geysers

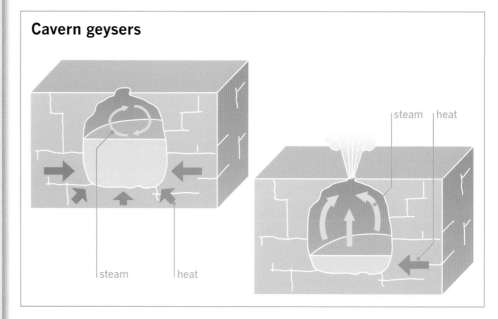

steam | heat

steam | heat

### Cavern and sump geysers

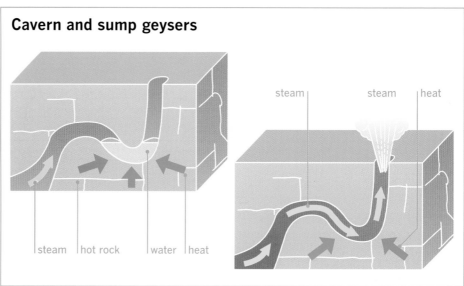

steam | steam | heat

steam | hot rock | water | heat

### Fumarole

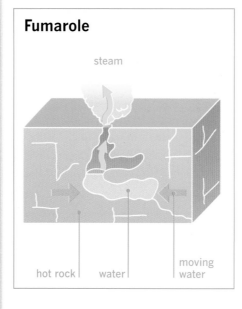

steam

hot rock | water | moving water

### Hot spring

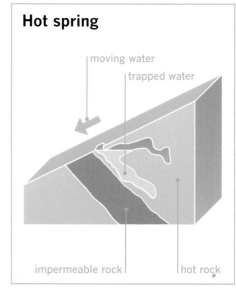

moving water

trapped water

impermeable rock | hot rock

# Sedimentary rocks: formation

**Key words**

*authigenesis*
*compaction*
*diagenesis*
*lithification*

## Compaction

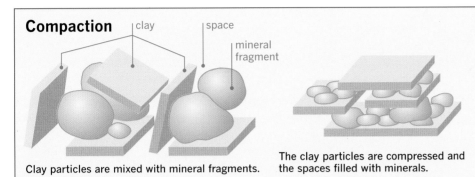

Clay particles are mixed with mineral fragments.

The clay particles are compressed and the spaces filled with minerals.

## Recrystallization

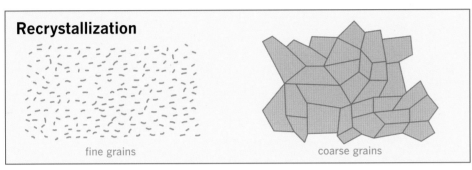

fine grains

coarse grains

## Solution

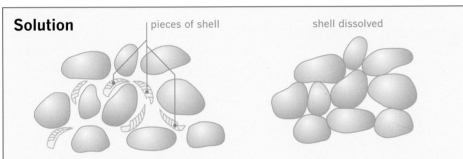

pieces of shell

shell dissolved

## Authigenesis

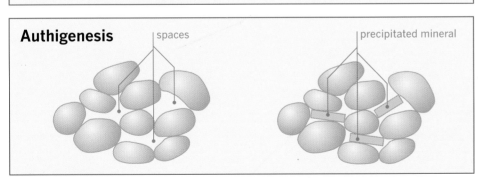

spaces

precipitated mineral

## Cementation

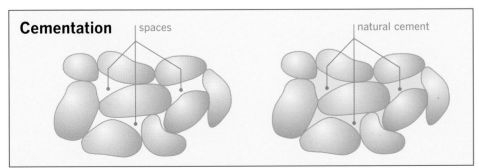

spaces

natural cement

### Rocks from sediments
- Buried sediments may undergo physical and chemical changes.
- Collectively called *diagenesis*, these changes can result in *lithification*—the conversion of loose sediments to solid sedimentary rock.

### Compaction
- Particles of sediment are forced closer together by the weight of sediment building up above them.

### Recrystallization
- Certain minerals in sedimentary deposits may be recrystallized, fine particles giving rise to coarse crystals. Thus lime mud forms calcite crystals, and amorphous silica forms quartz crystals.

### Solution
- Certain minerals in a sedimentary deposit may be dissolved away. Solution occurs in evaporites, limestones, and sandstones.

### Authigenesis
- *Authigenesis* is the precipitation of minerals within a sediment as this is being formed. They come from watery solutions percolating through pore spaces in the sediment.
- New minerals may replace those that have dissolved. For instance, clay minerals replace feldspars.

### Cementation
- Authigenic minerals filling pore spaces can cement the particles of sediment together, converting this to sedimentary rock.
- Major natural cements are calcium carbonate, iron oxides, and silica.

**Key words**

*breccia*
*clast*
*conglomerate*

# Sedimentary rocks: clastic

## Clastic sedimentary rocks

- Most sedimentary rocks form from particles eroded from rocks on land. Their main ingredients are *clasts* (rock fragments) of quartz, feldspar, and clay minerals. These range from tiny grains to boulders.

## Clastic rock textures

- Lutites (fine-grained particles) produce the sedimentary rocks mudstone, siltstone, and shale.
- The (medium-grained) arenites or sandstones include arkose, greywacke, and orthoquartzite.
- Rudites (coarse clasts) mixed with finer particles can be consolidated into *conglomerates*, with rounded fragments, and *breccias*, with sharp-edged fragments.
- Clasts of different sizes accumulate in different environments.

### Sedimentary rocks in Earth's crust

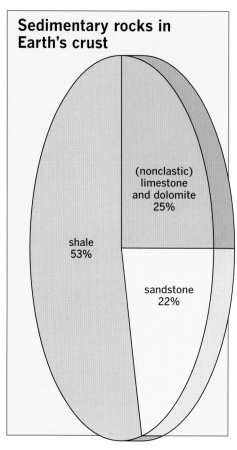

shale
53%

(nonclastic)
limestone
and dolomite
25%

sandstone
22%

### Clastic rock textures

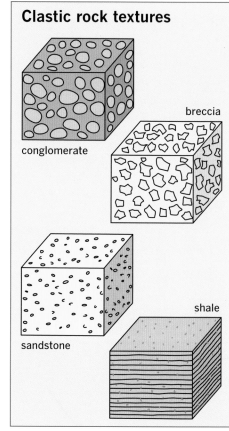

conglomerate

breccia

sandstone

shale

## Where rock-forming fragments accumulate

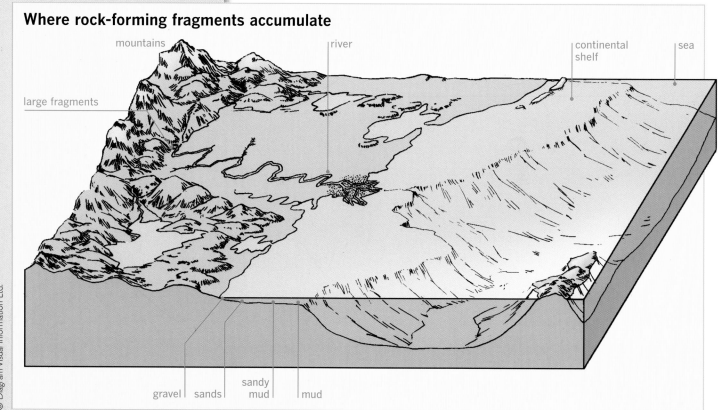

mountains

river

continental shelf

sea

large fragments

gravel | sands

sandy mud

mud

# Sedimentary rocks: organic and chemical

**Key words**

| | |
|---|---|
| coal | sediment |
| coral | |
| evaporite | |
| lignite | |
| limestone | |

## Shelly limestone (organic rock)

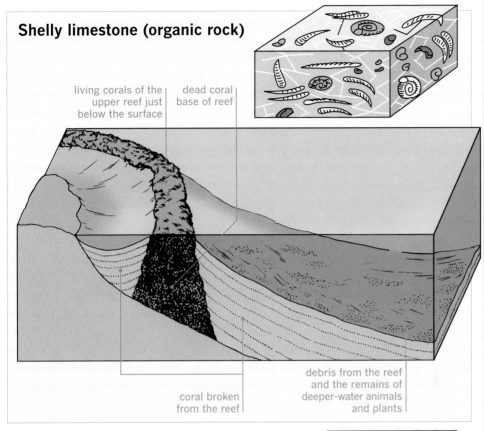

living corals of the upper reef just below the surface

dead coral base of reef

coral broken from the reef

debris from the reef and the remains of deeper-water animals and plants

## Evaporites (chemical rocks)

In a deepwater sea basin evaporation outstrips freshwater input. The basin water grows denser and sinks until evaporites are precipitated in the sequence **a**, **b**, **c**.

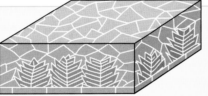

**c** halite (rock salt)

**b** gypsum

**a** dolomite

barrier sill partly shuts out the open sea

## Organic rocks

- Organic sediments produce the rocks we know as *coals* and shelly *limestones*.
- Coal forms as overlying *sediments* of compact dead swamp vegetation, converting it first to peat, then *lignite*, then coal.

## Limestone

- Marine organisms' shells rich in calcium carbonate form organic limestones.
- Reef limestones are largely made of coral polyps' skeletons.
- Coquina is a cemented mass of shelly debris.
- Chalk is a white powdery limestone formed from coccoliths—the shells of microorganisms.

## Rocks from chemicals

- Some rocks form from chemicals formerly dissolved in water.
- Examples are oolitic limestone, dolomite, gypsum, and halite (rock salt). These last three form one after another as *evaporites*.

© Diagram Visual Information Ltd.

## Key words

*bedding*
*sediment*

## Sedimentary rock layers

- Sedimentary rocks originate as sediments deposited in broadly horizontal sheets. These layers are known as beds or strata.
- Each stratum is separated from the next by a so-called *bedding* plane.
- Distinctive types of bedding can reveal the conditions under which sediments were laid down.

## Parallel bedding

- Parallel bedding layers contain particles distributed evenly within the bedding and occur when there is no wind or water turbulence.

## Graded bedding

- Graded bedding layers form in seas and rivers where the large, heavy particles of sediment have time to settle first. Subsequently, increasingly smaller and smaller pebbles and sand build a series of layers with the contents graded by size.

## Cross bedding (current bedding)

- Cross bedding is caused by overlapping layers of sand deposited by wind or moving water at an angle to underlying layers, such as when curved slopes develop on an old storm-beveled bedding plane.

# Sedimentary rocks: bedding

**Parallel bedding**

**Graded bedding**

**Cross bedding**
(current bedding)

ripples

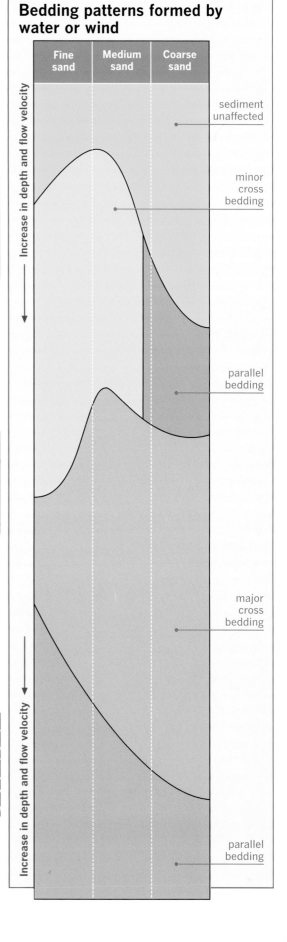

**Bedding patterns formed by water or wind**

| Fine sand | Medium sand | Coarse sand |
|---|---|---|

Increase in depth and flow velocity

sediment unaffected

minor cross bedding

parallel bedding

major cross bedding

parallel bedding

# Metamorphism

## How metamorphic rocks are formed

### Contact metamorphism
In contact metamorphism igneous rocks intrude through sedimentary rocks. Metamorphic rocks are formed at the point of contact.

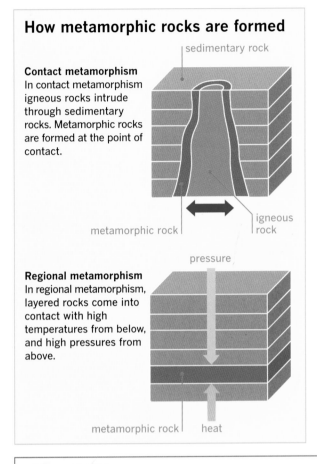

sedimentary rock

igneous rock

metamorphic rock

### Regional metamorphism
In regional metamorphism, layered rocks come into contact with high temperatures from below, and high pressures from above.

pressure

metamorphic rock | heat

## Foliation

In shale, the tiny flakes of mica are not arranged in a regular position. After the process of foliation, (i.e., alignment by directed pressure), they align to form layers, as happens in slate.

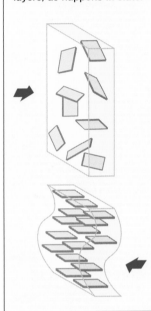

## Rocks remade

- Great heat and pressure alter igneous and sedimentary rocks into what is termed *metamorphic* ("changed shape") *rocks*.
- Metamorphic rocks' ingredients have undergone solid-state recrystallization to produce new textures or minerals.
- The greater the heat or pressure, the greater the change and the higher the grade of metamorphic rock produced.
- The best-known agents of change are contact and regional *metamorphism*.

## Contact metamorphism

- Contact or thermal metamorphism occurs when molten magma invades and bakes older rocks.
- Beyond a narrow baked zone extends a so-called contact *aureole* of altered rock.
- Regional metamorphism covers a far larger area, such as when colliding continental plates build mountains.
- Intensely altered rocks produced this way appear in the exposed roots of eroded old mountain ranges; the newer Alps and Himalayas; and in some old subduction zones.

## Six altered rocks

- Hornfels and slate are fine-grained metamorphic rocks.
- Marble and quartzite are granular metamorphic rocks.
- Schist and gneiss are examples of foliated metamorphic rocks.

## New rocks for old

Heat and pressure can transform original rocks into fine-grained granular or foliated rocks

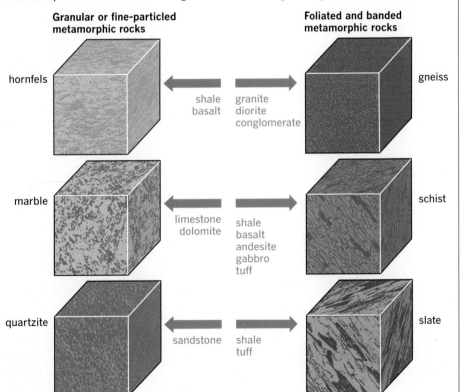

**Granular or fine-particled metamorphic rocks**

**Foliated and banded metamorphic rocks**

hornfels

shale
basalt

granite
diorite
conglomerate

gneiss

marble

limestone
dolomite

shale
basalt
andesite
gabbro
tuff

schist

quartzite

sandstone

shale
tuff

slate

© Diagram Visual Information Ltd.

### Key words

igneous rock
metamorphic
  rock
sedimentary rock

## New rocks from old

- A single type of *sedimentary* or *igneous rock* can produce a range of *metamorphic rocks*.
- Those produced depend upon the parent rock, the amounts of heat and pressure applied, and the fluids passing through the rock.
- Contact (thermal) metamorphism tends to produce rocks with fine-grained textures.
- Heat and pressure as in regional metamorphism produce coarse-grained rocks with foliated minerals—minerals flattened and aligned in bands at right angles to the stress applied.

## Progressive regional metamorphism

- The sedimentary rocks sandstone, limestone, and shale each turn into other rocks when subjected to intense heat and pressure.
- Sandstone becomes quartzite.
- Limestone becomes marble.
- Under increasing heat and pressure shale becomes first slate, then phyllite, then schist, then gneiss.
- Similarly, heat and pressure can convert certain different rocks to one type of metamorphic rock. Thus shale, basalt, and granite can all be converted into schist.

## Metamorphosis of shale

- Shale changes through four stages as it is subjected to heat and pressure. At five miles (8 km) and 3,632°F (2,000°C), the stone metamorphoses into slate. At more than 25 miles (40 km) and 14,432°F (8,000°C) the stone melts and forms molten rock.

# Progressive metamorphism

## Metamorphosis of shale

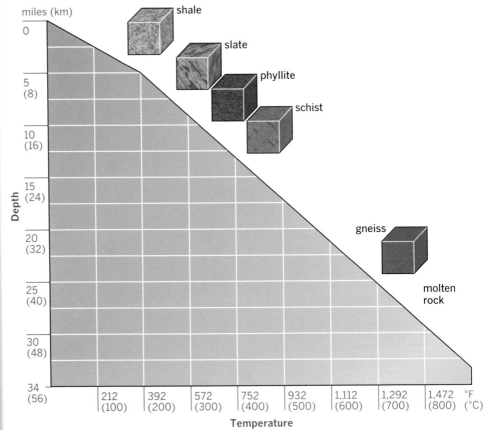

## Progressive regional metamorphism

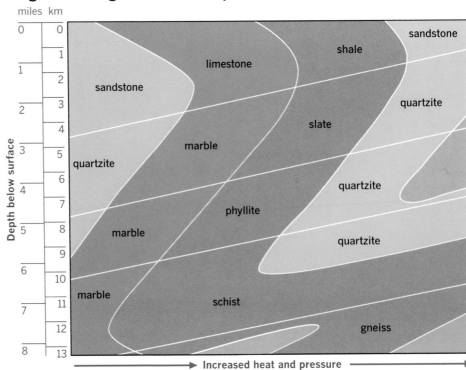

# The rock cycle

## The recycling of Earth's rock

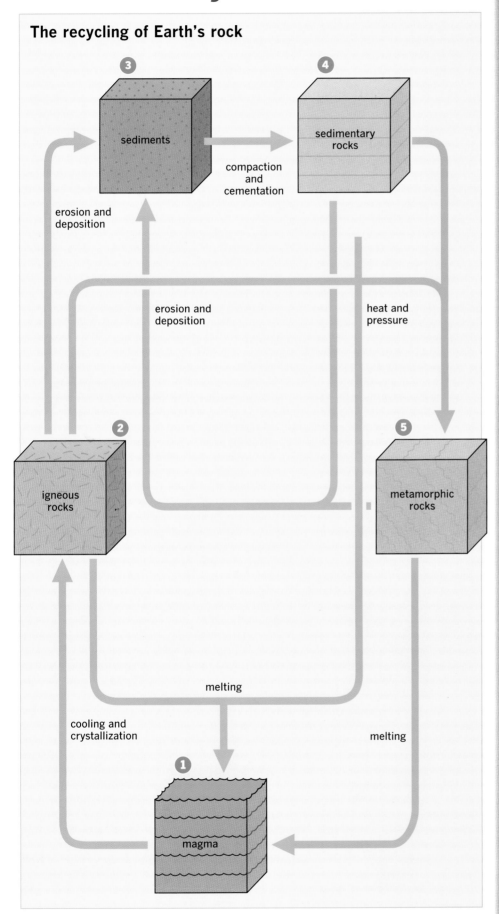

| Key words | |
|---|---|
| cementation | sediment |
| compaction | |
| lithosphere | |
| magma | |
| mantle | |

## Rocks recycled

- Internal and external forces together produce a rock cycle that constantly builds, destroys, and remakes Earth's crust.
- Internal forces are convection currents of magma (molten rock) in the mantle. Their circulation injects new, molten, rock into the crust's lithospheric plates and draws existing rocks into the mantle.
- The main external forces acting on Earth's crust are those of the weather:
- Water, ice, and wind erode rocks and redeposit them as sediments.

### ❶ Magma

- Magma within Earth's interior is the ultimate source of most rock forming Earth's lithospheric plates.

### ❷ Igneous rocks

- Magma that has risen, cooled, and crystallized forms igneous rocks.

### ❸ Sediments

- Igneous rocks subjected to erosion, transport, and deposition form layered sediments.

### ❹ Sedimentary rocks

- Sediments subjected to *compaction* and *cementation* form layers of sedimentary rock.

### ❺ Metamorphic rocks

- Sedimentary and igneous rocks subjected to great heat and pressure form metamorphic rocks.
- Metamorphic rocks that melt inside Earth's interior revert to magma.

## Key words

*continent*
*Pangaea*

### Continental fit

- In 1915 German meteorologist Alfred Wegener (1880–1930) proposed that the continents had drifted around the world.
- One clue was continental fit: South America and Africa almost fit together along the submerged rims of their continental shelves.

### A global jigsaw puzzle

- Like pieces of a gigantic jigsaw puzzle, most continents and part of Asia also seem to fit together.
- This boosted the belief that continents are fragments of a single prehistoric supercontinent, *Pangaea*.

# Continental drift: fit

### Continental fit

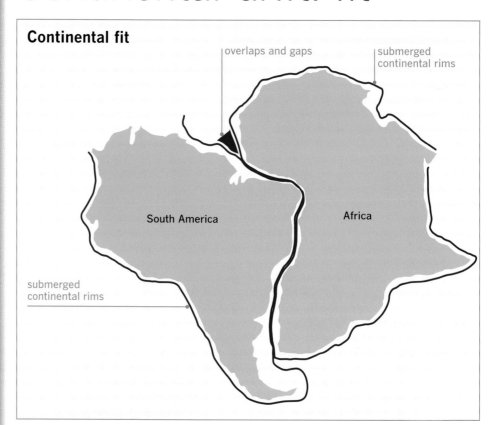

overlaps and gaps

submerged continental rims

South America

Africa

submerged continental rims

### Geographical evidence

Some continents' coasts would almost interlock if they were rearranged like pieces of a jigsaw puzzle. For instance, South America fits into Africa.

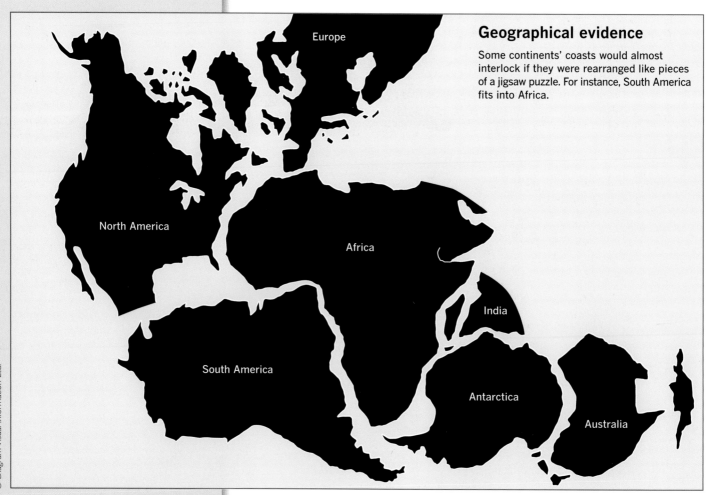

Europe

North America

Africa

India

South America

Antarctica

Australia

# Continental drift: geology

**Key words**

*craton*

## Geologic evidence

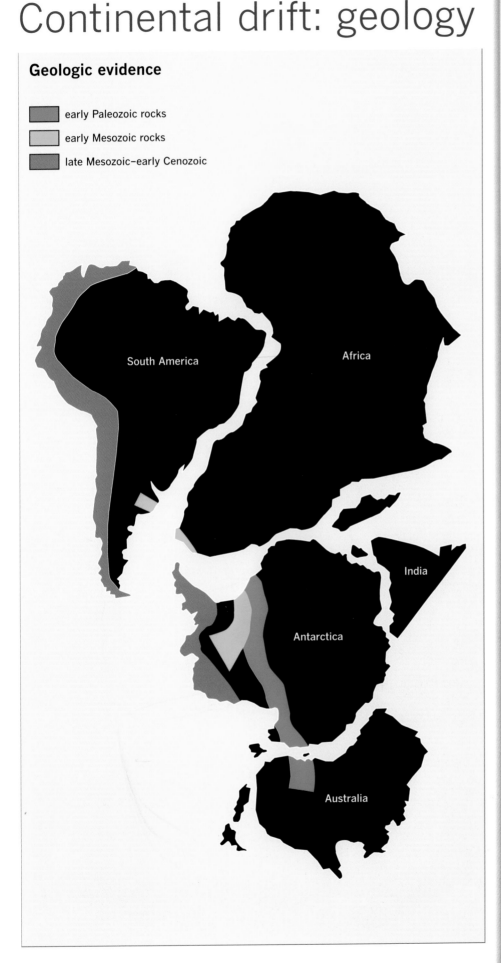

- early Paleozoic rocks
- early Mesozoic rocks
- late Mesozoic–early Cenozoic

South America

Africa

India

Antarctica

Australia

## Geologic evidence

- Three mountain-building phases successively tacked rocks onto the shields or *cratons* (ancient cores) of southern continents.
- These three old mountain zones survive as three belts of rocks of matching ages straddling the southern continents, if these are shown joined together in a particular way.
- Early Paleozoic mountains ran through Antarctica and Australia.
- Early Mesozoic mountains ran through South America, southern Africa, and Antarctica.
- Late Mesozoic and early Cenozoic mountains ran through South America and Antarctica.
- These geologic linkages suggest that southern continents were once joined before being separated by continental drift.

## Caledonian Mountains

- Geologic clues to past links between northern landmasses include rocks folded in early Paleozoic times into the Caledonian Mountains.
- The fold axes of this great chain passed through West Africa, northeast North America, Newfoundland, Ireland, Wales, Scotland, Greenland, and Norway.
- It is therefore logical to conclude that these places formed a continuous landmass before the Atlantic Ocean separated them.

## Key words

*continent*
*fossil*
*glacier*
*tillite*

## Permian land plants and animals

- Identical fossil land plants and animals appear in the southern continents, which are now widely separated by the sea.
- Examples are Glossopteris, a tree; Lystrosaurus, a synapsid; and Mesosaurus, a reptile.

## Climatic evidence

- Glacial deposits and rocks scratched by stones in moving ice show that ice covered huge tracts of the southern continents 300 million years ago. This suggests that these landmasses once lay in polar regions.
- The glacial deposits form boulder beds called *tillites*. These overlie pavements of solid rock scored by parallel scratches, or striations.

# Continental drift: biology

## Biological evidence

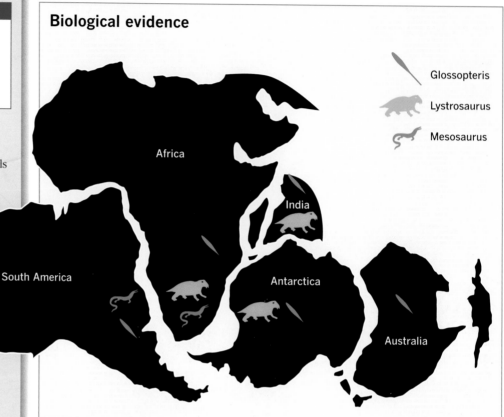

Glossopteris

Lystrosaurus

Mesosaurus

## Climatic evidence

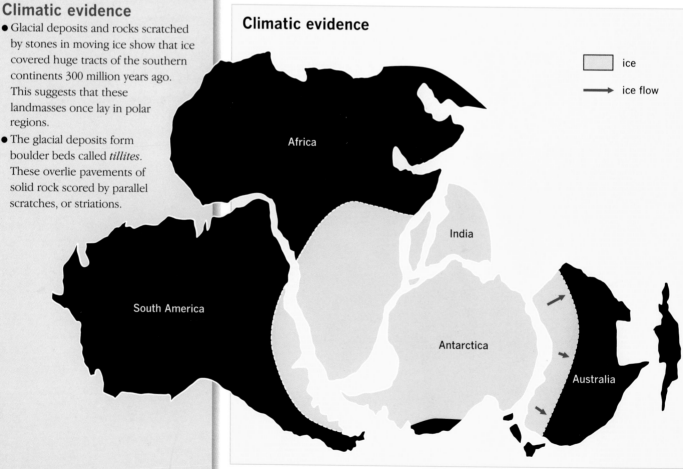

ice

ice flow

# Continental drift: polar paths

## Path of the North Pole

**Key words**

*continent*
*pole*

### North Pole

- Further proof of continental drift lies in paleomagnetic evidence.
- Some rocks contain magnetic grains aligned with the magnetic poles' positions when those rocks were formed.
- Studies of such alignments show the north magnetic pole apparently wandering across the North Pacific Ocean over the last 2,250 million years.
- Tests have shown that in fact it is the continents that have wandered.

### South Pole

- Paleomagnetic studies in different continents reveal two apparent polar wander paths, not one.
- South American rocks show a different polar wander path from that shown by the rocks of Africa.
- If both continents were joined, a single wander path appears, indicating that both continents were once joined but have since moved apart.

## Path of the South Pole

The South Pole's apparent path between 400 and 250 million years ago, if the continents were in their present positions.

The same path if the continents were joined.

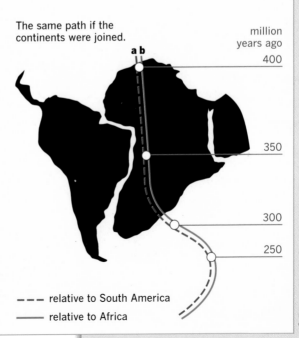

million
years ago
400
350
300
250

– – – relative to South America
——— relative to Africa

**Key words**

*continental drift*

## Three world maps

- Maps show the arrangements of landmasses at three stages in the past as envisaged in a 1915 publication by Alfred Wegener, a German meteorologist now famous as an early proponent of the theory of *continental drift*.
- Wegener showed Africa where it is today as a point of reference.
- Stippled areas indicate the presence of shallow seas.

## Late Carboniferous

- Late in the Carboniferous period there was only a single landmass, known as Pangaea (Greek for "all land"). One ocean, the Panthalassa (Greek for "all sea"), covered most of the rest of the world.

## Eocene epoch

- Wegener's map shows Pangaea beginning to break up in the Eocene epoch, early in the Cenozoic era. In fact break-up began much sooner, in the Triassic period.

## Early Pleistocene epoch

- By early in the Pleistocene epoch, the major continental landmasses of North and South America, Africa, Asia, Australia, and Antarctica are shown as having drifted apart. In fact they had virtually assumed their present positions well before this.

# Wegener's theory

**Late Carboniferous**

shallow seas

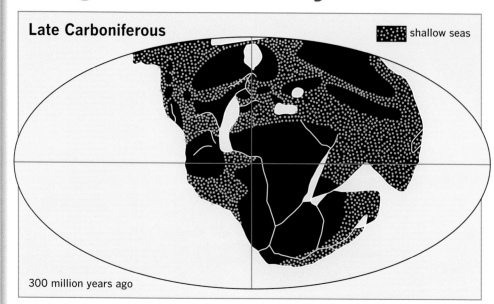

300 million years ago

**Eocene**

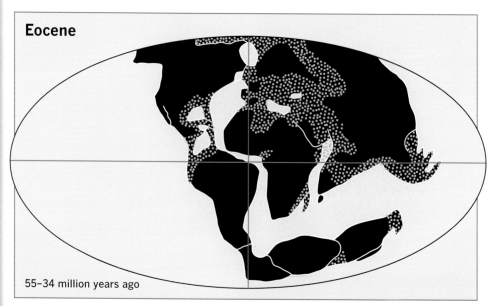

55–34 million years ago

**Early Pleistocene**

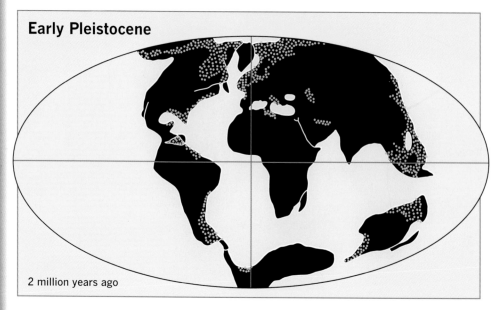

2 million years ago

# Continents: 250 million years ago

## 250 million years ago (Permian period)

— true continental rim    — modern continents

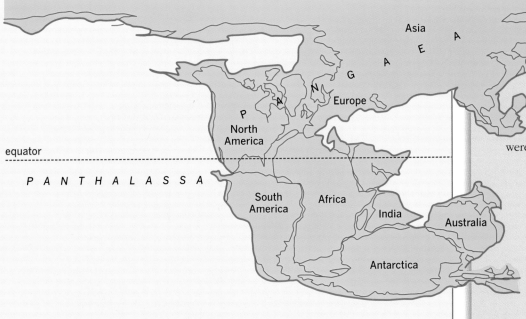

PANGAEA

Asia

Europe

North America

South America

Africa

India

Antarctica

Australia

PANTHALASSA

equator

## Land through time

- Geologists today can reconstruct the configuration of the world's landmasses by continental drift at intervals from 250 million years ago.

## Permian period

- In Permian times (about 290–248 million years ago) continents had fused into the single mighty landmass of Pangaea, surrounded by the immense Panthalassa Ocean.
- The continent of Europe collided with Siberia to form the Ural mountains, and other fusing lithospheric plates had formed most of the rest of Asia.
- Africa's (or South America's) collisions with Europe and North America pushed up Europe's Hercynian mountains and the Appalachians.

## Triassic Period

- Throughout the Triassic period (248–206 million years ago) the Pangaean landmass drifted north, but parts of Europe and North America still lay inside the tropics.
- Ice sheets that once covered the southern continents had melted, world climates ranged from warm to mild, and deserts were extensive.
- Pangaea now showed signs of breaking up. Where rising plumes of magma domed and split Earth's crust, rifts appeared in North America, Northwest Africa, and Western Europe.

## 220 million years ago (Triassic period)

Asia

PANGAEA

Europe

North America

equator

PANTHALASSA

South America

Africa

India

Australia

Antarctica

**Key words**
batholith
Gondwana
Laurasia
period

## Jurassic period

- In the Jurassic period (about 206–144 million years ago) Pangaea began breaking up into the continents we know today.
- The first split opened up what would become the North Atlantic Ocean.
- The resulting northern supercontinent is known as *Laurasia*, and the southern supercontinent as *Gondwana*.
- Rifting began separating Africa/South America from Antarctica/Australia but the Indian subcontinent was probably still stuck to East Africa.
- Mountains rose in western North America as the continent moved west and overrode an oceanic plate.
- Africa pushed against southern Europe, shedding minicontinents later tacked onto lands as far apart as Spain and the Arabian peninsula.

## Cretaceous period

- During the Cretaceous period Pangaea continued splitting into Laurasia and Gondwana, while both of these supercontinents were also fragmenting.
- Dramatic changes added land and mountains to North America. The overriding oceanic plates of western North America continued spawning a great island arc of batholiths and Andean-type volcanoes.

# Continents: 180 million years ago

## 180 million years ago (Jurassic period)

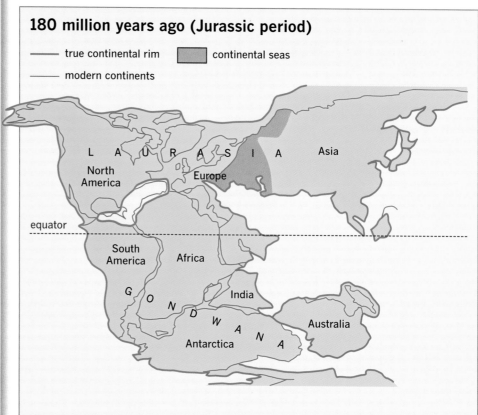

## 100 million years ago (Cretaceous period)

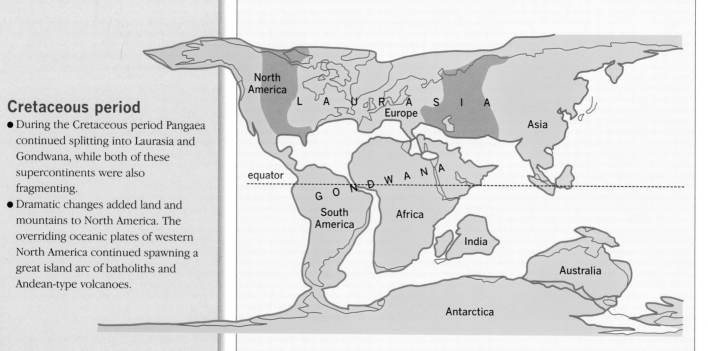

# Continents:
# 60 million years ago

**Key words**

*continent*
*epoch*
*period*

## 60 million years ago (Paleocene epoch)

— true continental rim    ▨ continental seas
— modern continents

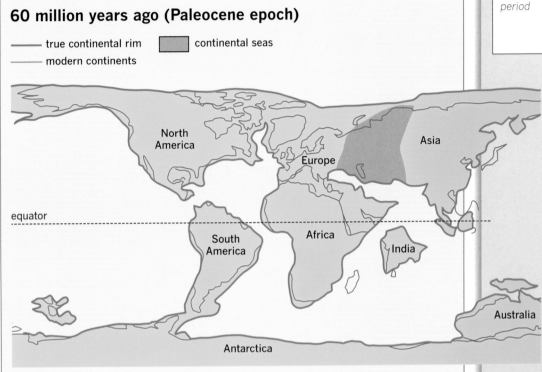

North America

Europe

Asia

equator

South America

Africa

India

Australia

Antarctica

## Today (Holocene epoch)

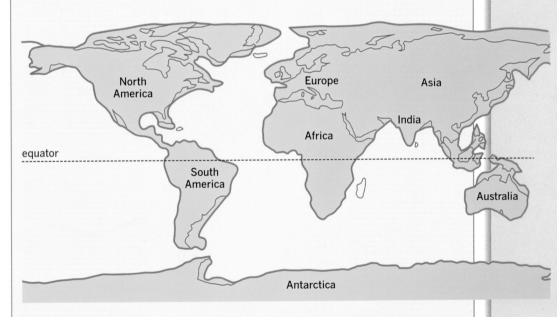

North America

Europe

Asia

India

equator

Africa

South America

Australia

Antarctica

## Paleocene epoch

- The Paleocene epoch (65–55 million years ago) saw continents taking on their present shapes and locations.
- Shallow seas that had invaded parts of North America, Africa, and Australia in the Cretaceous period now drained away.
- North America was still linked to Asia and Europe.
- South America was an island cut off from North America.
- The subcontinent of India was heading toward Asia.
- Everywhere, mammals filled ecological niches left vacant when all non-bird dinosaurs had died out at the end of the Cretaceous period.

## Holocene epoch

- In the Holocene epoch (present day), North America and Europe are separated by an ever-widening North Atlantic Ocean.
- South America and Africa are separated by an ever-widening South Atlantic Ocean.
- Greenland has been isolated from North America and Europe.
- India has impacted with Asia creating the vast Himalayan mountain range.
- North and South America have joined.
- Australia has separated from Antarctica and migrated northward.

**Key words**

*asthenosphere*
*plate tectonics*

## Lithospheric plate movement

● Earth's lithospheric plates float on the *asthenosphere* (the semifluid upper mantle). Their movement across Earth's surface is believed to be driven by convection currents in the mantle.

# Lithospheric plates

## How lithospheric plates are moving

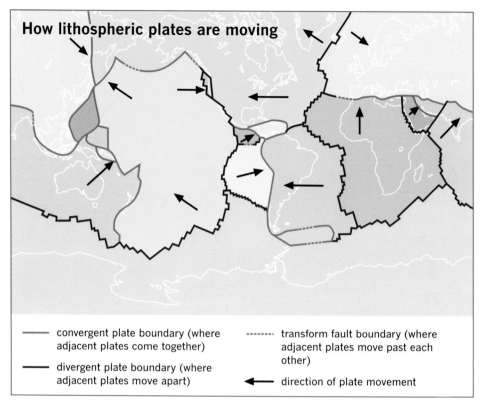

—— convergent plate boundary (where adjacent plates come together)

—— divergent plate boundary (where adjacent plates move apart)

------- transform fault boundary (where adjacent plates move past each other)

◄—— direction of plate movement

## Lithospheric plate names

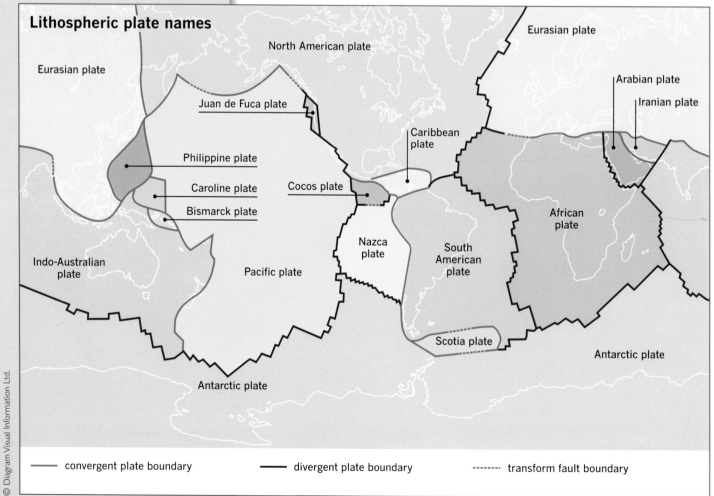

Eurasian plate

North American plate

Eurasian plate

Arabian plate

Iranian plate

Juan de Fuca plate

Caribbean plate

Philippine plate

Cocos plate

Caroline plate

Bismarck plate

African plate

Indo-Australian plate

Pacific plate

Nazca plate

South American plate

Scotia plate

Antarctic plate

Antarctic plate

—— convergent plate boundary

—— divergent plate boundary

------- transform fault boundary

# Plate tectonics

## Key words

*asthenosphere*
*lithosphere*
*plate tectonics*

**Spreading ridge**
Oceanic crust of plates **a** and **b** is spreading apart allowing magma from the mantle to escape onto the Earth's surface to form constructive margins.

**Subduction zone**
At the convergence of an oceanic crustal plate (**b**) and a continental crustal plate (**c**) an oceanic trench creates a destructive margin.

**Tectonic plates**

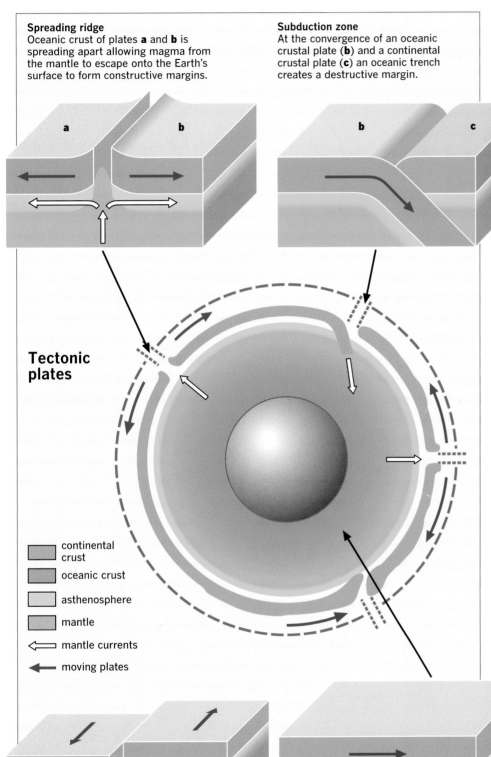

continental crust

oceanic crust

asthenosphere

mantle

⟵ mantle currents

⟵ moving plates

**Conservative margin**
Where two lithospheric plates slide past each other lithosphere is neither made nor lost.

**Convection within the mantle**
The directions of the oceanic and continental plates follow the direction of the upper movements of magma within the mantle.

## Earth's shifting surface

- *Plate tectonics* is the study of Earth's restless jigsaw of abutting, diverging, and colliding lithospheric plates.
- A section through Earth reveals the likely mechanisms that move lithospheric plates around, and balance the creation of new crust with the destruction of old crust drawn down into the mantle.

## Convection currents

- Each plate involves a slab of oceanic crust, continental crust, or both, coupled to a slab of rigid upper mantle. Collectively these plates make up the *lithosphere*.
- This rides upon the *asthenosphere*, a dense, plastic layer of the mantle.
- Heat rising through this layer from Earth's molten core and lower mantle seemingly produces convection currents that drive the plates above.

## Plate margins

- Plate movements produce several kinds of plate margins. Constructive margins are suboceanic spreading ridges where new lithosphere is formed between two separating oceanic plates.
- Oceanic trenches mark destructive margins—subduction zones where oceanic plates colliding with continental plates are pushed down below these.
- At conservative margins, plates slide past each other and lithosphere is neither made nor lost.
- At active margins oceanic and continental plate collisions spark off volcanoes and earthquakes.
- Passive margins are tectonically quiet boundaries between continental and oceanic crust.

# Crust and lithosphere

## Key words

*asthenosphere*
*lithosphere*
*mantle*

## Earth in section

- A segment cut through Earth from crust to core (below) would show the lithosphere then asthenosphere and lower mantle, followed by the dense molten outer core, then the inner core—immensely hot but kept solid by tremendous pressure from above.

## Lithosphere

- A section through the upper Earth shows thicknesses of oceanic crust, continental crust, and rigid upper mantle—layers that form the lithosphere.
- Below this lies a dense, plastic layer of the mantle—the asthenosphere.
- The relatively lightweight rocks of oceanic and continental crust float upon the mantle.

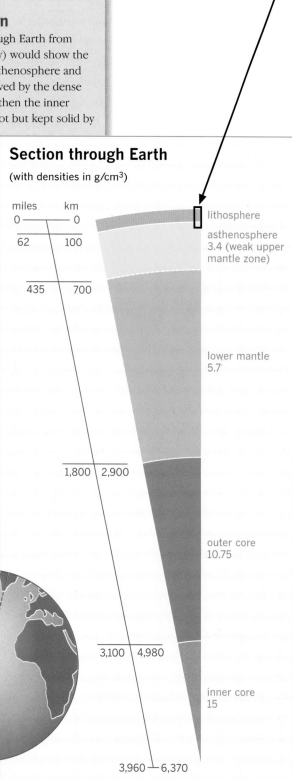

### Section through Earth

(with densities in g/cm³)

| miles | km |
|-------|------|
| 0 | 0 |
| 62 | 100 |
| 435 | 700 |
| 1,800 | 2,900 |
| 3,100 | 4,980 |
| 3,960 | 6,370 |

lithosphere

asthenosphere 3.4 (weak upper mantle zone)

lower mantle 5.7

outer core 10.75

inner core 15

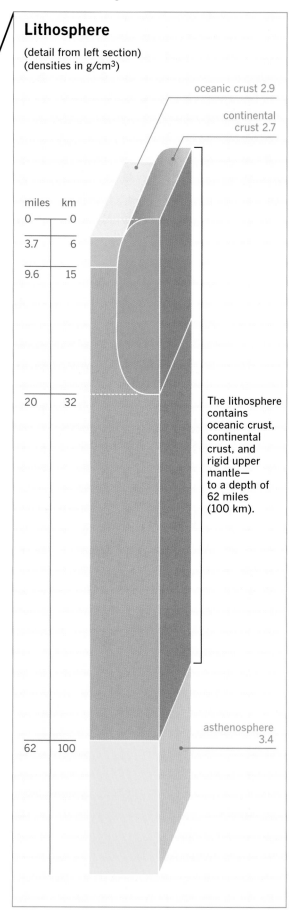

## Lithosphere

(detail from left section)
(densities in g/cm³)

oceanic crust 2.9

continental crust 2.7

| miles | km |
|-------|-----|
| 0 | 0 |
| 3.7 | 6 |
| 9.6 | 15 |
| 20 | 32 |
| 62 | 100 |

asthenosphere 3.4

The lithosphere contains oceanic crust, continental crust, and rigid upper mantle—to a depth of 62 miles (100 km).

# Oceanic crust

## Deep ocean sediments

■ silica    □ carbonates    ▨ sand and mud

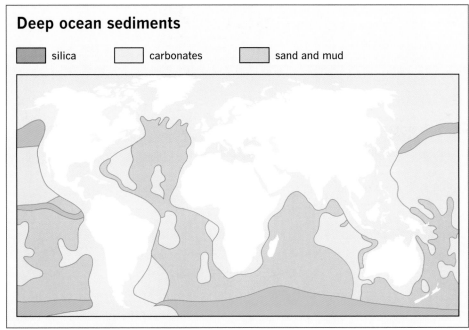

**Key words**

| | |
|---|---|
| basalt | silica |
| gabbro | sima |
| mantle | spreading ridge |
| oceanic crust | |
| sediment | |

## Oceanic crust
- Most oceanic crust is less than six miles (about 10 km) thick.
- Its rocks are richer in aluminum and calcium than the mantle, and their high silica and magnesium content has earned oceanic crust the name of *sima*.
- Oceanic crust has three layers: sediments overlying two layers of igneous rocks, the lower resting on the rigid upper mantle.

## Sediments
- Muds, sands, and other debris washed off continents lie thickly on continental shelves and nearby ocean floor.
- The open ocean's bed oozes rich in silica and carbonates (largely the remains of dead microorganisms from surface waters), clays, and, in places, nodules containing substances that include manganese.

## Basalt
- The second layer of oceanic crust is chiefly basalt, derived from the mantle and released at spreading ridges as rounded lumps of pillow lava.
- Analysis of the composition of basalt shows that it consists largely of the elements silicon and aluminum.

## Gabbro
- The third and lowest layer of oceanic crust is largely made of gabbro, a coarse-grained rock equivalent to the fine-grained basalt of the second layer.

## Rigid mantle
- Below and coupled to the bottom layer of the oceanic crust is the rigid upper mantle. This may consist largely of the dense igneous rock peridotite.

## Section through oceanic crust

## Composition of basalt

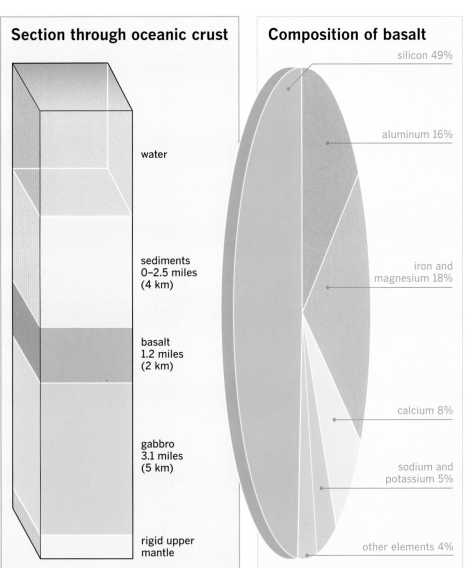

water

sediments
0–2.5 miles
(4 km)

basalt
1.2 miles
(2 km)

gabbro
3.1 miles
(5 km)

rigid upper
mantle

silicon 49%

aluminum 16%

iron and
magnesium 18%

calcium 8%

sodium and
potassium 5%

other elements 4%

**Key words**

*hot spot*
*seamount*
*volcano*

## The Hawaiian Islands and Emperor seamount chain

- For at least 70 million years a *hot spot* has been creating islands in the North Pacific, beginning with the construction of the Emperor chain (**a**).
- About 25 million years ago the lithospheric plate apparently changed direction (**b**) and construction of the Hawaiian Islands chain began (**c**).
- Today Hawaii is a volcanically active island, while to its southeast Loihi has yet to rise above sea level. As the Pacific lithospheric plate moves west it subsides so that islands are submerged and become seamounts.

## Volcanic island formation

**1** The lithospheric plate passes over a hot spot deep in the mantle.

**2** Magma finds its way up through the seafloor and erupts as a volcano.

**3** The active volcano builds a seamount. The lithospheric plate continues to move and the seamount breaks the surface of the sea to become an island.

**4** The island moves away from the hot spot with the lithospheric plate, and its volcanic activity ceases. Magma forces its way through the seabed again and begins to build another seamount. Over millions of years, a chain of islands is built.

# Hawaiian Islands

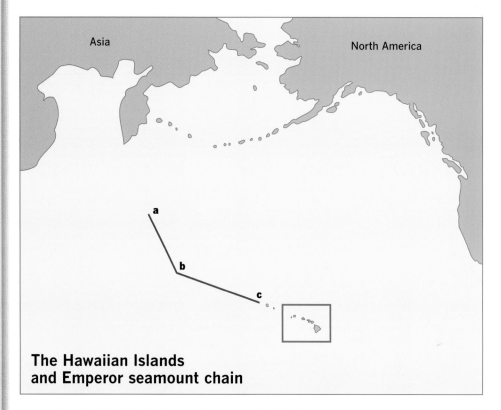

### The Hawaiian Islands and Emperor seamount chain

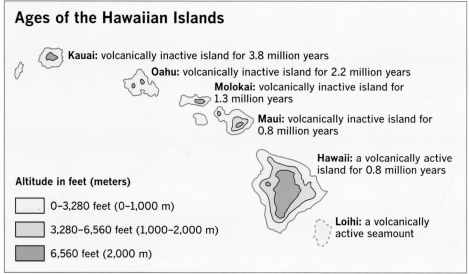

### Ages of the Hawaiian Islands

**Kauai:** volcanically inactive island for 3.8 million years

**Oahu:** volcanically inactive island for 2.2 million years

**Molokai:** volcanically inactive island for 1.3 million years

**Maui:** volcanically inactive island for 0.8 million years

**Hawaii:** a volcanically active island for 0.8 million years

**Loihi:** a volcanically active seamount

**Altitude in feet (meters)**

0–3,280 feet (0–1,000 m)

3,280–6,560 feet (1,000–2,000 m)

6,560 feet (2,000 m)

## Volcanic island formation

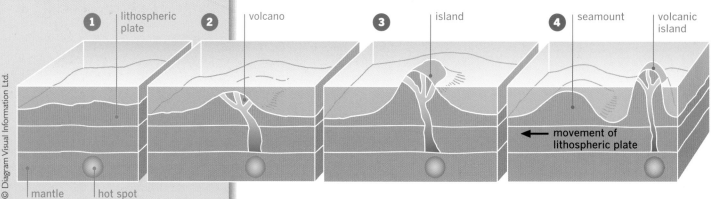

**1** lithospheric plate

**2** volcano

**3** island

**4** seamount / volcanic island

movement of lithospheric plate

mantle | hot spot

# Dating the seafloor

**Key words**

basalt
magnetometer
ocean

## Magnetic reversals

↗ normal polarity
↙ reversed polarity

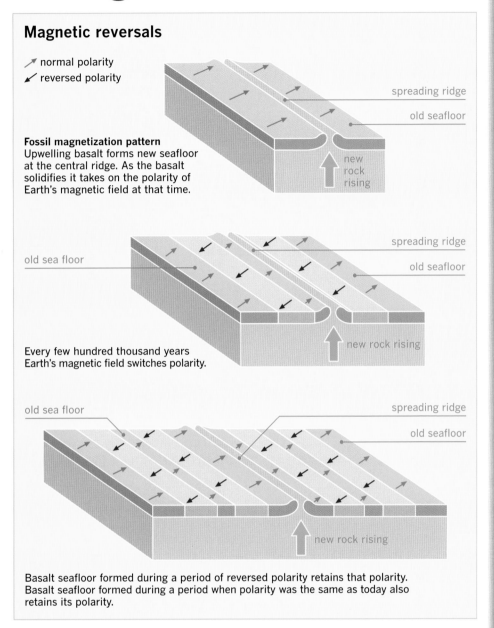

**Fossil magnetization pattern**
Upwelling basalt forms new seafloor at the central ridge. As the basalt solidifies it takes on the polarity of Earth's magnetic field at that time.

Every few hundred thousand years Earth's magnetic field switches polarity.

Basalt seafloor formed during a period of reversed polarity retains that polarity. Basalt seafloor formed during a period when polarity was the same as today also retains its polarity.

## Banded polarity

upwelling basalt    spreading ridge

million years ago | 4 | 3 | 2 | 1 | 0 | 0 | 1 | 2 | 3 | 4 |

Bands of reversed and normal polarity in the seafloor record polarity reversals over millions of years, and indicate rates of seafloor spread.

## Striped seafloor

- Great submarine ridges run across the floors of oceans.
- Magnetometer surveys across these ridges reveal patterns of magnetized striping in the basalt rock.

## Fossil magnetization

- Magnetized striping in seabed rocks preserves a record of past changes in Earth's magnetic field.
- Basalt rocks flanking an oceanic ridge contain particles aligned with Earth's "normal" geomagnetic field, the field that operates today. Thus the basalt must have solidified when Earth's magnetic field was as it is now.
- On each side of the oceanic ridge lies a band of rocks containing particles with a reversed magnetic alignment. This matching pair of bands must have formed when Earth's geomagnetic field had switched around.
- Beyond this pair of rock bands comes a succession of more matched pairs, with alternating "normal" and "reversed" polarity.

## Dating the ocean floor

- Magnetically striped seabed rocks show that new ocean floor appears at spreading ridges, then moves away from these on either side. So the oldest seafloor is that furthest from a spreading ridge.
- By dating reversals of Earth's magnetic field, geophysicists have shown that virtually no ocean floor is more than 2,000 million years old.

**Key words**

*asthenosphere*
*mantle*
*spreading ridge*

## New seafloor

- New seafloor forms where currents rising in the mantle hit the crust above.
- This helps to lift and split vast chunks of crust, but the resulting gaps are continuously plugged by molten rock originating in the mantle.
- Molten rock sticking to the edges of such rifts form vast underwater mountain chains, the *spreading ridges*.

## A ridge is born

- First, molten rock wells up from the upper mantle region called the asthenosphere.
- The upwelling molten mass pushes up a ridge in the oceanic crust.
- Gravity pulls the ridge flanks sideways and downwards, and the resulting tension opens two main cracks along the ridge.
- Between these cracks, the ridge's middle sinks to form a rift valley.
- Molten rock wells up through the main and lesser cracks, then cools and hardens to produce new ocean floor.
- As upwelling continues, the rifting is repeated. In time, rows of parallel ridges creep outwards from their starting point, gradually sinking to form the ocean's abyssal plains.

## Ridge features

- The main feature of a spreading ridge is its central rift valley.
- Another feature is that the ridge consists of short, straight, offset sections.
- Each section is offset at both ends from its neighbors by a transform fault that runs across the ridge.
- A spreading ridge cannot bend, but offsetting by transform faults allows a change in ridge direction.

# Spreading ridges

## Evolution of a spreading ridge

gabbroic lower crust, from lighter minerals solidifying as lower ocean crust

peridotite upper mantle, formed from dense minerals

asthenosphere (part-melted)

**1**

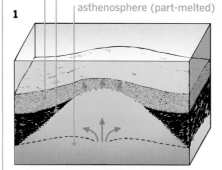

A rising mantle current partly melts and pushes up the oceanic crust above.

basalt and dolerite: fine-grained gabbroic rocks formed by fast cooling

**2**

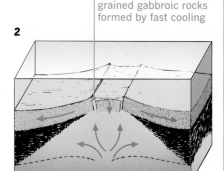

The bulging plate splits, and a central block subsides. Molten rock rises through cracks at the block's rims.

**3**

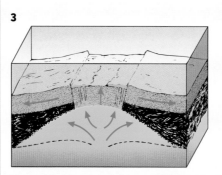

More molten rock plugs gaps left as tension pulls old crust apart.

**4**

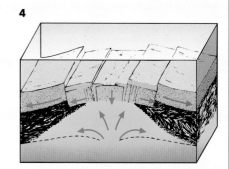

As new crustal blocks subside, fresh cracks appear. The process is repeated.

## Spreading ridge features

transform fault    central rift    spreading ridge

mantle    oceanic crust    rising current

# Continental crust

**Key words**

*craton*
*linear mobile belt*
*platform*
*shield*
*sial*

## Structural components of North America

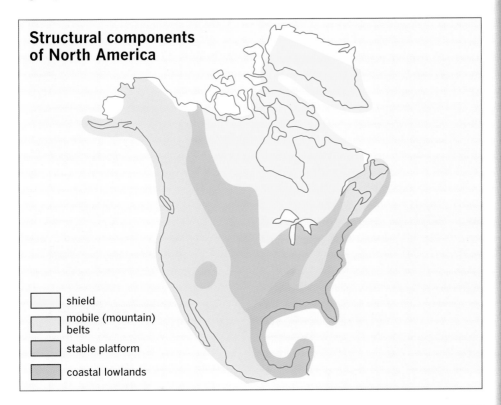

- shield
- mobile (mountain) belts
- stable platform
- coastal lowlands

## Elements in granite

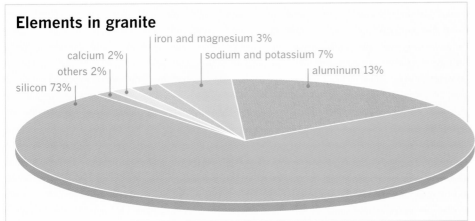

silicon 73%
others 2%
calcium 2%
iron and magnesium 3%
sodium and potassium 7%
aluminum 13%

## Continents

- Continents are the great landmasses above the level of the ocean basins.
- Continental crust is thicker, less dense, and more complex than oceanic crust.
- Continental crust is on average 20 miles (33 km) thick.
- The top nine miles (15 km) of crust consist of sedimentary, igneous, and metamorphic rocks rich in silicon and aluminum, which is why continental crust is often known as *sial*.
- A major constituent of continental crust is the igneous rock granite.
- The lower crust has denser igneous and metamorphic rocks.

## Structural components

- *Shields* are stable slabs—outcrops of ancient masses of crystalline rocks.
- *Platforms* are eroded shields overlain by younger rocks.
- *Cratons* are shields plus platforms.
- *Linear mobile belts* are belts of rock formed from island arcs, submarine plateaus, etc., swept up against preexisting microcontinents and forming lines of mountains.
- Sedimentary basins are depressions filled with sedimentary rocks.

## East–West section of the USA

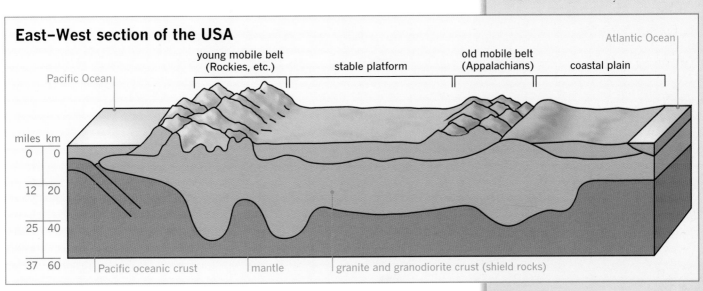

young mobile belt (Rockies, etc.)
stable platform
old mobile belt (Appalachians)
coastal plain
Atlantic Ocean
Pacific Ocean

| miles | km |
|---|---|
| 0 | 0 |
| 12 | 20 |
| 25 | 40 |
| 37 | 60 |

Pacific oceanic crust
mantle
granite and granodiorite crust (shield rocks)

# Continent growth

© Diagram Visual Information Ltd.

## Subduction and accretion

- Where a continental plate overrides an oceanic plate, some oceanic crust is subducted into the mantle but land is also tacked onto the continent.
- A volcanic island arc, offshore sediment, pieces of oceanic crust, and scraps of foreign continents may all be swept against the continent and welded on as mountains.
- Meanwhile, light, subducted rocks melting in the mantle may rise as a chain of continental volcanoes.
- Most of mountainous western North America consists of "add-ons"—suspect terrains—mighty slabs of alien rock that rotated and migrated north along the continent's western edge.

## Colliding continents

- New continental land is also formed where two continents collide.
- As an ocean shrinks between two continents, sedimentary rock layers overlying intervening oceanic crust are buckled into fold mountains that help to weld both continents together.
- Continental collision ends a so-called *Wilson cycle*.

## Modern continents

- All modern continents began as *microcontinents*—islands of old crystalline rock—to which younger rocks were later added.

## Oceanic plate subduction

**1**
Island arc and continent with offshore sediments advance on two plates, one subducting below the other.

**2**
Collision squeezes and rucks up sediments between island-arc volcanoes and a continent, producing a cordilleran mountain chain such as the Andes.

**3**
The old subduction zone gradually disappears.

**4**
The new subduction zone is formed.

## Colliding continents

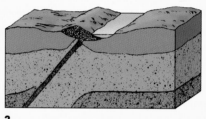

**1**
Continents advance on separate plates.

**2**
Collision rucks up marginal sediments and the ocean shrinks.

**3**
The oceanic crust between is subducted and the two continents collide, forming mountain ranges like the Alps or the Himalayas.

## Modern continents as the result of past accretions

oldest rocks     younger rocks     youngest rocks

# Isostasy

### Key words

*continental rim*
*crust*
*erosion*
*isostasy*

## Rival theories of how continents float on denser material

Densities are calculated in g/cm³.

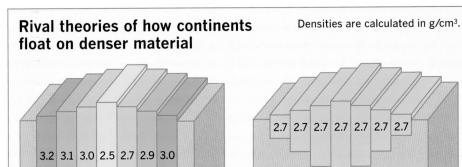

J.H. Pratt's now abandoned theory: blocks of different densities produce mountains of different heights.

G.B. Airy's now accepted theory: mountain heights vary with the depth (not density) of continental crust.

## Isostatic equilibrium

Densities are calculated in g/cm³.

**Continent before erosion**

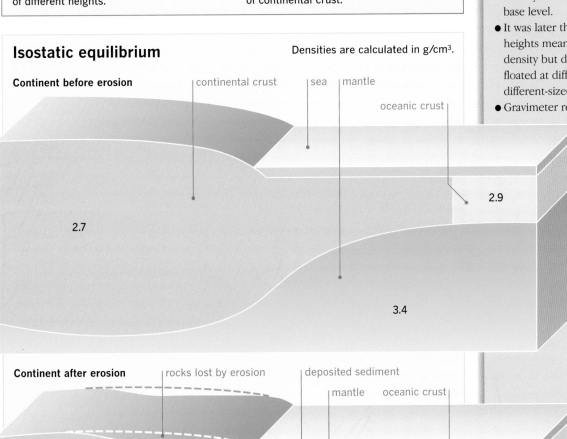

continental crust    sea    mantle

oceanic crust

2.9

2.7

3.4

**Continent after erosion**

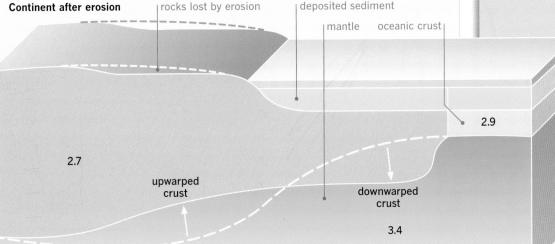

rocks lost by erosion    deposited sediment

mantle    oceanic crust

2.9

2.7

upwarped crust    downwarped crust

3.4

## Isostasy

- *Isostasy* is the state of balance of Earth's crust floating on the denser material of the mantle.
- In the nineteenth century it was argued that high and low mountains were blocks of rocks of different density floating above the same base level.
- It was later thought that different heights meant blocks had the same density but different thicknesses and floated at different depths (much like different-sized icebergs in the sea).
- Gravimeter readings showing local gravity anomalies confirm this view.

## Isostatic equilibrium

- Erosion and deposition can locally alter isostatic balance and cause warping—the gentle rise or fall of crust.
- Erosion that wears away a mountain mass reduces the weight of crust pressing on the underlying mantle, so the land surface bobs up.
- Deposition of eroded sediment can depress submerged parts of a continental rim.
- These upwarping and downwarping movements restore isostatic equilibrium.

## Key words

*batholith*
*lode*
*magma*
*ore*

## Ores and magma

- *Ores* are rocks rich enough in metals or certain other elements to be worth mining.
- Many ores originate where minerals crystallize in or near a cooling mass of molten magma.

## Ores and granite

- Ores also form where a molten granite batholith injects hot, mineral-rich fluids under pressure into rocks.
- As the fluids cool, their crystallizing minerals fill cracks, producing veins or groups of veins called lodes. Hot mineral-rich solutions losing heat and pressure as they filter out of granite replace nearby rocks with a sequence of tin, copper, lead, zinc, iron, gold, and mercury.

## Ores and sediments

- Ores of certain substances occur where these become concentrated in sediments and sedimentary rock.
- Iron eroded from an iron-rich mass of igneous rock may be redeposited as a precipitate below the sea.
- In the tropics, weathering breaks down rocks rich in aluminum silicate to yield bauxite, the raw material for aluminum.
- Percolating groundwater can deposit rich copper ores.
- Rivers and coastal waves sort particles of heavy minerals, dumping them on stream beds and beaches. Such placer deposits provide much of the world's tin; some gold and platinum; and diamonds and other gemstones.
- Useful nonmetallic sedimentary rocks and minerals include beds of gypsum, salt, and limestone.

# Ore

## Magma and ores

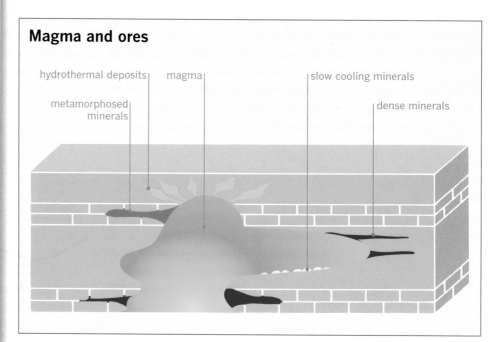

hydrothermal deposits | magma | slow cooling minerals

metamorphosed minerals | dense minerals

## Mineralized zones around granite

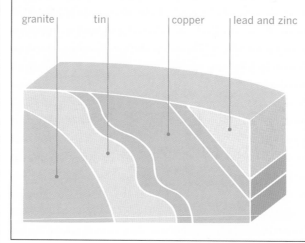

granite | tin | copper | lead and zinc

**Granite and ores**
Minerals derived from molten granite cool and crystallize at different temperatures in different zones.

## Exposure of iron

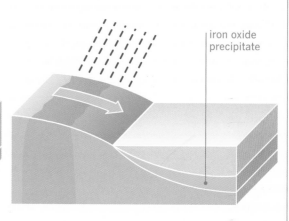

mountain | sea | iron oxide precipitate

iron-rich pluton

# Coal

## Stages of coal development

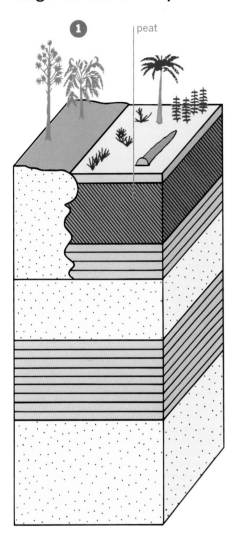

peat

Trees and vegetation die and rot in a swamp. The rotting remains form peat.

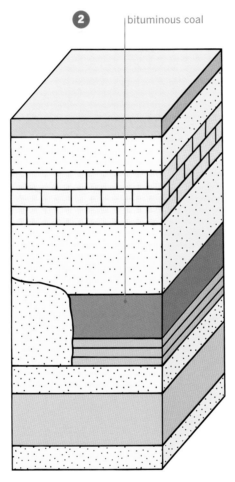

bituminous coal

Pressure and heat produced by the weight of rocks and soil above turn peat into bituminous coal.

| | water |
| | shale |
| | sandstone |
| | chalk |

### Key words

*anthracite*
*coal*
*peat*

## Products of pressure

● Intensifying pressure in the ground compacts buried vegetation and transforms it into peat.
● In time the peat becomes brown coal, then bituminous coal, and finally *anthracite*, a very hard form of coal.

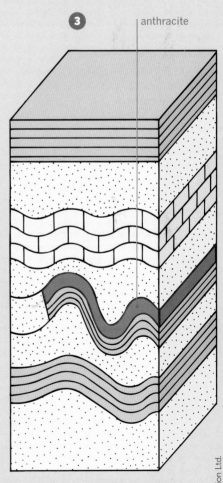

anthracite

Subsequent geologic forces distort the layer of bituminous coal into a tightly packed mass of anthracite.

## Key words

*anticline*
*fault*
*salt dome*
*unconformity*

## Formation of hydrocarbons

- Dead organisms sink to the seabed and partially decay (**a**). They are covered with sediment which in time, becomes rock (**b**).
- Under the effects of pressure and heat, bacterial action produces hydrocarbons, in the form of both gas and oil (**c**). These lie above a layer of water, and all three lie between particles of rock.

## Where oil and gas occur

- Movements of hydrocarbons through permeable rocks ultimately cause the gas and oil to be trapped in spaces between layers of rock.
- There are four main geological situations in which gas and oil are trapped: *anticlines*, *salt domes*, *faults*, and *unconformities*.
- An anticline is a curved fold structure: if formed by impermeable rock, it forms a simple cap that can trap oil and gas.
- A salt dome is the result of the vertical intrusion of a thick deposit of evaporite minerals into surrounding rock. This intrusion tends to form anticlines in the rock layers above.
- A fault is a crack in the crust that occurs due to differential movement within the crust. A fault can create a cavity beneath impermeable rock layers in which oil may accumulate.
- An unconformity represents a gap in the chronological sequence of rock layers.

## Recoverable oil

**Estimated percentage shares of world reserves (2003)**

| | |
|---|---|
| Middle East | 65.32 |
| Africa | 9.96 |
| Eastern Europe and CIS | 8.47 |
| Central and South America | 7.15 |
| North America | 3.95 |
| Asia and Australasia | 3.59 |
| Western Europe | 1.56 |

# Oil and gas

## Formation of hydrocarbons

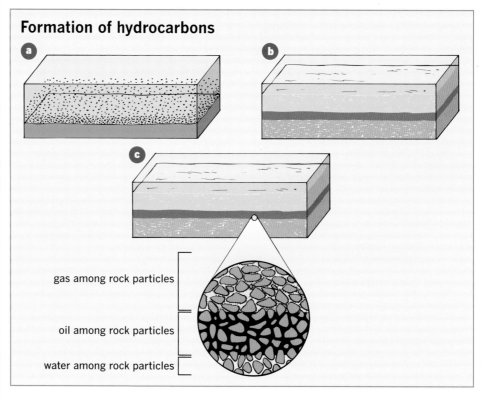

gas among rock particles

oil among rock particles

water among rock particles

## Where oil and gas occur

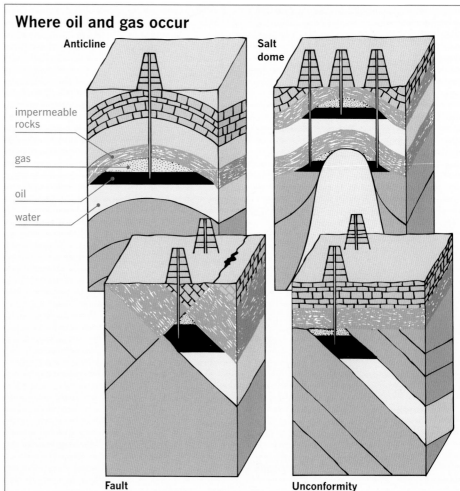

Anticline

Salt dome

impermeable rocks

gas

oil

water

Fault

Unconformity

# Atmosphere: structure

© Diagram Visual Information Ltd.

## Structure of the atmosphere

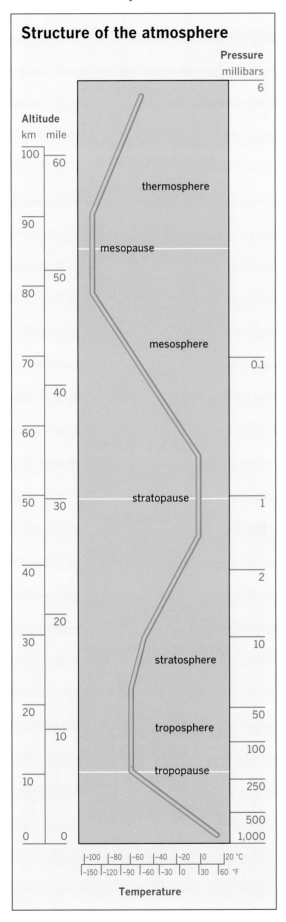

## Composition of the atmosphere

**Major components**

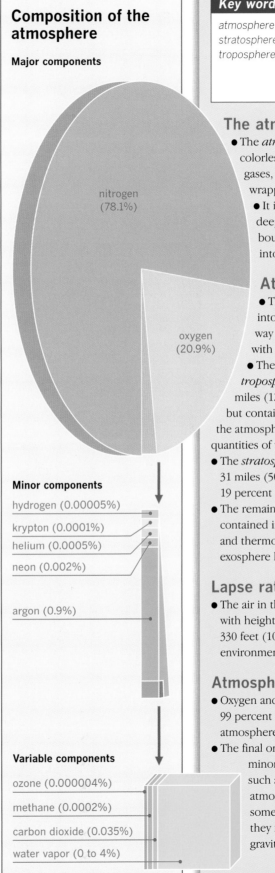

## The atmosphere
- The *atmosphere* is a blanket of colorless, odorless, and tasteless gases, water, and fine dust wrapped around Earth.
- It is about 430 miles (700 km) deep. It has no upper boundary and simply fades into space as it gets thinner.

## Atmospheric layers
- The atmosphere is divided into layers according to the way its temperature changes with height.
- The lowest layer, the *troposphere*, extends only seven miles (12 km) above the ground but contains more than 75 percent of the atmosphere's gas, and vast quantities of water and dust.
- The *stratosphere* extends up to 31 miles (50 km) and contains 19 percent of the atmosphere's gas.
- The remaining six percent of the gas is contained in the higher mesosphere and thermosphere layers, and the final exosphere layer.

## Lapse rate
- The air in the troposphere gets colder with height, losing 1°F (0.6°C) every 330 feet (100 m). This is known as its environmental lapse rate.

## Atmospheric composition
- Oxygen and nitrogen make up 99 percent of the gas in the atmosphere.
- The final one percent is composed of minor and variable components, such as hydrogen and neon. The atmosphere constantly loses some of these lighter gases as they float away from Earth's gravity.

## Key words

atmosphere
exosphere
ionosphere
mesosphere
stratosphere

thermosphere
troposphere

## Proportion of gases

- The proportion of gases in each layer of the atmosphere changes with height.
- Nitrogen and, to a lesser extent, oxygen, comprise most of the gases in the troposphere, stratosphere, *mesosphere*, and *thermosphere*, while the *exosphere* is composed of hydrogen and helium.

## The ionosphere

- The atmosphere comprises five different layers: the troposphere at the bottom, rising through the stratosphere, mesosphere, and thermosphere to the exosphere at the top.
- The *ionosphere* is a layer between 62 and 190 miles (100–300 km) within the thermosphere, where the density of ionized or electrically charged particles is very high. Some scientists consider the thermosphere and ionosphere to be identical.
- The ultraviolet rays and X-rays that flow from the Sun ionize the gas particles in the ionosphere.

## Total air mass

- Half the total air mass of the atmosphere is located in its first 3.5 miles (5.5 km). Ninety-nine percent lies below 20 miles (32 km), while only one percent is more than 20 miles (32 km) above the surface.

# Atmosphere: layers

## Relative proportions of gases in four layers

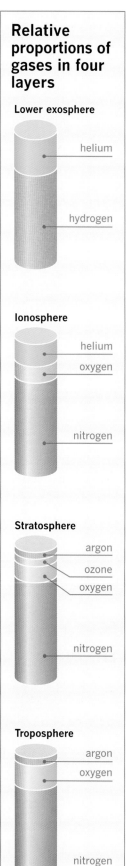

Lower exosphere

helium

hydrogen

Ionosphere

helium
oxygen

nitrogen

Stratosphere

argon
ozone
oxygen

nitrogen

Troposphere

argon
oxygen

nitrogen

## Atmospheric layers

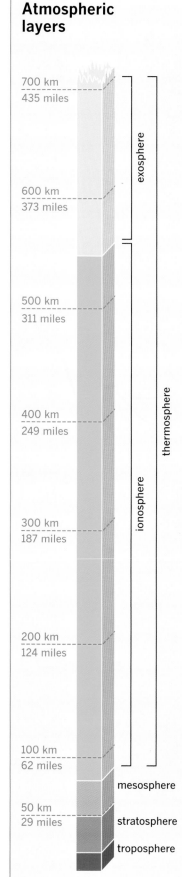

700 km
435 miles

600 km
373 miles

exosphere

500 km
311 miles

400 km
249 miles

thermosphere

300 km
187 miles

ionosphere

200 km
124 miles

100 km
62 miles

mesosphere

50 km
29 miles

stratosphere

troposphere

## Proportion of total air mass at different levels

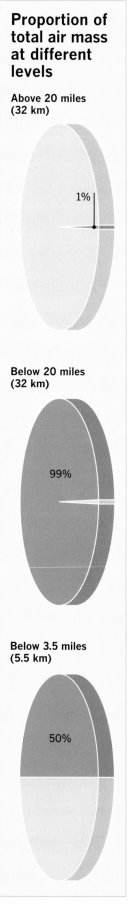

Above 20 miles
(32 km)

1%

Below 20 miles
(32 km)

99%

Below 3.5 miles
(5.5 km)

50%

# Radio waves

**Key words**

*radio wave*

## Shortwaves
present day and night

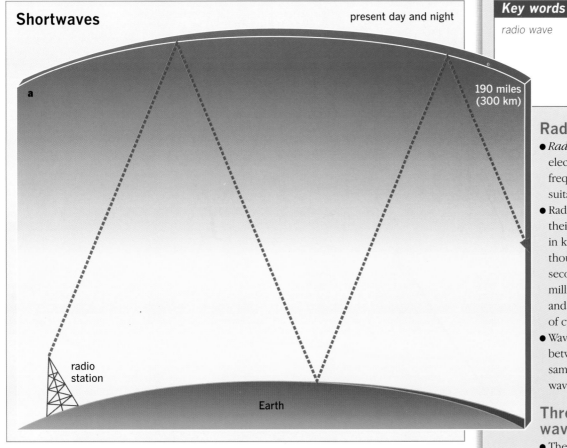

a

190 miles
(300 km)

radio station

Earth

## Mediumwaves
present by day and some hours after sunset

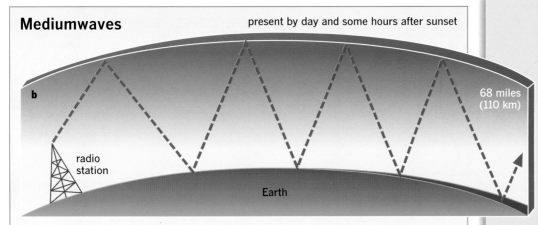

b

68 miles
(110 km)

radio station

Earth

## Longwaves
present by day

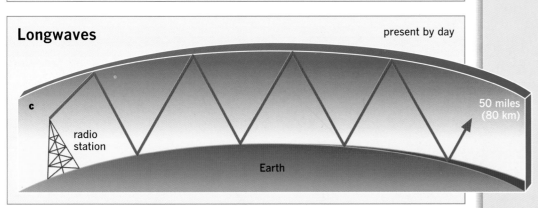

c

50 miles
(80 km)

radio station

Earth

**a–c** represent ionized layers reflecting radio waves

## Radio waves

- *Radio waves* are a range of electromagnetic waves with a frequency or wavelength suitable for communication.
- Radio waves are identified by their frequencies, expressed in kilohertz (kHz) or thousands of cycles per second; megahertz (MHz), millions of cycles per second; and gigahertz (GHz), billions of cycles per second.
- Wavelength is the distance between two points at the same phase in consecutive waves.

## Three main radio waves

- The three main types of radio wave are shortwaves, with a relatively high frequency, mediumwaves, and longwaves, with a relatively low frequency.
- Short waves have a frequency of 3–30 MHz and a wavelength of between 33–330 feet (10–100 m). They are reflected back to Earth from the top of the ionosphere, about 190 miles (300 km) up.
- Mediumwaves have a frequency of 300–3,000 kHz and a wavelength of 330 feet to 3,300 feet (100 m–1 km). They are reflected back to Earth at about 68 miles (110 km) up in the ionosphere.
- Longwaves have a frequency of 30–300 kHz and a wavelength of greater than 6.2 miles (10 km). They are reflected back to Earth at about 50 miles (80 km) at the bottom of the ionosphere.

**Key words**

*nitrogen cycle*

## Nitrogen

- The *nitrogen cycle* converts nitrogen in the atmosphere into ammonia, nitrates (a nitric acid salt), and proteins.
- Living things cannot exist without nitrogen, so the nitrogen cycle is essential for life.
- The atmosphere is about 80 percent nitrogen, but only bacteria can use nitrogen in this gaseous form. All other living things have to use compounds of nitrogen, such as nitrates.
- Most nitrates are produced by bacteria in the soil.

## The nitrogen cycle

- The cycle begins with ammonia, a compound of nitrogen, produced by lightning or by volcanoes, or in the soil by bacteria and fungi from dead animals and organisms and from animal droppings.
- Bacteria convert ammonia into nitrites, or salts of nitrous acid.
- Bacteria then convert nitrites into nitrates, or salts of nitric acid.
- The process of combining or fixing nitrogen with another element to form a nitrate compound is known as "nitrogen fixation."
- Nitrates are absorbed into plants through their roots.
- Plants convert nitrates into proteins.
- Animals obtain nitrogen by eating either protein-rich plants or other animals that eat plants.
- When living things die and decay, bacteria break down the nitrates and other compounds and return the nitrogen gas back to the atmosphere, a process known as "denitrification." This completes the nitrogen cycle.

# The nitrogen cycle

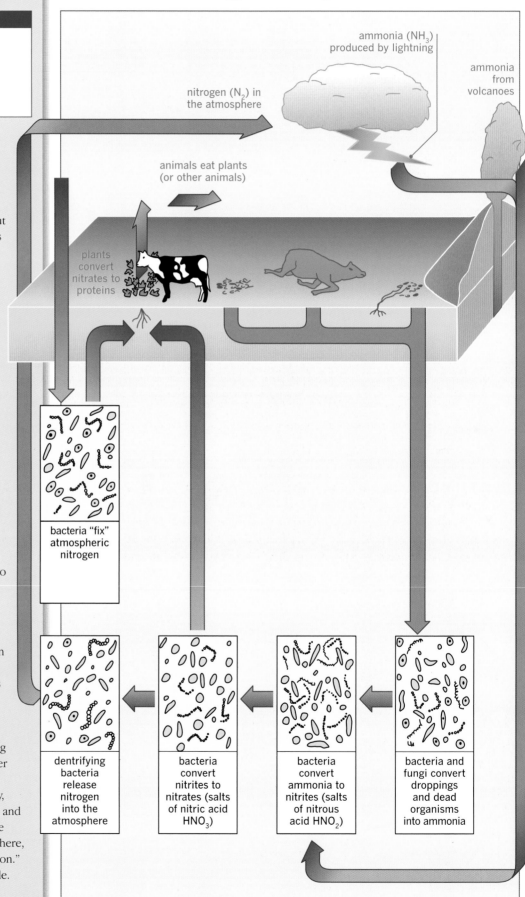

ammonia ($NH_3$) produced by lightning

ammonia from volcanoes

nitrogen ($N_2$) in the atmosphere

animals eat plants (or other animals)

plants convert nitrates to proteins

bacteria "fix" atmospheric nitrogen

dentrifying bacteria release nitrogen into the atmosphere

bacteria convert nitrites to nitrates (salts of nitric acid $HNO_3$)

bacteria convert ammonia to nitrites (salts of nitrous acid $HNO_2$)

bacteria and fungi convert droppings and dead organisms into ammonia

# The carbon and oxygen cycles

**Key words**

*atmosphere*
*limestone*

## Carbon and oxygen

- The carbon and oxygen cycles keep carbon and oxygen circulating through the atmosphere, the oceans, land, and living things.
- All living things contain the element carbon. Both carbon and oxygen are essential for life.
- Carbon exists as coal and oil deposits formed underground over millions of years by decomposed and compressed plant and animal remains, as a carbon dioxide solution in the sea, and as calcium bicarbonate in limestone.

## Photosynthesis

- Carbon forms carbon dioxide gas in the atmosphere. This gas is produced by volcanoes, by burning fossil fuels and wood, from decaying organic matter, and through plant and animal respiration.
- Carbon dioxide stored in the oceans is released into the atmosphere through evaporation, and eventually falls as a solution in rainwater; if it falls on land, it is then absorbed by plants.
- Carbon dioxide is removed from the atmosphere by plants and bacteria in a process known as photosynthesis.
- Plants use photosynthesis to produce organic compounds, such as carbohydrates, which become part of their tissue.
- When plants are eaten by animals, their carbon and carbohydrates are passed on.
- During respiration, animals use the carbohydrates from plants and release carbon dioxide back into the atmosphere.
- As a by-product, photosynthesis produces oxygen—essential for human and animal life—from plants.

## The carbon cycle

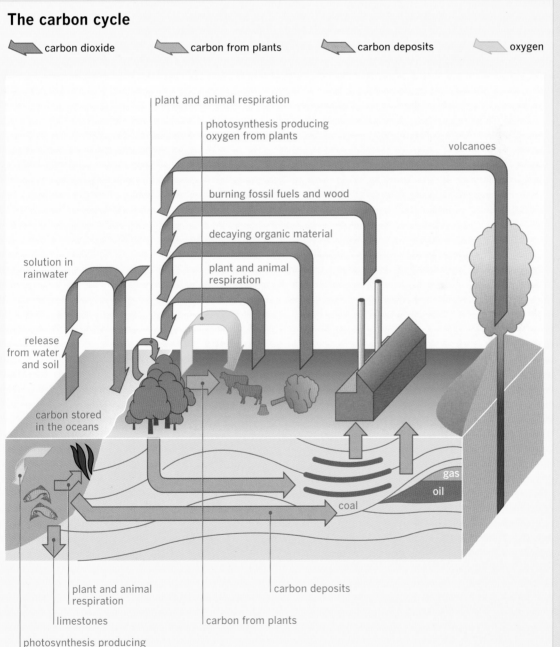

carbon dioxide    carbon from plants    carbon deposits    oxygen

plant and animal respiration

photosynthesis producing oxygen from plants

volcanoes

burning fossil fuels and wood

decaying organic material

plant and animal respiration

solution in rainwater

release from water and soil

carbon stored in the oceans

gas

oil

coal

plant and animal respiration

limestones

photosynthesis producing oxygen from plants

carbon deposits

carbon from plants

### Key words

*atmosphere*
*convection*

# Heat transfer processes

## Heat transfer

- Heat transfer is the process in the atmosphere by which many different types of radiation from the Sun reach Earth.
- Radiation from the Sun, including heat and light, travels in very small waves, with 41 percent of it visible as light.
- Only 47 percent of solar radiation reaches the ground, while 19 percent is retained by the atmosphere on the way. The remaining 34 percent is reflected back into space.

## Longwave radiation

- Fifty percent of the Sun's radiation that reaches Earth is longwave radiation. This consists of waves such as infrared waves too long for our eyes to see, though we may feel their heat.
- Longwave radiation is reflected off the ground and heats the lower layers of the atmosphere by convection.
- Convection occurs when a pocket of air expands as it warms, causing it to rise because it is less dense than the surrounding air.
- A small amount of the air is heated by conduction, or direct contact with the hot Earth. This effect is negligible, as the air is a good insulator.

## Shortwave radiation

- The remaining nine percent of solar radiation is shortwave radiation, such as gamma and ultraviolet rays, and X-rays. These waves cannot be seen but they can affect the human body's tissues.

### Longwave radiation

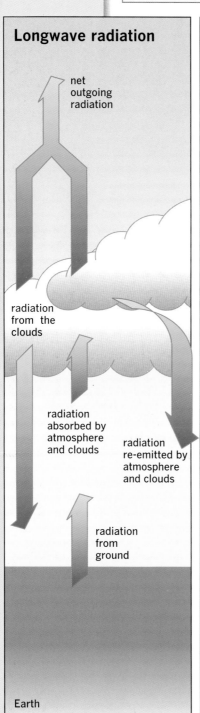

net outgoing radiation

radiation from the clouds

radiation absorbed by atmosphere and clouds

radiation re-emitted by atmosphere and clouds

radiation from ground

Earth

### Shortwave radiation

incoming solar radiation

UV radiation absorbed by ozone layer

radiation reflected by atmosphere and clouds

radiation reflected by ground

radiation absorbed by ground

Earth

### Other processes

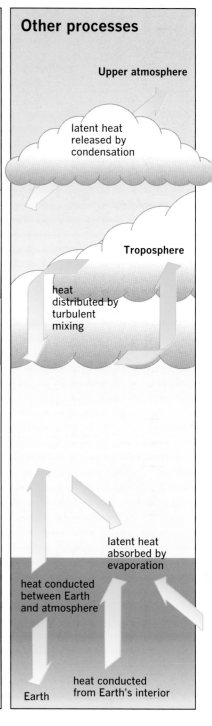

**Upper atmosphere**

latent heat released by condensation

**Troposphere**

heat distributed by turbulent mixing

latent heat absorbed by evaporation

heat conducted between Earth and atmosphere

heat conducted from Earth's interior

Earth

# Sunshine

## The Sun's rays

in polar latitudes

in mid latitudes

in the tropics

in mid latitudes

in polar latitudes

North Pole

atmosphere

equator

South Pole

Key words

*equinox*
*insolation*
*solstice*
*tropic*

## Insolation

- The amount of heat from the Sun reaching the top of the atmosphere is known as *insolation*. It depends on the angle of Earth to the Sun and so varies with latitude and season.
- Half of Earth's surface is exposed to the heat of the Sun at any one time, depending on whether it is day or night.
- Insolation is at its maximum in the tropics either side of the equator, and during the summer months.
- On average, the tropics receive almost two and a half times as much radiation per day as the poles. This is because low-angle solar radiation near the poles is spread over a larger area than the radiation arriving near the equator, so its heating effect is reduced.

## Temperature zones

- The world is divided into three main temperature zones either side of the equator: the polar regions above the Arctic and below the Antarctic circles; the temperate zones between these circles and the two tropics; and the two tropics either side of the equator.
- For three months, the zone in which the Sun is directly overhead moves north until around June 22 when it reaches a line of latitude called the Tropic of Cancer.
- The Sun then moves south for the next six months, crossing the equator around September 23, until it reaches a line of latitude called the Tropic of Capricorn around December 22.
- An *equinox* occurs when the Sun is directly overhead at the equator. A *solstice* occurs when the Sun is directly overhead at a tropic.

## Resulting temperature zones

North Pole

Arctic Circle

polar region

temperate zone

Tropic of Cancer

northern tropics

southern tropics

equator

Tropic of Capricorn

temperate zone

polar region

Antarctic Circle

South Pole

# Temperature belts

**Key words**

Nothern
  Hemisphere
Southern
  Hemisphere

## Temperature belts

- The amount of heat from the Sun reaching the ground depends on the angle of Earth to the Sun, so varies with latitude and season.
- The Southern Hemisphere is therefore warm when the Northern Hemisphere is cool in January during the southern summer, while the reverse is true in July during the northern summer.
- Air temperature is measured either on the Fahrenheit scale, where water freezes at 32°F and boils at 212°F, or on the Celsius (centigrade) scale, where water freezes at 0°C and boils at 100°C.

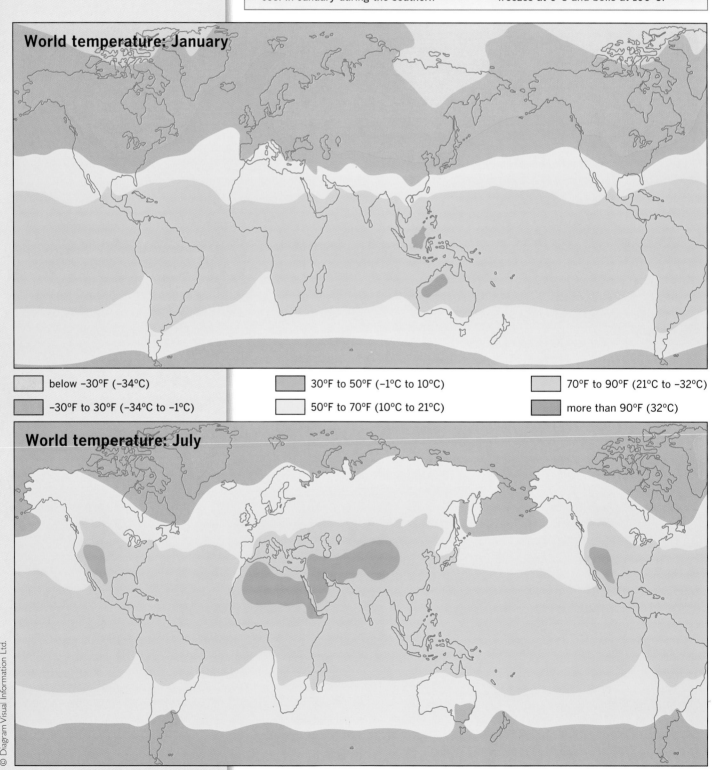

**World temperature: January**

| | below −30°F (−34°C) | | 30°F to 50°F (−1°C to 10°C) | | 70°F to 90°F (21°C to −32°C) |
|---|---|---|---|---|---|
| | −30°F to 30°F (−34°C to −1°C) | | 50°F to 70°F (10°C to 21°C) | | more than 90°F (32°C) |

**World temperature: July**

# Pressure belts

## Changing pressure

- Cold air is denser than warm air. This causes a high-pressure zone at the cold poles known as the *polar high*, and a low-pressure belt at the warm equator known as the *equatorial low*.
- There are also subtropical highs 30° north and south of the equator, where the air is squashed by sinking air, and subpolar lows around 55° N and 55° S.
- The system of pressure belts around Earth moves from 6° to 10° north or south following the seasonal movements of the Sun.

### Key words

*equatorial low*
*polar high*

**Pressure: January**

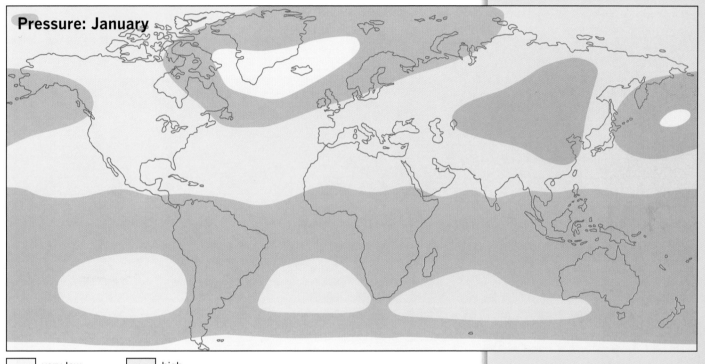

| | very low | | high |
|---|---|---|---|
| | low | | very high |

**Pressure: July**

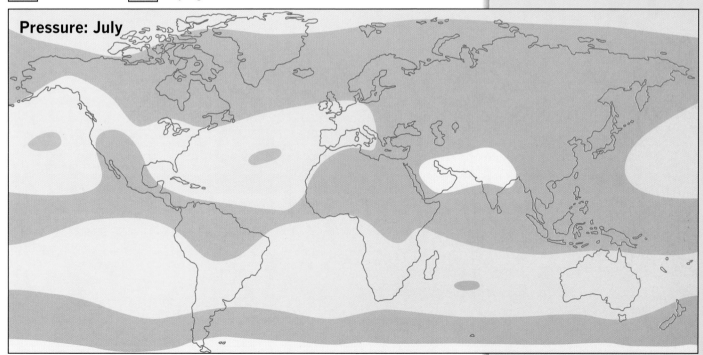

# The Coriolis effect

## Stationary world

- Winds blowing in various directions can be represented on an imaginary nonrotating globe.
- The *Coriolis effect* (named for Gustave-Gaspard de Coriolis, 1792–1843) refers to the apparent deflection of moving objects produced by Earth's rotation.
- The effect applies to objects, such as winds and ocean currents, moving long distances where there is a north–south component.
- Winds and ocean currents are deflected to the right (clockwise) in the Northern Hemisphere and to the left (counterclockwise) in the Southern Hemisphere. There is no deflection at the equator.

## Spinning world

- The same winds show the deflections caused by the Coriolis effect on a rotating planet.

## Resultant winds

- Winds blow from areas of high pressure to areas of low pressure.
- The Coriolis effect deflects these winds and produces the angled paths of Earth's dominant wind systems.

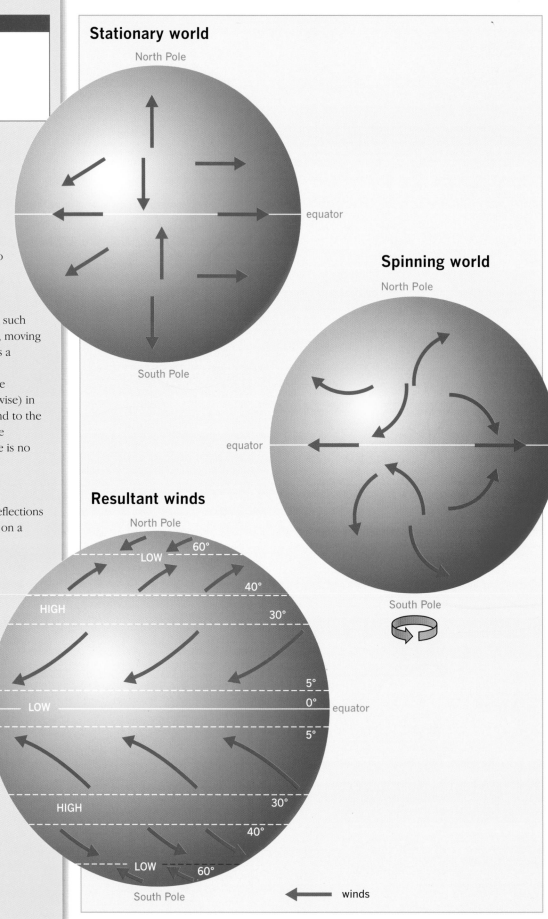

**Stationary world**

**Spinning world**

**Resultant winds**

# Wind circulation

## Air circulation

- The world's winds are part of a global system of air circulation that moves warm air from the equator to the poles, and cold air from the poles to the equator, maintaining a balance of temperatures around the world.
- Due to the Coriolis effect, warm wind rises in one direction and cold wind falls in the other in a circular movement known as a *cell*.

- There are three major cells in each hemisphere: the Hadley cell above the trade winds, the midlatitude or Ferrel cell above the westerlies, and the polar cell above the polar easterlies.
- Between the cells are zones of light winds: the doldrums at the equator and the horse latitudes between the trade winds and the westerlies.

**Key words**

*equator*
*pole*

## Principal surface winds and pressure zones

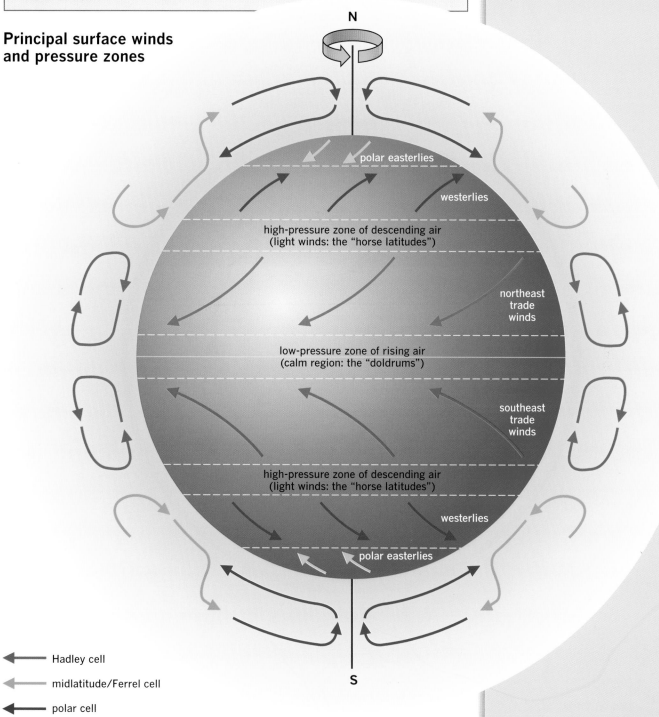

N

polar easterlies

westerlies

high-pressure zone of descending air
(light winds: the "horse latitudes")

northeast trade winds

low-pressure zone of rising air
(calm region: the "doldrums")

southeast trade winds

high-pressure zone of descending air
(light winds: the "horse latitudes")

westerlies

polar easterlies

S

← Hadley cell

← midlatitude/Ferrel cell

← polar cell

# Jet streams

## Key words

*jet stream*

## Jet streams

- *Jet streams* are narrow belts of strong westerly winds that blow up to 230 miles per hour (370 kmph) at an altitude of up to 12.4 miles (20 km).
- The two main jet streams are the subtropical jet stream between the Hadley and midlatitude cells, and the polar front jet stream between the midlatitude and polar cells.

## Rossby waves

- The polar jet stream undulates around the world in four to six giant waves, each about 1,240 miles (2,000 km) long.

## Tracks of winter jet streams

subtropical jet stream

polar front jet stream

## Location of jet streams in the atmosphere

polar front jet stream

polar cell

Ferrel cell

North Pole

60° N

subtropical jet stream

30° N

Hadley cell

equator

**Heights**   12.4 miles   6.2 miles   Earth's
              (20 km)      (10 km)     surface

## Formation of upper air waves

**1** Jet stream begins to undulate.

**2** Rossby waves form.

**3** Waves become more pronounced.

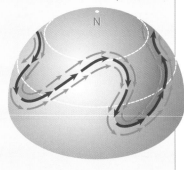

**4** Warm and cold air cells form.

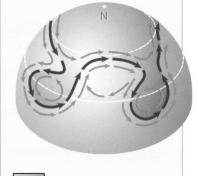

cold air ⬅ jet axis

warm air ⬅ wind

# Coastal breezes

## Coastal breezes

- Seawater has a higher heat capacity than land. Given the same conditions of solar irradiation, seawater both gains and loses heat energy more slowly than adjacent land. This difference in thermal characteristics gives rise to coastal breezes that change direction during a 24-hour period.

- Coastal breezes vary markedly in intensity and regularity, depending on the location and time of year. They are most pronounced in the tropics and subtropics, and in temperate latitudes during the summer.

### Key words

*monsoon*

## Sea breeze

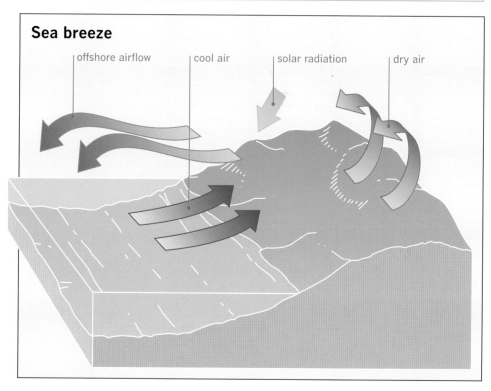

offshore airflow · cool air · solar radiation · dry air

## Land breeze

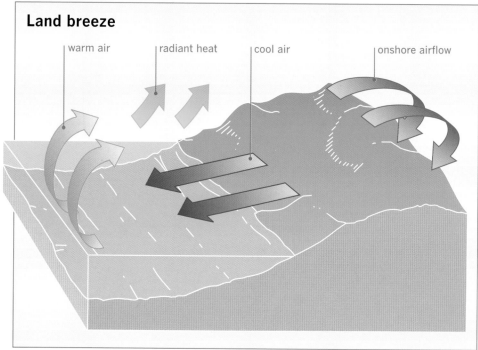

warm air · radiant heat · cool air · onshore airflow

## Sea breezes

- On a bright sunny day the land warms more quickly than the nearby surface water of the sea.
- Solar radiation is absorbed by both sea and land, but the heat capacity of the land is less and it warms up more quickly.
- Dry air close to the land surface warms quickly and rises.
- Cool, moist air close to the sea surface moves ashore to replace the rising air. A cool onshore sea breeze is thus generated during the day.
- Aloft, an offshore airflow descends to complete the cycle.

## Land breeze

- At night, the land cools faster than the nearby ocean surface.
- Radiant heat energy is lost more rapidly from the land than from the sea.
- Warm moist air close to the ocean surface rises.
- Cool air from the land moves offshore to replace the rising air. A cool offshore land breeze is generated at night.
- Aloft an onshore airflow descends to complete the cycle.

## Monsoon winds

- Massive sea breezes known as *monsoon* winds blow off the Indian Ocean into India and southeast Asia during summer as the interior of the Asian continent heats up.
- Monsoon winds bring heavy rains with them.
- Monsoon winds may be partly caused by seasonal changes in the subtropical jet stream.

© Diagram Visual Information Ltd.

**Key words**

*anemometer*
*hurricane*

## The Beaufort scale

- The Beaufort scale is named for Admiral Francis Beaufort (1774–1857), the British hydrographer (ocean surveyor) who devised it in 1805. The scale was modified in 1926.
- The scale measures the speed or force of the wind: how fast the air is moving.
- Wind speeds are measured at 33 feet (10 m) above the ground, to remove the effect of any obstructions or disturbances at ground level.

## The scale

- Beaufort numbers 0 to 11 represent a different strength of wind from less than one mile per hour (1 kmph) through 72 miles per hour (115 kmph).
- Beaufort numbers 12–17 represent increasing strengths of *hurricanes*. Such strong winds are very rare except in the tropics, where they can cause great loss of life and catastrophic structural damage.
- The characteristics and possible effects of each wind strength are listed to enable observers to identify it easily without the aid of an *anemometer*, a device used for measuring wind speed.

# The Beaufort scale of wind speeds

| Beaufort number | | Description | Characteristics | Range: miles per hour | Range: kmph |
|---|---|---|---|---|---|
| 0 | | Calm | No wind; smoke rises vertically. | less than 1 | less than 1 |
| 1 | | Light air | Smoke drifts with air; weather vanes do not move. | 1–3 | 1–5 |
| 2 | | Light breeze | Wind felt on face; leaves rustle; weather vanes move. | 4–7 | 6–11 |
| 3 | | Gentle breeze | Leaves and twigs move; light flags are extended. | 8–12 | 12–19 |
| 4 | | Modererate breeze | Small branches sway; dust and loose paper blown about. | 13–18 | 20–28 |
| 5 | | Fresh breeze | Small trees sway; waves break on lakes. | 19–24 | 29–38 |
| 6 | | Strong breeze | Large branches sway; umbrellas difficult to use. | 25–31 | 39–49 |
| 7 | | Near gale | Whole trees sway; difficult to walk against the wind. | 32–38 | 50–61 |
| 8 | | Gale | Twigs break off trees; very difficult to walk against the wind. | 39–46 | 62–74 |
| 9 | | Strong gale | Chimneys, roof slates and roof shingles blown off buildings. | 47–54 | 75–88 |
| 10 | | Storm | Trees uprooted; extensive damage to buildings. | 55–63 | 89–102 |
| 11 | | Severe storm | Widespread damage. | 64–72 | 103–115 |
| 12–17 | | Hurricane | Extreme destruction. | more than 73 | more than 117 |

# Humidity

**Key words**

absolute humidity
condensation
 nucleus
humidity
relative humidity

## Relative humidity
**Spring day in Washington, D.C.**

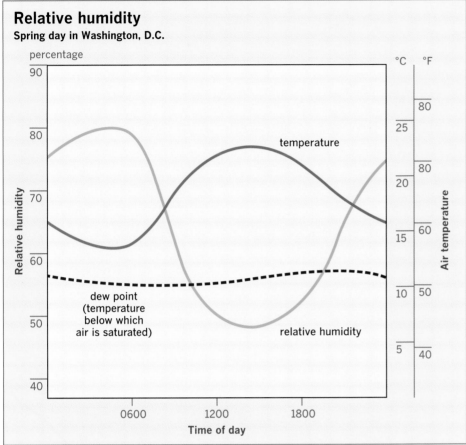

## Absolute humidity

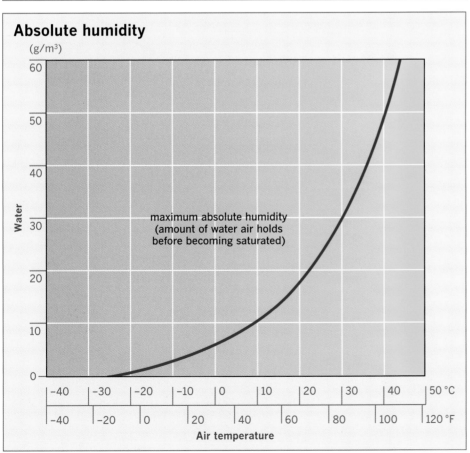

## Humidity

- *Humidity* is the amount of water vapor in the air.
- The air is almost always moist, even when it is not raining, because it contains water vapor.
- Water vapor fills the spaces between the air molecules. When all these spaces are filled and the air can absorb no more vapor, it is said to be "saturated."
- "Saturation point" is the limit to the amount of water that air can absorb.
- Air expands when it gets warmer. As it does so, the space between the air molecules expands and the air can absorb more vapor.
- Air contracts as it cools, packing the molecules together more tightly. This forces the water vapor out, condensing it into drops of liquid water, which then form clouds, fog, mist, dew, and rain.
- Condensation is the change of a gas to a liquid. Water vapor condenses into water droplets when the air cools to dew point at 100 percent *relative humidity* (rh).
- The vapor condenses around *condensation nuclei*: minute airborne particles of dust or sea salt. If the air is very clean, the vapor may not condense even when the air is saturated. If the air is very dirty, water vapor may condense before the dew point is reached.

## Measuring humidity

- *Absolute humidity* is the total moisture in a given volume of air expressed in grams per cubic meter.
- A "specific humidity" is the vapor contained in 2.2 pounds (1 kg) of air expressed in grams.
- *Relative humidity* (rh) is the moisture in the air expressed as a percentage of the maximum amount that air can hold at that temperature.

**Key words**

*advection fog*
*fog*
*radiation fog*

## Fog

- *Fog* is a dense cloud of water droplets close to the ground.
- Fog is defined as existing where visibility falls below 0.62 miles (1 km).

## Radiation fog

- In normal atmospheric conditions, a layer of warm air covers the warm ground. A layer of cold air sits above it.
- On nights that are cold, clear, and calm the ground radiates the heat it has absorbed during the day back into the air, and loses its warmth.
- This causes an inversion of temperature, with a layer of warm air sitting above the ground trapped below a layer of cold air.
- As the ground cools, the air above it cools to its dew point: the point at which water vapor condenses into water droplets.
- These water droplets form a dense cloud called *radiation fog*.
- Cold air flows downhill under gravity, which is why radiation fog is often found in valleys and hollows.
- In summer, radiation fog disperses quickly when the Sun rises. In fall and winter, the fog is trapped by the temperature inversion and may persist all day.

## Advection fog

- *Advection fog* is formed when a mass of warm moist air flows over a cooler surface. This reduces the temperature of its lower layers in a temperature inversion. When the air mass reaches dew point, condensation occurs.
- Advection fog often occurs when warm sea air moves over a cold land surface, or when warm land air flows over a cold sea.

# Fog

## Normal atmospheric conditions

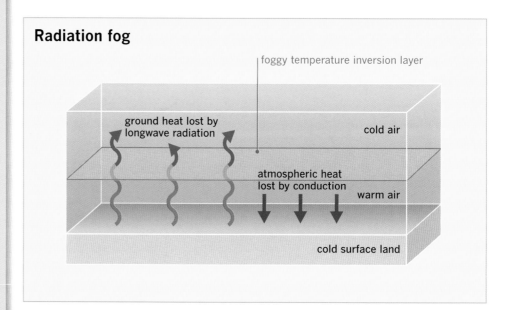

## Radiation fog

## Advection fog

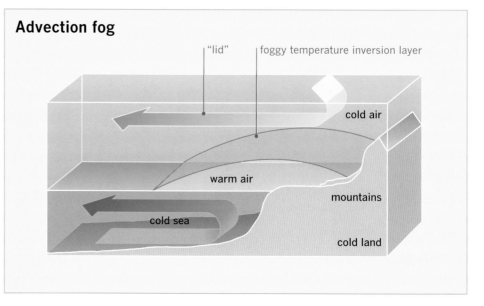

# Cloud types

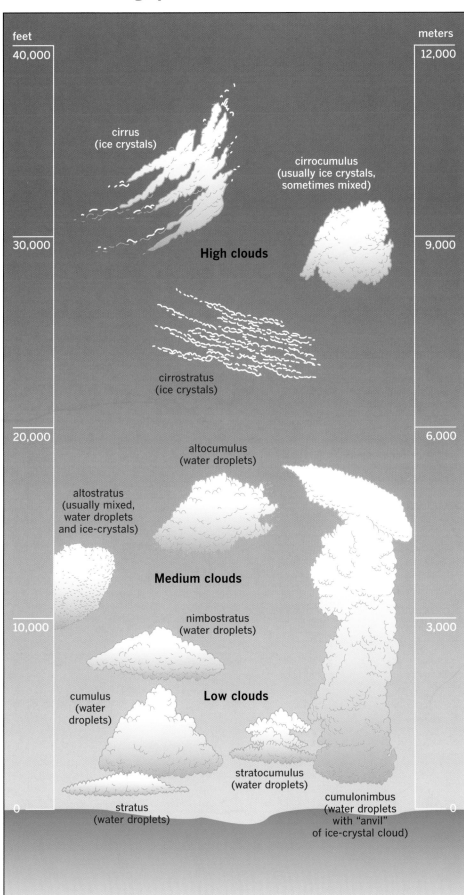

feet
40,000

30,000

20,000

10,000

0

meters
12,000

9,000

6,000

3,000

0

cirrus
(ice crystals)

cirrocumulus
(usually ice crystals,
sometimes mixed)

**High clouds**

cirrostratus
(ice crystals)

altocumulus
(water droplets)

altostratus
(usually mixed,
water droplets
and ice-crystals)

**Medium clouds**

nimbostratus
(water droplets)

cumulus
(water
droplets)

**Low clouds**

stratocumulus
(water droplets)

stratus
(water droplets)

cumulonimbus
(water droplets
with "anvil"
of ice-crystal cloud)

© Diagram Visual Information Ltd.

## Key words

*altocumulus*
*altostratus*
*cirrus*
*cumulonimbus*
*nimbostratus*

## Clouds

- A *cloud* is a mass of tiny particles of water and ice held in suspension by the vertical movement of air.
- Clouds are formed by water vapor condensing around airborne nuclei such as dust and smoke particles.
- There are numerous types of cloud, although meteorologists commonly use 10 main categories to describe them, classified according to their height and shape.

## High clouds

- High *cirrus* clouds form at high altitudes, between 20,000 and 40,000 feet (6,000–12,000 m), where the air is extremely cold.
- Cirrus clouds are usually formed of ice crystals. Strong winds blow them into wispy formations.
- The long trail of ice crystals seen behind a jet aircraft at this height is called a contrail, formed by the exhaust of hot gas and water vapor emitted from the engine freezing in the cold air.

## Medium clouds

- Medium clouds form at altitudes between 6,500 and 20,000 feet (2,000–6,000 m).
- *Altocumulus* and *nimbostratus* clouds are formed of water droplets. *Altostratus* clouds are a mixture of water droplets and ice crystals.

## Low clouds

- Low clouds form below 6,500 feet (2,000 m), although the anvil or cap of a *cumulonimbus* cloud can reach up to 20,000 feet (6,000 m).
- Low clouds are formed of water droplets, though the cumulonimbus has a cap of ice crystals.
- Strong updraughts of moist air create towering cumulonimbus clouds that bring heavy rain, thunder, and lightning.

# Rain, snow, and sleet

**Key words**

*precipitation*

## Precipitation

- Rain, snow, and sleet are all forms of *precipitation* falling to the ground from clouds.
- Precipitation occurs when water droplets or ice crystals become so heavy that the air can no longer support them.

## Rain and drizzle

- Raindrops that fall from nimbostratus clouds measure 0.04–0.08 inches (1–2 mm) across. Raindrops that fall from cumulonimbus clouds can be 0.2 inches (5 mm) or more across.
- Drizzle consists of water drops 0.008–0.02 inches (0.2–0.5 mm) across and usually falls from stratus clouds.
- Raindrops increase in size as they fall through a cloud, hitting and absorbing microscopic cloud droplets as they drop, thus increasing in size.

## Snow and sleet

- Snow consists of ice crystals. They are arranged in many different geometric shapes that vary according to the temperature at which they fall.
- Sleet is a mixture of rain and snow, or partly melted snow.
- Snowflakes grow inside a cloud, the ice crystals merging with water molecules in the cloud.

### Raindrop growth by collision and coalescence

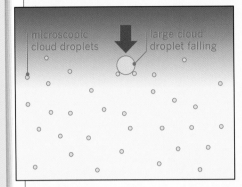

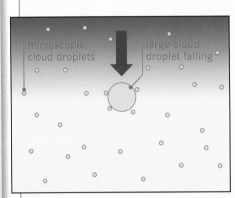

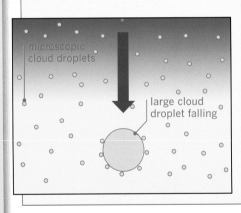

### Growth of snowflake

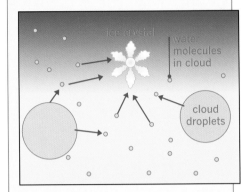

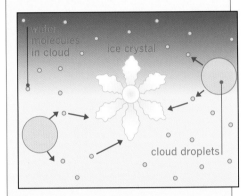

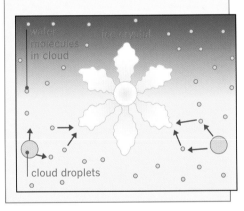

### Sleet formation

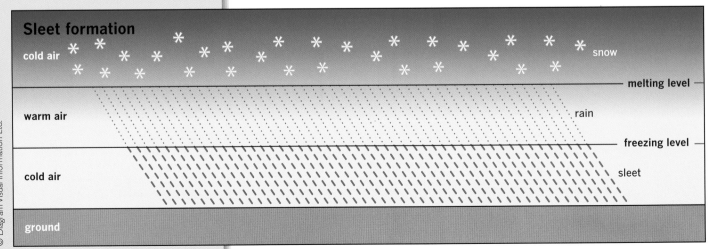

# Rain types

## Cyclonic rain

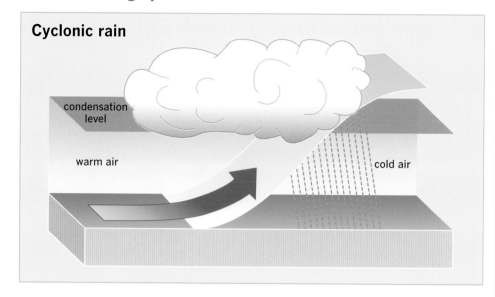

condensation level

warm air

cold air

## Convectional rain

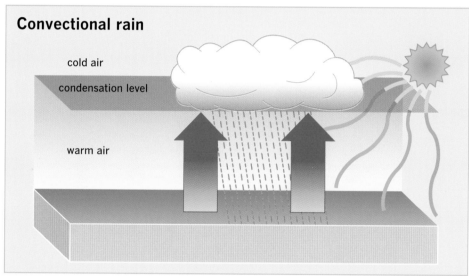

cold air

condensation level

warm air

## Orographic rain

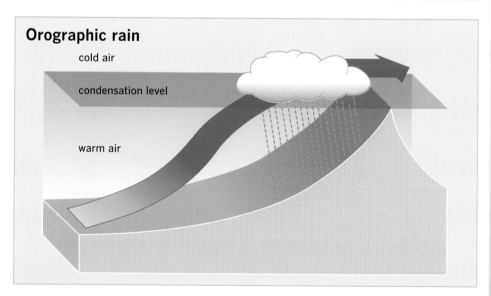

cold air

condensation level

warm air

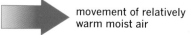

movement of relatively warm moist air

### Key words

*convectional rain*
*cyclonic rain*
*orographic rain*
*rain shadow*

## Rainfall

- Rain occurs when a mass of warm moist air is swept up into a cloud. Here the air cools and the water vapor in the air condenses into water droplets and falls as rain.

## Cyclonic rain

- *Cyclonic* or frontal *rain* occurs when warm air rises in warm and cold fronts, causing it to condense as clouds and fall as rain.
- A warm front is a boundary between warm and cold air masses where the warm air is advancing. As it does so, the warm moist air rides slowly over the cold air, creating a long, gently sloping front that brings steady rain.
- A cold front is a boundary between warm and cold air masses where the cold air is advancing. The mass of cold air undercuts the warm air, forcing it to rise sharply. Tall thunderclouds often develop, bringing short but heavy rain showers.

## Convectional rain

- *Convectional rain* occurs when masses of warm, moist, rising air form cumulonimbus clouds. The water vapor condenses into water droplets and falls as rain.

## Orographic rain

- *Orographic rain* occurs when warm, moist air is driven by the wind up the side of a hill or mountain, causing it to condense into clouds and fall as rain on the summit.
- The air warms and dries as it descends the leeward side of the mountain, creating an effect known as a *rain shadow*.

© Diagram Visual Information Ltd.

## Key words

*cumulonimbus*

## Thunderstorms

- A thunderstorm is a storm that brings lightning, thunder, and torrential rain.
- Thunderstorms are associated with cumulonimbus or "thunderhead" clouds. These clouds can reach up to 9–11 miles (15–18 km) into the sky and have anvil-shaped heads made entirely of ice crystals.

# Thunderstorm

## Thunder and lightning

- Thunderclouds are formed by strong updrafts of air, such as those that form along cold fronts. They also form over ground heated by the Sun, which is why thunderstorms often occur in the tropics during the afternoon.
- Violent air currents sweep ice crystals up and down inside a thundercloud. Water freezes round these crystals to form hail pellets more than 0.2 inches (5 mm) across.
- The violent air currents also cause the hail pellets to collide with water droplets, which thereby becoming charged with static electricity. Heavier, negatively charged particles sink to the bottom of the cloud; lighter, positively charged particles rise to the top, creating a difference in charge within the cloud.
- If this charge builds up enough, it is discharged within the cloud as lightning. Sheet lightning rises from the base to the top; forked lightning extends the quickest way down from the cloud to the ground.
- Thunder is a rumbling shock wave caused by lightning powering through the air, heating it up to more than 45,000°F (25,000°C). The heated air expands so quickly that it sends out a shock wave we hear as a thunderclap.
- Because light travels faster than sound, we first see the lightning and then hear the thunder, roughly three seconds later for every 0.62 miles (1 km) we are from the storm.

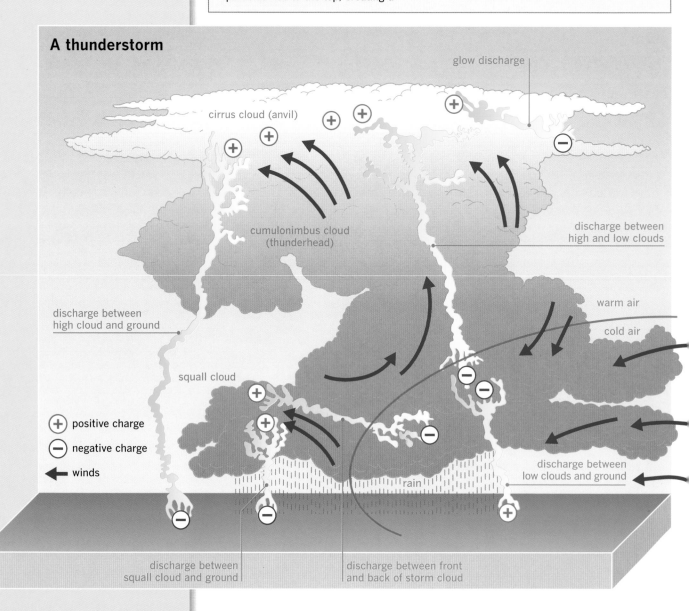

**A thunderstorm**

glow discharge

cirrus cloud (anvil)

cumulonimbus cloud (thunderhead)

discharge between high and low clouds

discharge between high cloud and ground

warm air

cold air

squall cloud

⊕ positive charge

⊖ negative charge

← winds

rain

discharge between low clouds and ground

discharge between squall cloud and ground

discharge between front and back of storm cloud

# Cyclones

## Key words

*cyclone*
*hurricane*

## Advancing front

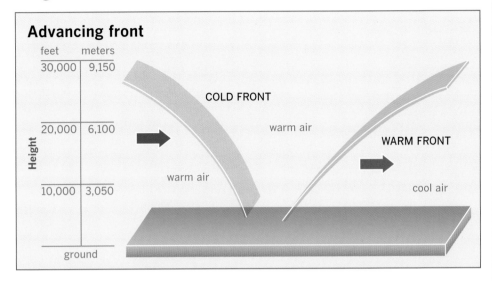

| feet | meters |
|---|---|
| 30,000 | 9,150 |
| 20,000 | 6,100 |
| 10,000 | 3,050 |

Height

COLD FRONT

warm air

WARM FRONT

warm air

cool air

ground

## Cloud types

As a cyclone (depression) passes over an observer on the ground, the air masses, fronts, and associated cloud types and weather arrive in this order:

**Ci** cirrus
**Cs** cirrostratus
**As** altostratus
**Ac** altocumulus
**Cb** cumulonimbus
**Cu** cumulus
**St** stratus
**Ns** nimbostratus

short showers   heavy showers   prolonged rain

## Growth of a cyclone

- A *cyclone* is an area of local pressure, often called a "depression" or a "low."
- In the Northern Hemisphere, a cyclone occurs when warm, moist, and less dense maritime air meets cold polar air to its north. This situation is reversed in the Southern Hemisphere.
- As the two masses of air collide, a bulge or depression is formed on the front or boundary between the two. As this depression deepens, a mass of warm air is trapped between the advancing warm and cold fronts.
- The cold air chases the warm air in a spiral, causing the front to split into two arms.
- Eventually, the cold front catches up and merges with the warm front, creating an occluded front that slowly disappears.
- A *hurricane* is a storm that results from a cyclone forming in tropical regions.

## The growth of a cyclone

← warm air      ← cold air

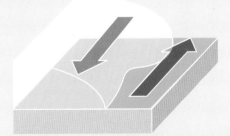

In the Northern Hemisphere, the depression starts as a kink in the front (boundary) between cold polar air to the north and warmer, moist maritime air to the south. The situation is reversed in the Southern Hemisphere.

As the depression deepens, a warm sector is trapped between advancing warm and cold fronts.

The mature depression has characteristic clouds and associated weather. Later, the cold front will catch up with the warm front creating an occluded front that will eventually dissipate.

## Key words

*cyclone*
*hurricane*
*typhoon*

## Hurricanes

- A *hurricane* is a violent tropical maritime storm, known as a tropical *cyclone* in the Indian Ocean and a *typhoon* in the Pacific.
- Hurricanes revolve counterclockwise in the Northern Hemisphere and clockwise in the Southern Hemisphere.
- A hurricane develops from a cluster of thunderstorms that build up over a warm, tropical sea. As the storms combine, they tighten into a spiral with a central calm ring of low pressure known as the "eye." Here the wind speed is less than 16 miles per hour (25 kmph).
- A hurricane can be as wide as 375 miles (600 km), as high as 10 miles (16 km), and can last for several days.
- The strongest winds—sometimes more than 100 miles per hour (160 kmph)—are found at the base of the storm just outside the eye.
- Heat from the warm sea provides the energy to drive the storm, which moves in a westerly direction over the sea, picking up strength as it moves.

# Hurricanes

## Hurricane structure

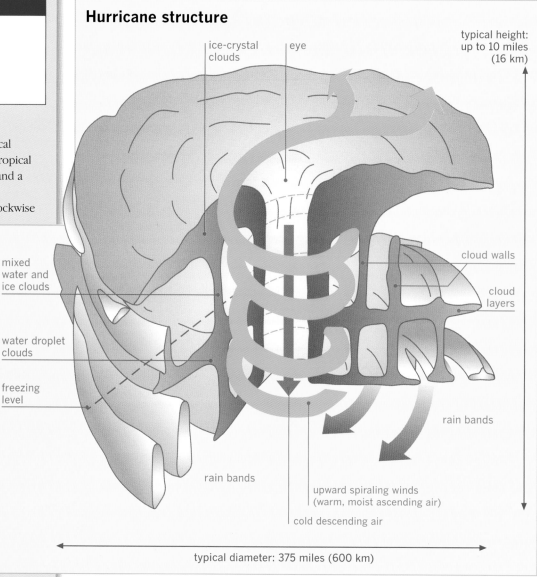

ice-crystal clouds

eye

typical height: up to 10 miles (16 km)

cloud walls

cloud layers

mixed water and ice clouds

water droplet clouds

freezing level

rain bands

rain bands

upward spiraling winds (warm, moist ascending air)

cold descending air

typical diameter: 375 miles (600 km)

## Principal hurricane tracks and regional names

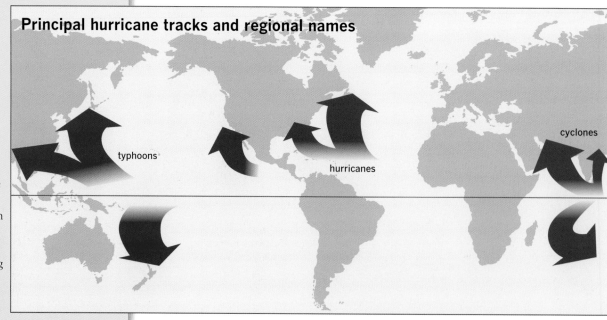

typhoons

hurricanes

cyclones

# Tornadoes

**Key words**

*tornado*
*waterspout*

## Distribution of tornadoes across the USA

**Annual average over a 12-year period**

| | | |
|---|---|---|
| fewer than 10 | 50 to 100 | more than 200 |
| 10 to 50 | 100 to 200 | |

## Tornado frequency

**Number of tornadoes**

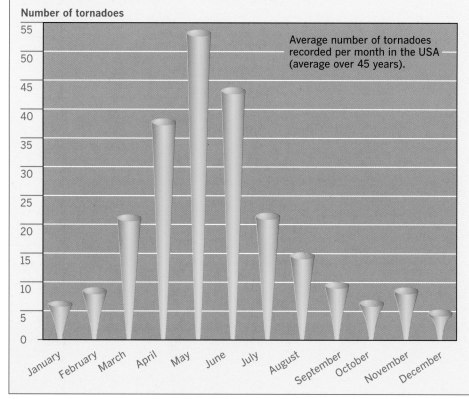

Average number of tornadoes recorded per month in the USA (average over 45 years).

## Tornado formation

- A *tornado* is a column of spiraling wind formed around a very low-pressure center.
- Although the precise causes of tornado formation are not fully understood, they appear to develop when a layer of warm moist air at low level lies under a layer of dry air at a higher level.
- A thunderstorm, an intense cold front, or the Sun heating up the ground can then trigger the formation of a rapidly rotating, rising column of air, with winds blowing up to 250 miles per hour (400 kmph). The winds form a counterclockwise spiral with violent downdrafts—a tornado.
- Air surrounding the tornado is sucked into the funnel of the spiral, taking with it any objects in its path.
- A tornado is usually very narrow, but its base may be as wide as 330 feet (100 m), resulting in a very narrow path of destruction. Tornadoes are erratic and unpredictable in their behavior.

## Tornado location

- Tornadoes can form in any low and midlatitude country, but the largest number are recorded in the Midwest of the United States, notably in the "Tornado Alley" that stretches from the Texas Pandhandle northeast through Oklahoma and into Kansas.

## Waterspouts

- A *waterspout* is formed at sea when seawater is drawn up into a tornado. Because water is heavier than air and strong updrafts less common over water than land, waterspouts are gentler than tornadoes and last longer.

**Key words**

*anticyclone*
*Coriolis effect*
*cyclone*
*hurricane*
*tornado*

## Cyclones

- Air pressure varies considerably from place to place as solar radiation—heat, light, and other rays from the Sun— makes the air warmer in some places than others.
- The term *cyclone* is used for any revolving weather system in which air is warm and less dense than the surrounding air. Converging air spirals in at the base of the system and rises, creating a low-pressure area at ground level. Normal cyclones, also called depressions or lows, often bring wet unsettled weather.
- As a result of the Coriolis effect, the air spirals into a cyclonic system counterclockwise in the Northern Hemisphere and clockwise in the Southern Hemisphere.
- Hurricanes and tornadoes are extreme forms of cyclones.

## Anticyclones

- *Anticyclones*, with descending air creating high pressure at ground level, bring settled weather with light winds and often little cloud.
- As a result of the Coriolis effect, the air spirals out of an anticyclonic system clockwise in the Northern Hemisphere and counterclockwise in the Southern Hemisphere.

# Pressure systems

### Cyclones

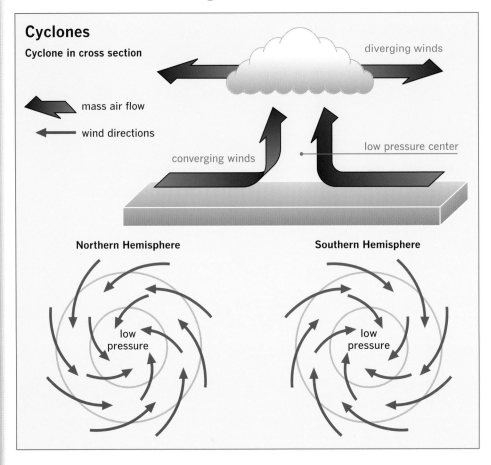

### Anticyclones

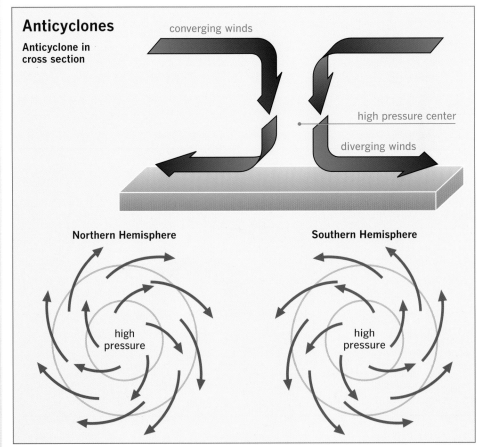

# Air masses

## Principal air masses over North America

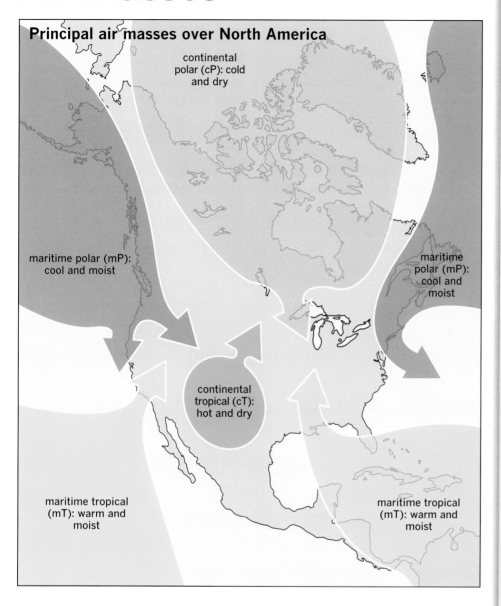

continental polar (cP): cold and dry

maritime polar (mP): cool and moist

maritime polar (mP): cool and moist

continental tropical (cT): hot and dry

maritime tropical (mT): warm and moist

maritime tropical (mT): warm and moist

### Key words

*air mass*

## Air mass

- An *air mass* is a large section of the atmosphere where the air is uniformly warm, cold, wet, or dry. An air mass may stretch over many thousands of miles and can stay in place for many days or weeks. This creates stable, unchanging weather.
- An air mass forms when air stays long enough over the sea or a plateau of land to take on its humidity and temperature.
- Meteorologists classify air masses according to where they form and whether they are warm, cold, moist, or dry.
- Maritime air masses (*m*) form over oceans and have high moisture content. Continental air masses (*c*) form over land and are dry. Masses forming in polar regions (*P*) are cold, while those forming in tropical areas (*T*) are warm.

## North America

- The continental polar or arctic air mass (*cP*) forms over the Arctic Ocean; it is described as continental because the ocean is frozen solid for much of the year. This air mass is very dry and cold and can bring clear skies and extremely low temperatures.
- The maritime polar air mass (*mP*) forms over the north Atlantic and Pacific oceans and is cool and moist. It brings cloudy skies, rain, and snow along cold fronts.
- The maritime tropical (*mT*) air mass forms over the tropical and subtropical Pacific Ocean and Caribbean Sea and is warm and moist. It usually brings long rain showers along warm fronts. It also causes thick advection fogs to form along the coast as the warm, moist air moves over cooler land surfaces.
- The continental tropical (*cT*) air mass forms over the subtropical Midwest and is warm and dry. It brings hot, dry weather with clear skies for days at a time.

## Classification of air masses

| Group | Subgroup | Source region | Properties at source |
|---|---|---|---|
| Polar (including arctic) | continental polar (cP) | Arctic, northern Eurasia, northern North America, Antarctic | cold, dry, and stable |
| | maritime polar (mP) | oceans poleward of 40–50° | cool, moist, and unstable |
| Tropical (including equatorial) | continental tropical (cT) | low latitude deserts | hot, dry, and stable |
| | maritime tropical (mT) | tropical and subtropical oceans | warm, moist, and unstable |

© Diagram Visual Information Ltd.

**Key words**

*atmosphere*
*ocean*

## The importance of water

- Water is vital for life on planet Earth. Most organisms comprise at least two thirds water.
- The distribution of water on land largely determines the occurrence and abundance of terrestrial flora and fauna.
- Water dissolves many kinds of substance and is a major transporter of chemicals between land and sea.
- Water is the planet's most potent heat transporter. It acts as a massive heat sink that carries tropical heat to temperate and polar regions.
- The presence of water in the atmosphere generates weather and climate. Clouds, for example, form from condensing water droplets. They trap sunlight, release precipitation, and act as a heat-insulating layer around Earth.
- Water heats up and cools down slowly, thereby moderating temperature changes in coastal areas.
- Water—as liquid or ice—is a powerful erosive force that shapes the planet's surface.

# Water

## The partition of surface water

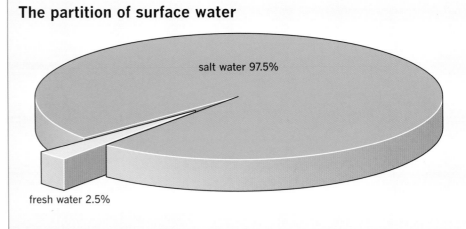

salt water 97.5%

fresh water 2.5%

The oceans cover 71% of Earth's surface: 139 million square miles (361 million km²).

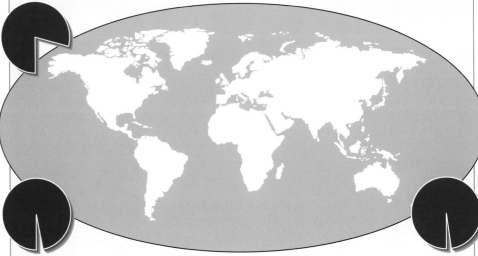

The oceans contain more than 97% of Earth's surface water: 323 million cubic miles (1,348 million km³).

Of all Earth's living space, 98% is found in the oceans.

## The partition of water on Earth's surface

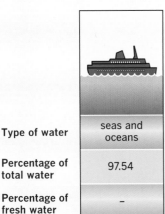
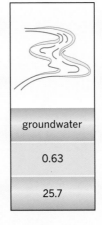
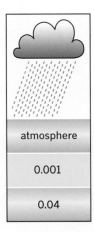

| Type of water | seas and oceans | ice | groundwater | freshwater lakes | atmosphere |
|---|---|---|---|---|---|
| Percentage of total water | 97.54 | 1.81 | 0.63 | 0.009 | 0.001 |
| Percentage of fresh water | – | 73.9 | 25.7 | 0.36 | 0.04 |

These figures do not include the tiny fraction of available water contained within living organisms.

# Oceans

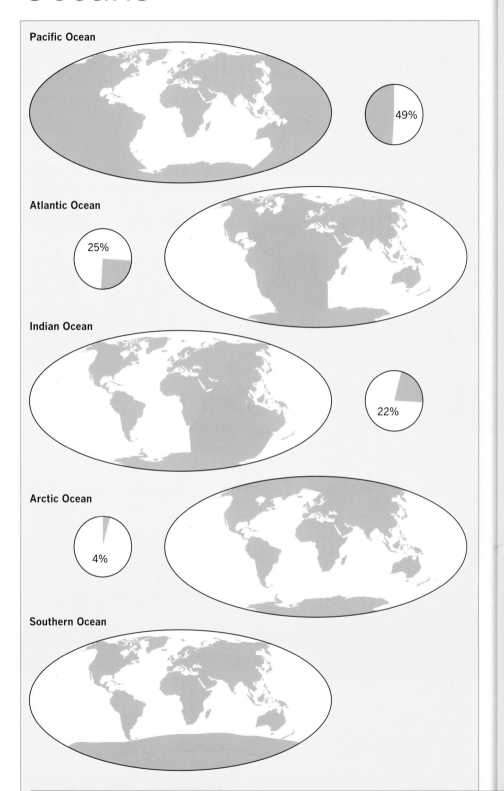

**Pacific Ocean**

49%

**Atlantic Ocean**

25%

**Indian Ocean**

22%

**Arctic Ocean**

4%

**Southern Ocean**

## The Ocean

- The term *Ocean* refers to the continuous expanse of seawater that covers 71 percent of the planet. It also refers to its major subdivisions contained within ocean basins.
- A *sea* is a more contained expanse of water. Some seas, such as the Caspian, are entirely landlocked.
- Seawater contains 96.5 percent water; the rest is mainly dissolved mineral salts, the most common of which is sodium chloride (table salt). Seawater also includes calcium, magnesium, potassium, sulfur, and traces of most other elements found on land.
- The percentages shown against the ocean maps to the left indicate the proportion of the total world ocean area made up by each named ocean (excluding adjacent seas).
- The world's four oceans occupy 129,425,150 square miles (335,220,000 km²) of the world's surface. They have an average depth of 12,240 feet (3,730 m).
- Their total volume is 304,288,000 cubic miles (1,281,396,920 km³).

## The Southern Ocean

- The Southern Ocean refers to the most southerly reaches of the Pacific, Atlantic, and Indian oceans beyond the Antarctic convergence at latitudes 50–55° S.
- Although the Southern Ocean is contained within ocean basins, its boundaries are not delineated by landmasses and it is not usually regarded as a true ocean.

| Ocean (excluding seas) | Area in square miles (km²) | | Mean depth in feet (m) | | Volume in cubic miles (km³) | |
|---|---|---|---|---|---|---|
| Pacific Ocean | 63,800,000 | (165,250,000) | 14,040 | (4,280) | 169,610,000 | (707,270,000) |
| Atlantic Ocean | 31,830,000 | (82,440,000) | 10,920 | (3,330) | 65,830,000 | (274,525,000) |
| Indian Ocean | 28,355,000 | (73,440,000) | 12,760 | (3,890) | 68,510,000 | (285,681,000) |
| Arctic Ocean | 5,440,150 | (14,090,000) | 3,240 | (988) | 3,338,000 | (13,920,920) |

© Diagram Visual Information Ltd.

**Key words**

epilimnion
hypolimnion
thermocline

## Ocean temperatures

- Ocean temperatures vary around the world. The oceans are warmest at the equator, where the Sun's heat is strongest, and become steadily cooler toward the poles. Parts of the Arctic Ocean are permanently frozen.
- The world's ocean temperatures are classified as either tropical, temperate, or polar. Both tropical and temperate oceans have warm and cool areas.

## Thermal stratification

- Thermal stratification is the layering of ocean temperatures by depth. This occurs because the Sun's heat has limited penetration in the water. As a result, seawater gets colder with depth.
- The surface temperature of tropical oceans can reach 77°F (25°C). At 3,300 feet (1,000 m) beneath the surface, the temperature falls to 41°F (5°C). Below this depth, the temperature continues to fall, reaching as low as 34–36°F (1–2°C).
- There are three layers within seawater. The *epilimnion* is the top, thin, and warm layer continually stirred by the wind, waves, and the Sun's heat.
- The middle layer is the *thermocline*, in which the temperature drops sharply.
- The bottom layer is the *hypolimnion*, where the water is cold, dark, and stagnant.

# Ocean temperatures

## Tropical

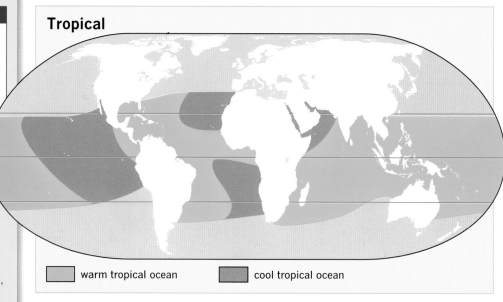

☐ warm tropical ocean    ☐ cool tropical ocean

## Temperate

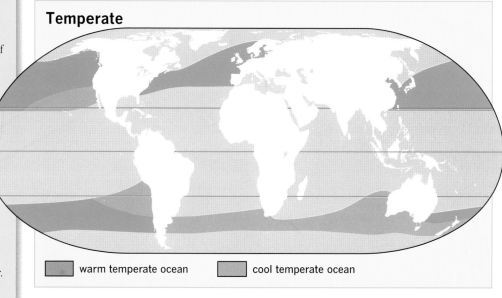

☐ warm temperate ocean    ☐ cool temperate ocean

## Polar

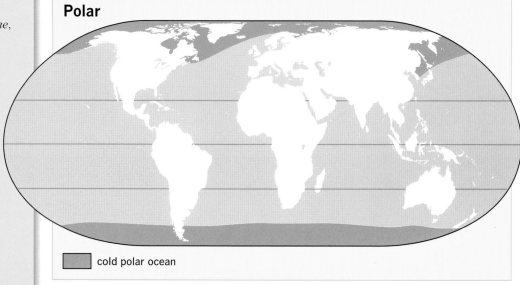

☐ cold polar ocean

# The ocean floor

### Key words

| | |
|---|---|
| abyssal plain | seamount |
| continental rise | spreading ridge |
| continental shelf | trench |
| continental slope | |
| guyot | |
| island arc | |

## Ocean floor features

### Trenches and volcanoes

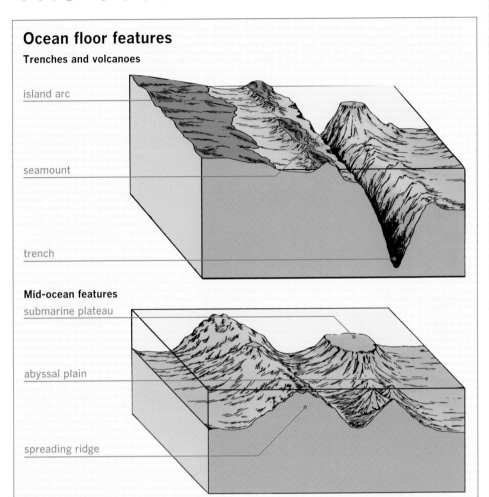

island arc

seamount

trench

### Mid-ocean features

submarine plateau

abyssal plain

spreading ridge

### Continental shelf

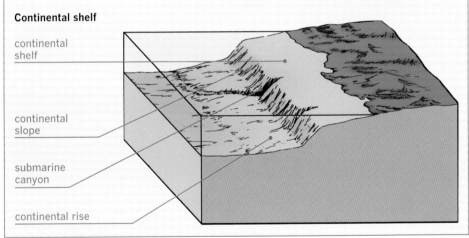

continental shelf

continental slope

submarine canyon

continental rise

## Trenches and volcanoes

- A *trench* is a deep, steep-sided trough in the deep ocean floor.
- At 35,840 feet (10,924 m) below sea level—deep enough to submerge Mount Everest—the Mariana Trench in the Pacific Ocean is the deepest part of any ocean in the world.
- An *island arc* is a curved row of volcanic islands, usually on the continental side of a trench.
- A *seamount* is a submarine volcano 3,300 feet (1,000 m) or more above its surroundings. A *guyot* is a flat-topped seamount that was once a volcanic island.

## Mid-ocean features

- A submarine plateau is a high, seafloor tableland.
- An *abyssal plain* is a sediment-covered deep-sea plain about 11,500–18,000 feet (3,500–5,500 m) below sea level.
- A *spreading ridge* is a submarine mountain chain generally 10,000 feet (3,000 m) above the abyssal plain. A huge system of submarine ridges extends more than 37,000 miles (60,000 km) through the oceans.

## Continental shelf

- A *continental shelf* is a continent's true but submerged and gently sloping rim. It descends to an average depth of 650 feet (200 m).
- Continental shelves occupy about 7.5 percent of the ocean floor.
- A *continental slope* is a relatively steep slope descending from the continental shelf. These slopes occupy about 8.5 percent of the ocean floor.
- A submarine canyon is a deep cleft in the continental slope, cut by river water flowing out to sea.
- A *continental rise* is a gentle slope below the continental slope.

## Profile of an ocean

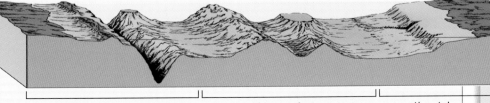

trenches and volcanoes    mid-ocean features    continental shelf

## Key words

*ocean*

## Sonar techniques

- Sonar (SOund NAvigation and Ranging) is the use of sound to discover the location and distribution of underwater objects or oceanic features.
- Sonar can also be used to produce images and measure the speed of objects. Sound can be used in this way as it travels more efficiently through water than it does through air.
- The first real scientific work on sonar systems was carried out in the 1930s. There are two main types: passive and active sonar.

## Acoustic Doppler Current Profilers

- Acoustic Doppler Current Pofiler (ADCP) systems became a widely used oceanographic tool in the 1980s. They use sound to measure current direction and speed, by making use of the doppler shift.
- The doppler shift is the fact that sound waves change in pitch if the water through which they are traveling is in motion. The size and direction (up or down) of the shift can be used to calculate current speed and direction. ADCPs are either mounted on the bottom of a ship, or anchored on the seabed.

# Seafloor profiling

## Passive sonar

Passive sonar detects sound waves given off by objects. It involves listening to underwater sounds from marine animals such as whales and from submarines or other underwater vessels.

Ancient mariners used to listen to whale song through the hulls of their ships, but it was not until WWI that a simple underwater microphone was made to listen out for enemy submarines.

Passive sonar can determine primarily the direction of objects. Submersibles and submarines mainly use passive sonar as it does not reveal their position underwater.

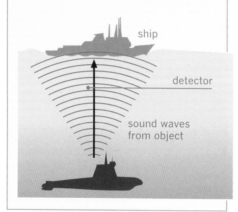

## Active sonar

With active sonar, sound is emitted into the ocean in short bursts or "pings" and the reflections are detected.

The distance to an object is calculated from the echo transmission and return interval, and the speed of sound in water (about one mile per second, 1.6 kmps).

Active sonar is mostly used by surface ships, not submersibles.

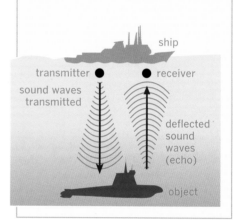

## Types of active sonar

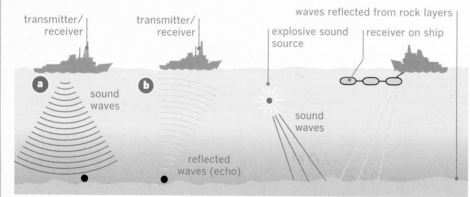

### a Echo sounders

Weak, high-frequency pings are used to discover distances to objects.

Echo sounders are suspended from ships, lowered onto the sea from helicopters, or attached to buoys, which transmit the recordings by radio to ships or shore stations.

### b Seismic reflection profilers

These mostly use high-energy, low-frequency explosives to create sound waves, which are reflected from rock layers in the seabed. They can detect the thickness of rock beds and indicate the type of rock.

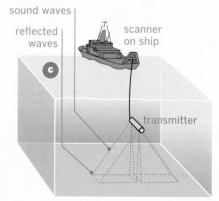

### c Side-scan sonars

These cameras build up a picture or image of surfaces or objects. They are used to map the topography of the seabed.

Strips of seabed up to 37 miles (60 km) wide and 16,400 feet (5,000 m) long can be mapped at a time.

Side-scan sonar can also be used to study fish populations, including their volume, species, and age.

# Tides

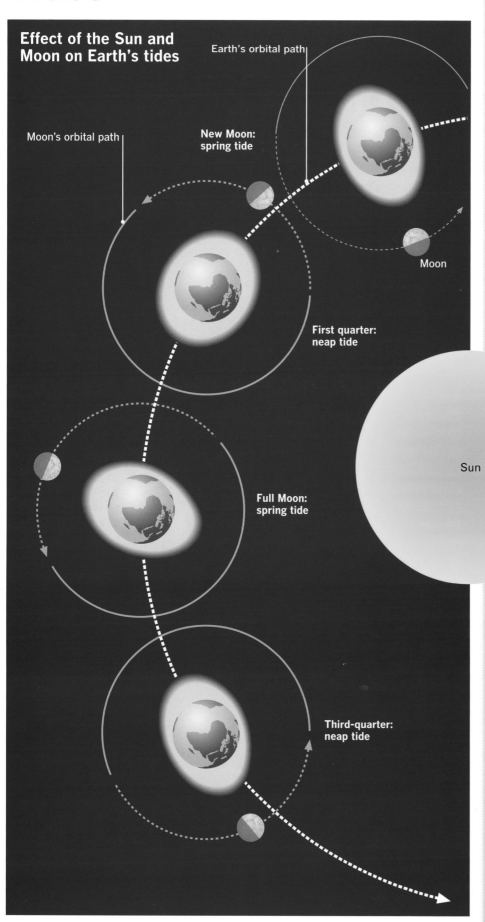

**Effect of the Sun and Moon on Earth's tides**

Earth's orbital path

Moon's orbital path

**New Moon: spring tide**

Moon

**First quarter: neap tide**

**Full Moon: spring tide**

Sun

**Third-quarter: neap tide**

Key words

*equinox*
*neap tide*
*perigee*
*spring tide*

## Spring and neap tides

- Spring and neap tides are generated by the gravitational attraction of the Sun adding to, or counteracting the effect of, the Moon's gravitational attraction.

- When the Sun and Moon are aligned, their gravitational attractions are added and create a higher-than-normal high tide and a correspondingly lower-than-normal low tide. Such large-range tides are *spring tides*. These occur at the full Moon and the new Moon.

- When the Sun and Moon are at right angles (90 degrees) relative to Earth, their gravitational attractions have opposing effects. This creates lower than normal high tides and higher than normal low tides. Such small-range tides are *neap tides*. These occur when the Moon is in its first and third quarters.

- In a lunar month (29.5 days) there are two sets of spring tides and two sets of neaps, with tides of intermediate size in between.

## Unusually large spring tides

- The term "spring tide" derives from the greatest tides of the year, which occur at the vernal (spring) and autumnal equinoxes. At these times, a lunar *perigee* (Moon closest to Earth) and an equinox (Sun directly overhead at the equator) coincide to create spring tides. These spring tides have on average a 20 percent wider tidal range than normal.

## Key words

equator
gyre
ocean
salinity

### Deep-ocean currents

- Water circulates slowly far below the surface of the ocean as a result of differences in water temperature and *salinity*, the amount of mineral salts dissolved in seawater.
- Cold polar waters sink slowly toward the seabed and flow toward the equator, a process known as "subsidence." Currents can also rise from the deep.

### Surface currents

- A surface current is a mass of seawater flowing just below the ocean's surface.
- Winds can disturb ocean waters to a depth of about 330 feet (100 m). This sets currents in motion that can flow for thousands of miles. The direction of these surface currents mainly depends on the prevailing winds and their direction.
- Currents do not flow in straight lines, but are pulled into curves by the Coriolis effect and the shape of the ocean floor. In the subtropics, currents form large circles known as *gyres*.

# Ocean currents

## Deep-sea circulation in the Atlantic Ocean

- **a** Antarctic intermediate water
- **b** Antarctic bottom water
- **c** North Atlantic deep water
- **d** Mediterranean water

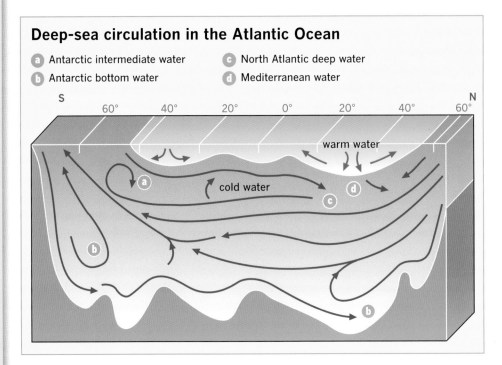

## Surface currents

- **a** Kamchatka
- **b** Kuro Siwo
- **c** North Pacific
- **d** California
- **e** North equatorial
- **f** Equatorial countercurrent
- **g** South equatorial
- **h** East Australian
- **i** West wind drift
- **j** Peru (Humboldt)
- **k** Labrador
- **l** East Greenland
- **m** Gulf Stream
- **n** North Atlantic drift
- **o** Canaries
- **p** North equatorial
- **q** Guinea
- **r** South equatorial
- **s** Brazil
- **t** Falkland
- **u** Benguela
- **v** Aguilhas
- **w** Monsoon drift
- **x** South equatorial
- **y** West Australian
- ← warm currents
- ← cold currents

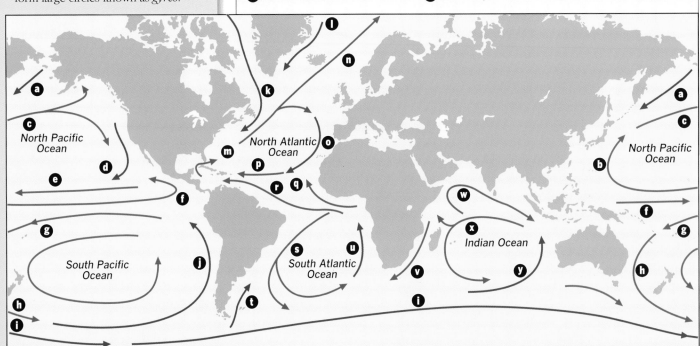

# Wave features

© Diagram Visual Information Ltd.

## Wave features

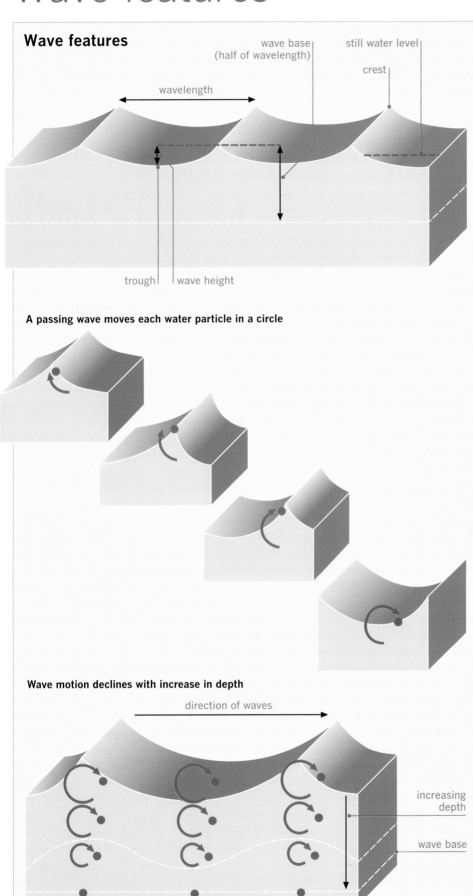

wave base
(half of wavelength)

still water level

crest

wavelength

trough  wave height

**A passing wave moves each water particle in a circle**

**Wave motion declines with increase in depth**

direction of waves

increasing
depth

wave base

## Waves

- A wave is a regular undulation of the surface of the sea, caused by the wind. When wind blows across the sea, it breaks the surface up into ripples. If the wind is strong enough and blows far enough across the water, the ripples build up into waves.

## Length and height

- The length of a wave is measured by the distance between two *crests*. The height of a wave is measured between the *trough* and crest of a wave. The base of a wave is half its wavelength.
- The length and height of a wave depend not only on the wind but also on its *fetch*, the distance the wind has to build up a wave. In a large ocean such as the Pacific, the fetch is so great that swells, or huge, regular, unbroken waves, develop that can travel for thousands of miles before they reach the coast.

## Wave motion

- The water in a wave stays in the same place even though the wave itself travels long distances. As a wave passes through, it moves each water particle in a circle. As waves reach the shore, the water particles are moved in a more elongated shape.

## Wave dimensions

- Water particles at greater depth move in smaller circles. At a certain depth, they are not moved by the wave at all. This depth is known as the "wave base."
- The depth of the wave base is equal to half the wave's length: it is not directly related to the height of the wave.
- An ocean swell with long wavelengths but low wave heights will have a much deeper wave base than tall waves with short wavelengths.

## Key words

*backwash*
*breaker*
*swash*
*tsunami*

## Breakers

● A *breaker* is a wave that spills over and breaks up on the shore.

● As a wave moves into shallow water, the wave base touches the rising seabed and hinders the circulation of water inside the wave. This causes the wavelength and speed to decrease as the waves become closer together and the wave height increases.

● Eventually the wave height increases so much that the top spills over. The wave then rushes up the beach as *swash* and falls back as *backwash*.

## Tsunamis

● A *tsunami* is a huge wave set off by a submarine earthquake. *Tsunami* is Japanese for "harbor wave."

● Tsunamis can also be caused by violent volcanic eruptions at or below sea level.

● It is incorrect to describe a tsunami as a "tidal wave," as its cause has nothing to do with tides.

## The cause of tsunamis

● Shock waves from an earthquake create a tsunami wave on the surface that in mid-ocean has a wave height of approximately three feet (1 m) and a wavelength often in excess of 125 miles (200 km).

● Although barely visible at sea, the tsunami moves at speeds of 435 miles per hour (700 kmph) or more and can travel for several thousand miles.

● As the tsunami approaches land, it loses speed but gains height, often reaching 100 feet (30 m) or more by the time it breaks on the shore. A tsunami causes massive destruction in low-lying areas and can lead to huge loss of life.

# Wave types

## How breakers form

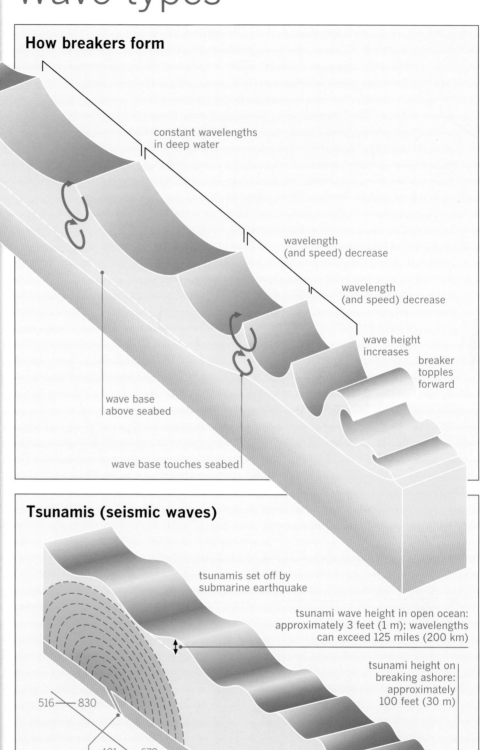

constant wavelengths in deep water

wavelength (and speed) decrease

wavelength (and speed) decrease

wave height increases

breaker topples forward

wave base above seabed

wave base touches seabed

## Tsunamis (seismic waves)

tsunamis set off by submarine earthquake

tsunami wave height in open ocean: approximately 3 feet (1 m); wavelengths can exceed 125 miles (200 km)

tsunami height on breaking ashore: approximately 100 feet (30 m)

516 — 830

421 — 678

297 — 478

93 — 150

30 — 48
miles per hour    kmph

**Decreasing speeds**

submarine earthquake

# Bays and headlands

## Coastal erosion types

**1** On a newly established shoreline, erosion-resistant rock types are commonly interspersed with less resistant rocks. In time, resistant rocks form headlands separated by bays eroded from weaker rock.

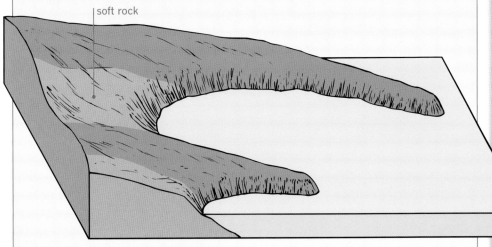

soft rock

**2** Eventually, promontories or headlands are severely eroded by waves. Sea caves and blowholes form, and then sea arches.

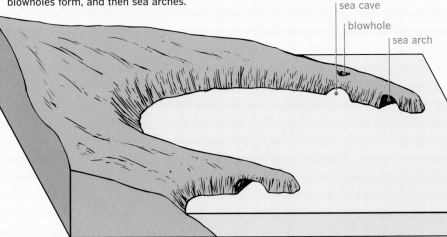

sea cave

blowhole

sea arch

**3** When sea arches collapse, sea stacks are left.

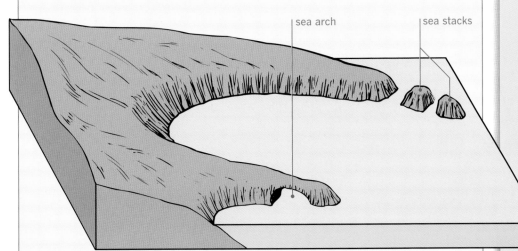

sea arch

sea stacks

### Key words

| | |
|---|---|
| bay | peninsula |
| bight | point |
| blowhole | promontory |
| gulf | |
| headland | |

## Bays and headlands

- A *bay* is a wide, curving indentation in a coastline with a headland at either side. A cove is a small, narrow bay, often on a rocky coast, while a *gulf* is an inlet of the sea with a large area, generally more indented and enclosed than a bay. A *bight* is a huge bay.
  - An area of high land jutting out into the sea is called a *headland* or *promontory*. A *peninsula* is a long, narrow piece of land ending in a headland; a *point* is at the very end of the headland.

## Changing coastline

- Coastal landscapes change very quickly as waves beat against the coastline, eroding it in places and moving sand and shingle elsewhere along the coast.
- The force of the waves against a rocky headland or cliff can be considerable, especially during a storm. The constant pounding of seawater, sand, and shingle against the rocks soon wears them down and splits them apart.
  - In places, waves can erode the bottom of a cliff to create a sea cave. If there is a fault at the back of the cave, the force of the waves compresses the air and forces air and spray up into the fault. This eventually breaks through to the top of the cliff to create a *blowhole*.
- Waves can sometimes cut through a headland to create a sea arch. In time, the arch will collapse, leaving a series of freestanding stacks. Waves will eventually erode these into stumps of rock.

# Sea cliffs

© Diagram Visual Information Ltd.

**Key words**

*tide*

## Sea cliffs

● A sea cliff is a steep rock face
formed by the action of the
waves undercutting a slope of
rock. As the waves wear back
the cliff, they create a broad
platform of rock between the
high and low tide marks.

## Cliff and wave-cut platform

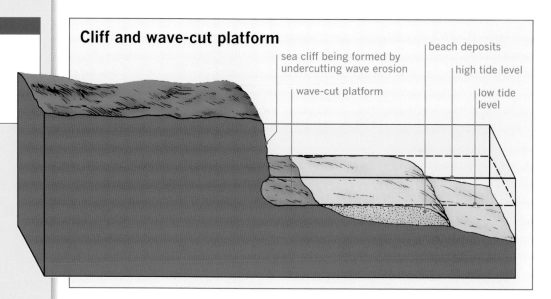

sea cliff being formed by
undercutting wave erosion

beach deposits

high tide level

wave-cut platform

low tide
level

## Coastal erosion: cliffs

**Cliff retreat**

**Boulder beach**

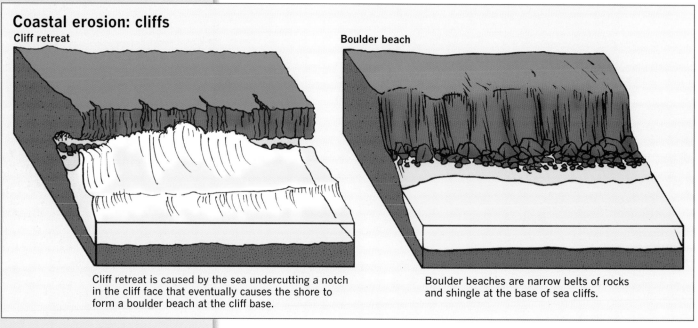

Cliff retreat is caused by the sea undercutting a notch
in the cliff face that eventually causes the shore to
form a boulder beach at the cliff base.

Boulder beaches are narrow belts of rocks
and shingle at the base of sea cliffs.

## Coastal rock layers

**Gentle cliff slopes**

**Steep cliffs**

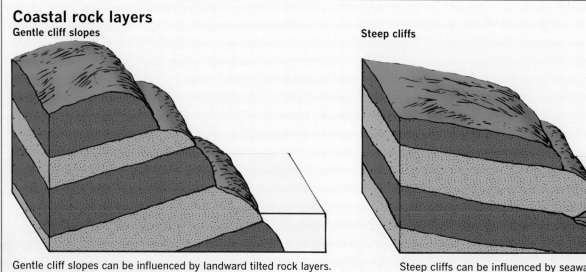

Gentle cliff slopes can be influenced by landward tilted rock layers.

Steep cliffs can be influenced by seaward-tilted rock layers.

# Waves and beaches

## Coastal deposition

**Destructive wave (plunging breaker) on steep shingle beach**

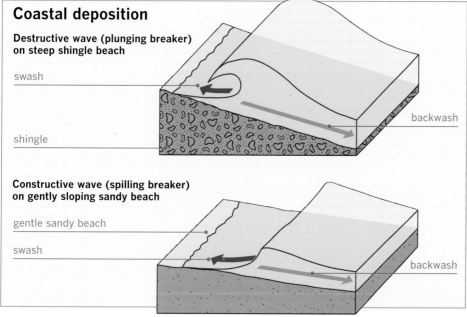

swash

shingle

backwash

**Constructive wave (spilling breaker) on gently sloping sandy beach**

gentle sandy beach

swash

backwash

## Beach features

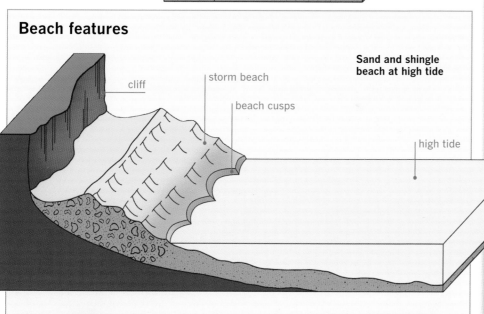

cliff

storm beach

beach cusps

**Sand and shingle beach at high tide**

high tide

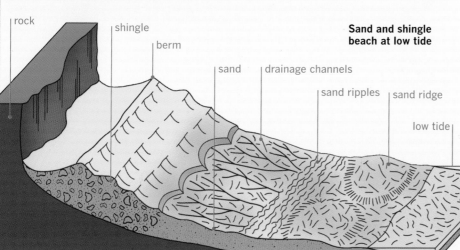

rock

shingle

berm

sand

drainage channels

sand ripples

sand ridge

**Sand and shingle beach at low tide**

low tide

## Types of wave

- A wave's energy is dispelled as it rushes up the beach as *swash* and then drains back as *backwash*. Both swash and backwash can carry material such as sand and shingle over a beach.
- A constructive wave has a stronger swash than a backwash—more material is moved up the beach by the swash than back again by the backwash. A destructive wave has a stronger backwash than a swash—less material is moved up the beach by the swash than back again by the backwash. Constructive waves therefore build up a beach while destructive waves break it down.
- A spilling breaker is a low constructive wave that breaks gradually on a gently sloping, shallow sandy beach. A plunging breaker is a high destructive wave that curls over and crashes onto a steeper shingle shore. Surging breakers are constructive waves that steepen to a peak and then surge up the beach.

## Tidal differences

- A *storm beach* is a band of sand and shingle thrown above high-tide mark by waves during a storm.
- A beach ridge or *berm* is a mass of sand and shingle on a beach parallel with the high-water mark that indicates the limit of the swash at each high tide. A beach ridge will thus form at the highest spring tide; below it will be a descending series of ridges marking each subsequent high tide down to the neap tide.
- A beach cusp is one of a series of scallop-shaped deposits of sand and shingle scooped out by waves striking the beach at an angle.
- As the tide retreats, it carves drainage channels, sand ripples, and sand ridges out of the beach down to the low-water mark.

**Key words**

*groin*
*longshore drift*

## Longshore drift

- *Longshore drift* is the slow shifting of sand and shingle along a beach when waves strike it at an angle.
- Waves striking a beach at an oblique angle carry material up the beach with their swash at that same angle. The waves' backwash then carries that material straight back down the beach. In this way, sand and shingle are carried slowly along the beach in a zigzag pattern.

## Groins

- Longshore drift can erode a beach and pile up the sand and shingle further along the coast in an unsuitable place, such as a harbor mouth or a river estuary. To prevent this, wooden, stone, or concrete barriers called *groins* are built at regular intervals along the beach, effectively creating a series of miniature bays.

## Bay beaches

- Before entering a bay, waves reach headlands, and their energy is therefore concentrated there. Material eroded from a headland is often washed into the bay, forming a bay-head beach.
- Waves hitting a coastline will slow first at the headland and then curve into the bay, a process known as "wave refraction." Once in the bay, the waves will have little impact on that part of the bay beach sheltered by the headland.
- If the waves then strike the bay beach at an angle, longshore drift will erode the beach toward the opposite headland.

# Longshore drift

## Coastal deposition by longshore drift

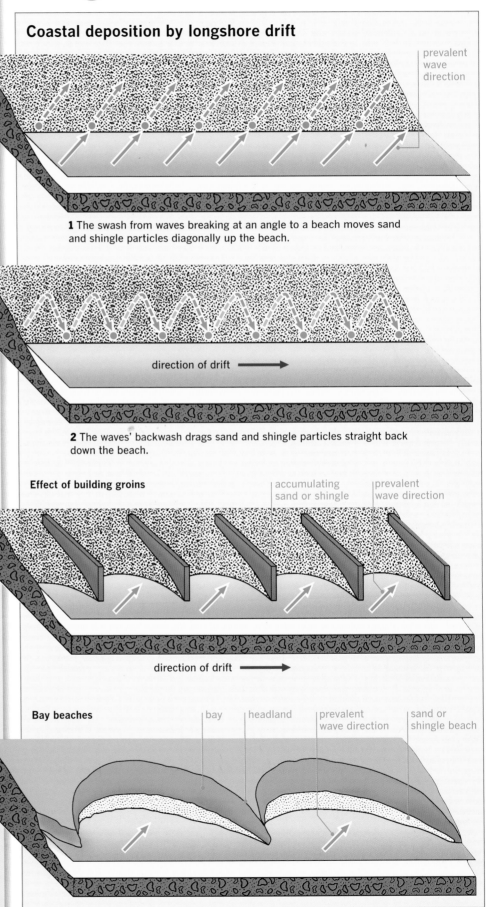

**1** The swash from waves breaking at an angle to a beach moves sand and shingle particles diagonally up the beach.

**2** The waves' backwash drags sand and shingle particles straight back down the beach.

**Effect of building groins**

**Bay beaches**

# Spits and bars

**Key words**

bar
spit
tombolo

## Features of a deposition dominated shore

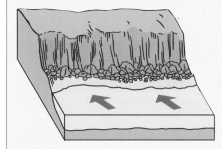

**Boulder beach**
A boulder beach is a narrow belt of boulders and shingle at the base of a sea cliff.

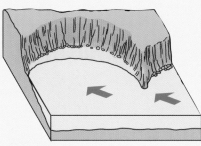

**Bay-head beach**
A bay-head beach is a sandy crescent lying in the bay between two rocky promontories.

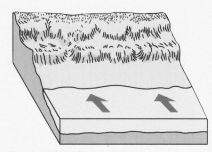

**Lowland beach**
A lowland beach is broad, gently sloping, sandy, and usually features a strip of shingle on the upper shore backed by dunes of windblown sand.

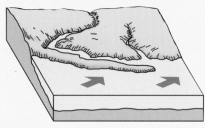

**Spit**
A spit forms from sediment deposited on the down-current side of a promontory.

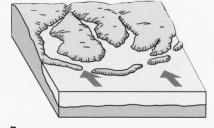

**Bar**
A bar is a spit or double-spit that entirely or almost entirely closes off a bay. Bars also form as offshore strips of sand or shingle parallel to the coast.

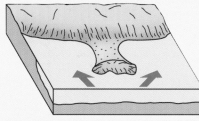

**Tombolo**
A tombolo is formed when sediment accumulates to form a causeway between the mainland and a near-shore island.

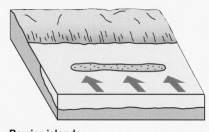

**Barrier islands**
These may originate from spits or bars, or from engulfed coastal sand dunes. They are characteristic of the east and southeast coast of the United States, between Long Island, New York, and southern Texas.

## Features of a deposition-dominated shore

● Depositional (deposition-dominated) shores receive sediment from eroding parts of the coastline, discharging rivers, and biogenous sediments (those of biological origin) in local shallow waters.

● Longshore currents and longshore drift generate characteristic coastal features, particularly where the coastline is irregular and the water is relatively shallow.

## Deposition beaches

● Boulder and bay-head beaches are both built up by deposits carried up the beach by the swash.

● A sandy, gently sloping lowland beach has a characteristic strip of shingle on the upper shore and is backed by dunes of windblown sand.

## Spits and bars

● A *spit* is a narrow bank of sand projecting out from a bend in the coast, formed by longshore drift washing sand along the coast and depositing it as a sand spit. This often occurs across a river mouth, where the waves meet deeper water and slow down, depositing the sand across the mouth.

● If a spit extends to an island, it creates a sandy causeway linking the island to the mainland known as a *tombolo*.

● A *bar* is a spit that almost or entirely closes off a bay. Bars can form as offshore strips of sand or shingle parallel to the coast.

● Barrier islands can originate from spits, bars, or engulfed coastal sand dunes that have been eroded to form sandy islands just off the coast.

**Key words**

coast

# Raised coastlines

## Emergent highland coasts

- Emergent highland coasts feature raised beaches. A raised beach, often covered with shells or shingle, stands perched high and dry above sea level.
- The raised beach is an old shoreline and adjoining wave-cut rock platform, up to 2,600 feet (792 m) across.
- Inland, above the raised beach, rises an old sea cliff, perhaps pierced by wave-cut caves.
- Below the raised beach, a new sea cliff and wave-cut platform form the seaward boundary.
- Successive land movements can create a series of raised beaches, one above the other. Many form where land depressed by ice has re-emerged after the ice has melted.

## Emergent lowland coasts

- Emergent lowland coasts are coastal plains that slope gently to the sea and are rimmed by marshes, sandy beaches, bars, lagoons, and spits.
- The plains are uplifted continuations of the shallow offshore continental shelf, and thus may be floored by seashells, sand, and clay consolidated into limestone, sandstone, and shale.
- Inland, the plains may end abruptly below a line of hills marking the old coastline.

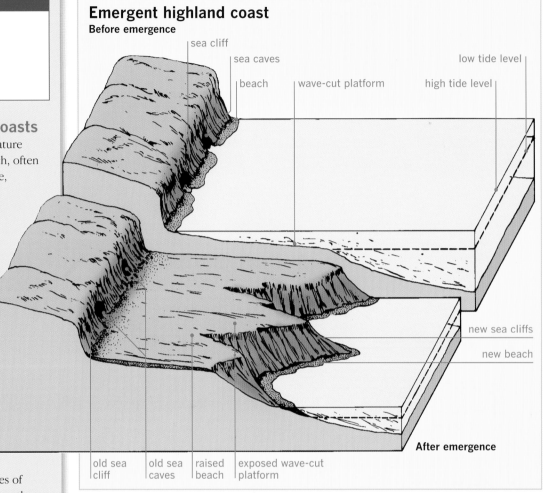

**Emergent highland coast**
Before emergence

sea cliff
sea caves
beach
wave-cut platform
low tide level
high tide level

new sea cliffs
new beach

After emergence

old sea cliff
old sea caves
raised beach
exposed wave-cut platform

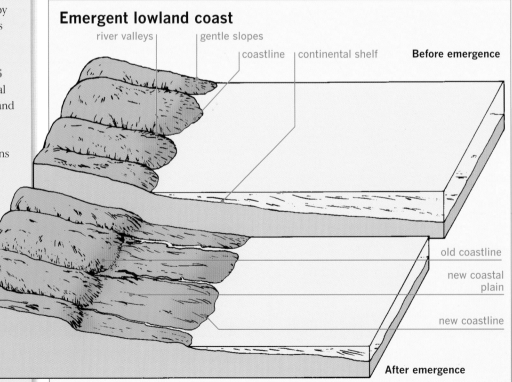

**Emergent lowland coast**

river valleys
gentle slopes
coastline
continental shelf
Before emergence

old coastline
new coastal plain
new coastline

After emergence

# Submerged coastlines

## Submerged coastline types

### Ria coasts

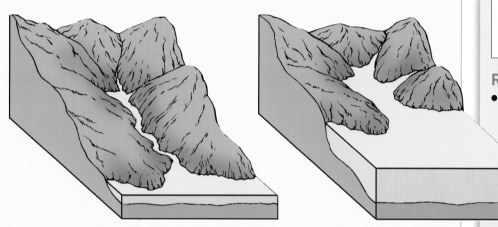

### Fjord coasts

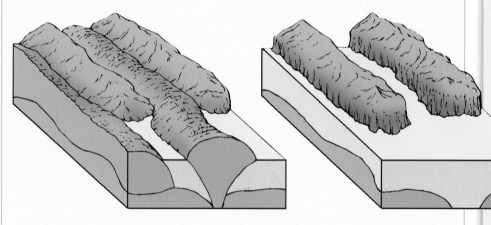

### Longitudinal coasts

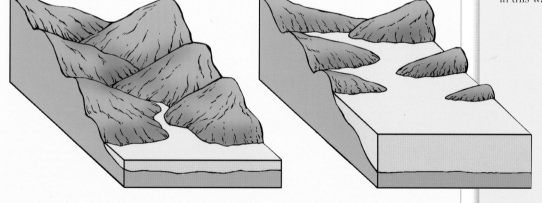

**Key words**

fjord
longitudinal
  coastline
moraine
ria

## Ria coasts

- *Rias* are drowned river valleys forming long, funnel-shaped, branching inlets.
  - They meet the sea at right angles and have a V-shaped cross profile.
  - Rias abound in southwest England, southwest Ireland, and Japan.

## Fjord coasts

- *Fjords* are submerged, glacially deepened inlets with sheer, high sides, a U-shaped cross profile, and a submerged seaward sill largely formed of end *moraine*.
- Fjords occur in Norway, south Alaska, British Columbia, south Chile, Greenland, and New Zealand's South Island.

## Longitudinal coasts

- *Longitudinal coastlines* (also known as drowned concordant, Dalmatian, or Pacific coastlines) feature mountain ridges that are parallel to the sea.
- Flooding forms valleys into sounds and isolated ridges as long, narrow offshore islands.
- Croatia's Dalmatian coast and many British Columbian islands are shaped in this way.

# Coral reefs

## The coral polyp

- A *coral reef* is an underwater ridge created by the coral polyp, a tiny sea creature.
- Coral polyps protect themselves by secreting calcium carbonate to form a hard skeleton around their soft, cylindrical bodies. They spend their entire lives in one place, fixed to the skeletons of other living and dead polyps. Gradually, a reef of countless dead polyp skeletons builds up.

## Fringing reef

- A fringing reef is a narrow coral reef attached to the shore as a continuous wave-washed platform, or separated from it by a narrow, shallow lagoon.

- Fringing reefs abound off the Bahamas and Caribbean islands.

## Barrier reef

- A barrier reef is a broad coral platform separated from the coast by a wide deep lagoon or strait of water. Some barrier reefs were formed on flat coasts where the sea level has subsequently risen after the end of the last ice age, submerging the reef. The coral has then kept growing to keep pace with the rising water, creating the great depth many barrier reefs attain.

- The world's largest barrier reef is the Great Barrier Reef off the northeast coast of Australia, which stretches for 1,260 miles (2,027 km) and varies in width from 18–95 miles (30–150 km).

## Coral reef types

**Fringing reef**

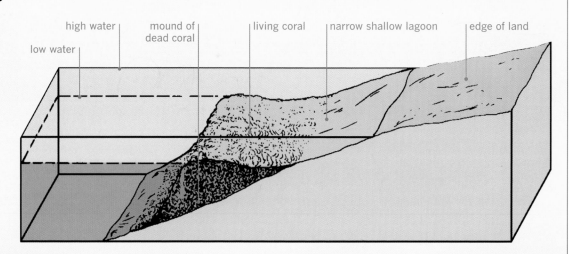

high water · mound of dead coral · living coral · narrow shallow lagoon · edge of land · low water

**Barrier reef**

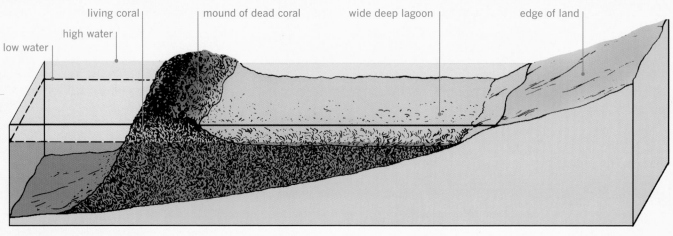

living coral · high water · low water · mound of dead coral · wide deep lagoon · edge of land

# Atolls and guyots

## Atoll

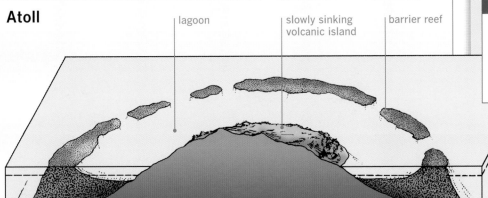

lagoon — slowly sinking volcanic island — barrier reef

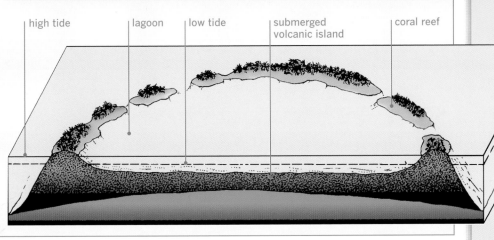

high tide — lagoon — low tide — submerged volcanic island — coral reef

### Atolls

- An *atoll* is a ring-shaped island made of a coral reef surrounding a lagoon.
- The origins of atolls are still unclear, but it is thought that the coral reef starts as a fringing reef around a volcanic island.
- As the volcano subsides, or the sea level rises at the end of an ice age, a seawater lagoon forms inside the ring of coral, turning the fringing reef into a barrier reef.
- After the volcanic island subsides completely beneath the sea, the ring of coral reef known as an atoll is left.
- Over time, vegetation grows on the atoll, while the sea has eroded the coral into fine sand.
- Coral atolls are particularly common in the Pacific and Indian oceans.

### Guyots

- A *guyot* is a flat-topped volcanic seamount; a lone mountain standing on the seafloor, totally submerged by the sea.
- Once an active volcano formed at an oceanic spreading ridge and standing above sea level, wave action has subsequently eroded and flattened its summit.
- As the ocean crust moves beneath it, the flat-topped volcano is submerged and thereafter considered a guyot.

## Guyot

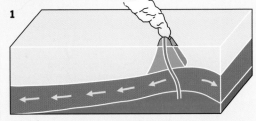

**1** A volcanic island is formed at an oceanic spreading ridge.

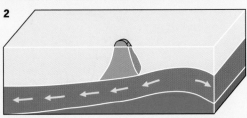

**2** The volcanic island moves away from the spreading ridge, and as it sinks, wave action erodes its top.

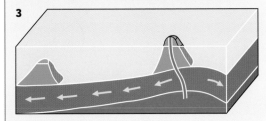

**3** The submerged island moves further away from its source and the top is flattened to form a guyot: a flat-topped seamount. Meanwhile a new volcanic island is formed at the spreading ridge.

© Diagram Visual Information Ltd.

**Key words**

denudation
erosion
scree
talus
weathering

## Weathering

- When rock is exposed on Earth's surface, wind, rain, and other physical or chemical processes gradually break it down in a process known as *weathering*.
- The three main types of weathering are mechanical, organic, and chemical.
- Only rocks on the surface are usually affected by weathering, but water filtering down through the ground can weather rocks as deep as 600 feet (185 m). In general, the more extreme the climate, the faster weathering takes place.

## Mechanical weathering caused by low temperatures

- Extremes of heat and cold can break down rock by the simple mechanical process of expansion and contraction.
- In cold regions, low temperatures can fracture rock when intrusive rainwater entering cracks in the surface of a rock expands once frozen.
- As the frozen water expands, it begins to fracture the rock, causing small fragments to break away. Most of these fragments will stay in the same place.
- However, wind, rain, ice, and waves from the sea can all carry these fragments away by *erosion*. These eroded fragments are then carried to another site and deposited as sediment.
- The combined result of weathering and erosion is known as *denudation*. Over millions of years denudation can destroy even the strongest rock.

## Scree

- Severe shattering by frost can produce huge piles of rock fragments known as *scree* or *talus* that form scree slopes at the bottom of a rock or hill face.
- Frost can also shatter mountaintops into jagged peaks.

# Mechanical weathering

## Effects of low temperatures

In cold regions, frost and ice action at night or in winter help to break down surface rocks.

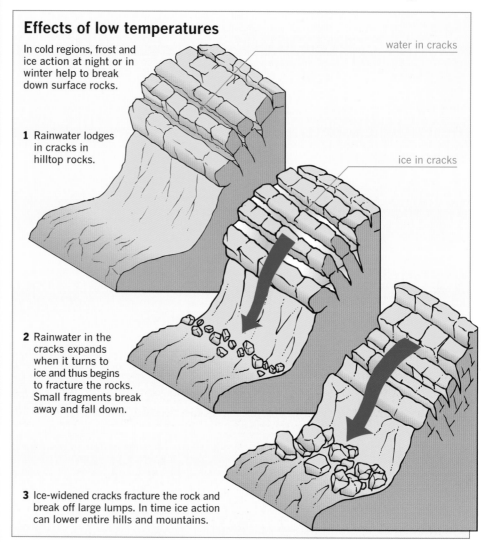

water in cracks

ice in cracks

**1** Rainwater lodges in cracks in hilltop rocks.

**2** Rainwater in the cracks expands when it turns to ice and thus begins to fracture the rocks. Small fragments break away and fall down.

**3** Ice-widened cracks fracture the rock and break off large lumps. In time ice action can lower entire hills and mountains.

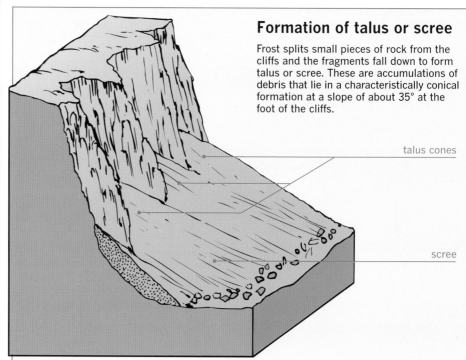

## Formation of talus or scree

Frost splits small pieces of rock from the cliffs and the fragments fall down to form talus or scree. These are accumulations of debris that lie in a characteristically conical formation at a slope of about 35° at the foot of the cliffs.

talus cones

scree

# Mechanical and organic weathering

**Key words**

chelation
insolation
thermoclastic
  erosion
weathering

## Effects of high temperatures

High temperatures cause rock to expand and sometimes to fracture, causing mechanical weathering.

**1** Desert rock expands in hot sunshine.

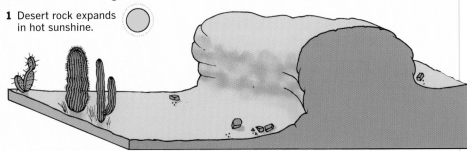

**2** At night rock cools and contracts.

**3** Alternate high daytime and low nighttime temperatures result in pieces of rock breaking off.

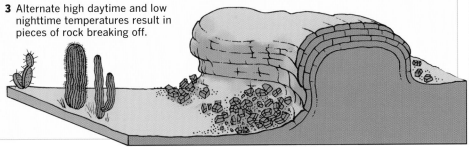

## Organic weathering

Vegetation produces organic acids that help to break up surface rocks already weakened by mechanical and chemical weathering. Tree roots widen cracks in rock, letting in air and water. Burrowing animals contribute to weathering by loosening surface materials.

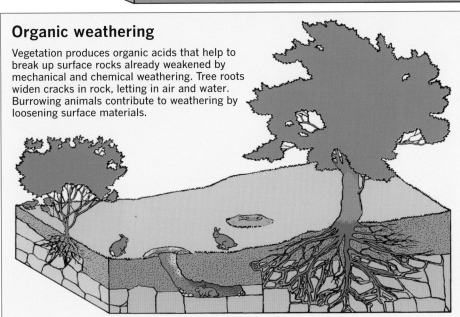

## Mechanical weathering

● Mechanical weathering breaks down a rock into smaller and smaller pieces. Each piece has the same characteristics as the original, larger rock. In this respect, mechanical weathering differs from chemical weathering, in which the rock's chemistry is altered.

## Mechanical weathering caused by high temperatures

● Rocks in hot places such as deserts expand during the heat of the day and contract in the cooler temperatures of the night. This process is known as "insolation" or *thermoclastic erosion*.

● Although insolation is significant in weathering rocks in hot places, it is probably less important than chemical weathering.

## Organic weathering

● Organic or biological weathering is the breaking down of rock by living organisms. These might include tree or plant roots or burrowing animals.

● Although the actions of living organisms are important in weathering, the acids produced by these organisms—especially those produced once they are dead and decaying—play a much more important role.

● The process by which rocks are eaten away by acids from soil humus is known as *chelation*.

**Key words**

*carbonation*

## Chemical weathering

- Chemical weathering is the breaking down of rocks by chemical reactions, usually involving water, as many substances dissolved in rainwater form weak acids. These acids slowly attack rocks and dissolve the minerals that hold the rock grains together.
- Water seeping through cracks in a rock can chemically weather rocks below ground. The boundary between the weathered rock above and the deeper, unweathered rock below is known as the basal weathering front. This can be as much as 200 feet (60 m) below ground.

## Carbonation

- The chemical breakdown of rocks by carbonic acid is known as *carbonation*.
- Carbonic acid is formed by carbon dioxide in the air dissolving in rainwater. This weak acid quickly eats away limestone, the most permeable of all rocks because it has a well-developed joint system.
- Carbonic acid eats away limestone to form bare limestone pavements with clints (ridges), grikes (grooves), and sinkholes (swallowholes). As water flows into a sinkhole, it forms a funnel-shaped hollow or doline, up to 330 feet (100 m) across. Under the sinkhole, chemical weathering of the rock may form deep potholes with deep waterfalls.
- Underground, the water carves galleries and tunnels. Dissolved calcium bicarbonate from the rock forms insoluble calcite, which builds stalactites, stalagmites, and terraced ledges called "gours."

# Chemical weathering

## How caves are formed

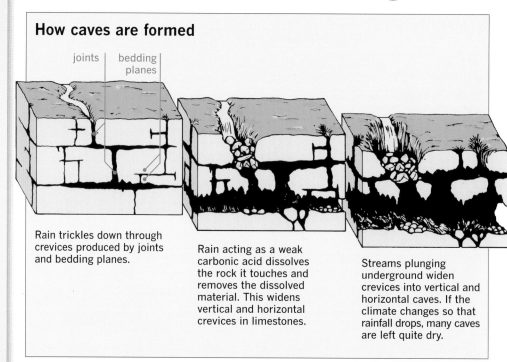

joints    bedding planes

Rain trickles down through crevices produced by joints and bedding planes.

Rain acting as a weak carbonic acid dissolves the rock it touches and removes the dissolved material. This widens vertical and horizontal crevices in limestones.

Streams plunging underground widen crevices into vertical and horizontal caves. If the climate changes so that rainfall drops, many caves are left quite dry.

## Exploring a limestone cave system

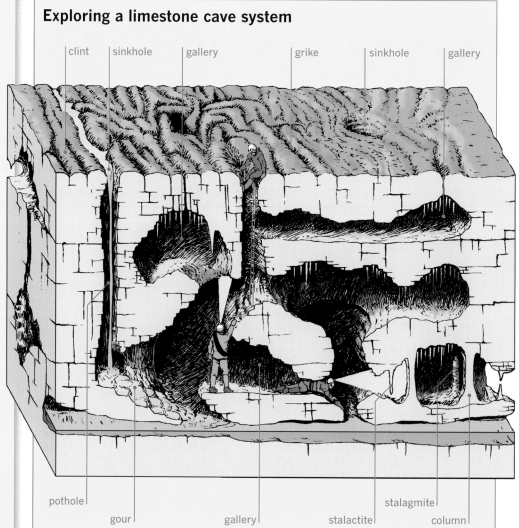

clint    sinkhole    gallery    grike    sinkhole    gallery

pothole    gour    gallery    stalactite    stalagmite    column

# Chemical weathering: hydration

**Key words**

granite
hydration
kopje
tor

## Unweathered granite mass

Granite can be destroyed by hydration, a process in which some minerals take up water and expand, breaking up the rock that contains them. Hydration starts to act as rainwater trickles down through joints in the rock.

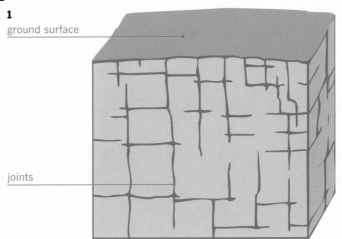

1

ground surface

joints

## After subsurface weathering

Hydration widens the joints in the granite, splitting it up into blocks separated by loose mineral fragments. The former ingredients of granite loosen and fall out as the rock decomposes.

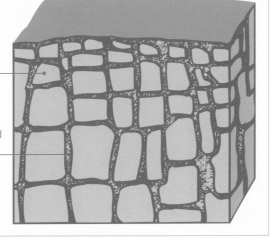

2

granite split into blocks

disintegrated or decomposed granite

## Tor

Tors are massive blocks of weathered granite that stand above the surrounding landscape. They crown hilltops where the surrounding surface has been worn down by erosion.

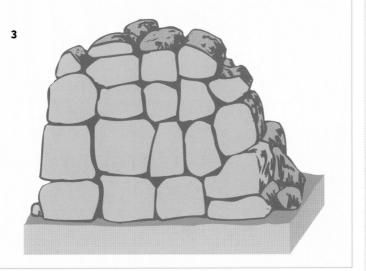

3

### Hydration

- *Hydration* is the breakdown of rocks as they absorb water.
- During this absorption, rocks swell and soften, leaving them weaker.
- Hydration is therefore as much a process of mechanical weathering as it is of chemical weathering.

### Weathering granite

- *Granite* is one of the hardest of rocks, but its high feldspar content makes it susceptible to chemical weathering and hydration.
- In addition, the many joints in granite enable hydration to carry on well below the surface.
- Hydration in granite occurs as rainwater trickles down through its joints. Some minerals in granite take up rainwater and expand, thus breaking up the granite block that contains them.
- As the joints widen, the granite block is split up into smaller blocks separated by mineral fragments. These fragments become loose and fall out as the rock gradually decomposes.
- As the weathered rock is washed away, the original granite block is exposed as a rocky outcrop known as a *tor*. These are usually found on the top of smooth, grassy hills.
- Torlike features found in the tropics are known as *kopjes*.

**Key words**

*granite*
*hydration*
*sand*
*soil*

## Breakdown of granite

- There are many different types of granite, but it is largely composed of quartz, with varying amounts of feldspar, biotite (a form of mica), and amphibole, a silicate mineral.
- As hydration takes place, some of the minerals in the granite expand and are washed out as the rock gradually decomposes.
- The minerals are then dissolved and crushed, leaving the quartz crystals intact. This is then commonly known as *sand*.

## Evolving texture of sand

- When sand becomes mixed with stones, silt, and clay, it forms *soil*: a loose mixture of small rock particles and rotting organic matter that covers the ground.
- Silt may be removed from the soil by the winnowing effects of wind and water.
- Further sorting separates stones, sand grains, and clay particles, and progressively wears down the size and angularity of the quartz crystals.
- Eventually only sand remains. Its grains are now a much finer texture than the quartz crystal residue originally derived from the granite: the finest, most rounded sand particles are those abraded by rubbing against rocks and each other in deserts.

# From granite to sand

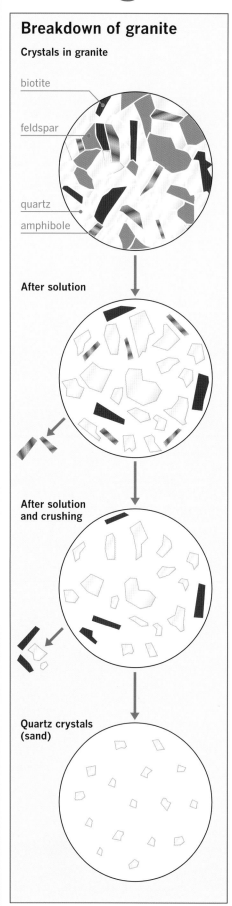

### Breakdown of granite

**Crystals in granite**

biotite
feldspar
quartz
amphibole

**After solution**

**After solution and crushing**

**Quartz crystals (sand)**

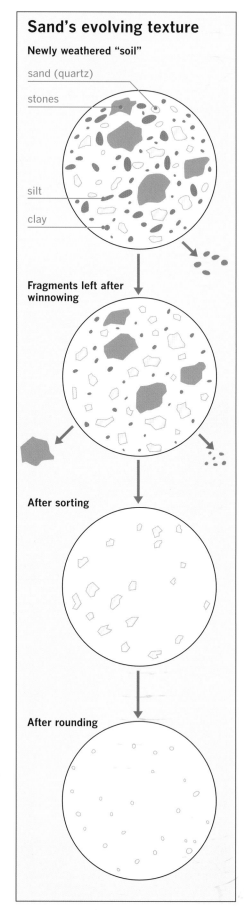

### Sand's evolving texture

**Newly weathered "soil"**

sand (quartz)
stones
silt
clay

**Fragments left after winnowing**

**After sorting**

**After rounding**

# Soil formation

## Soil formation

**First stage**

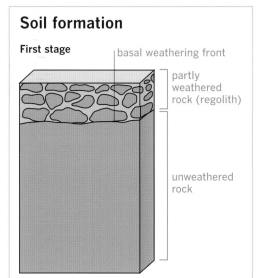

basal weathering front

partly weathered rock (regolith)

unweathered rock

**Immature soil**

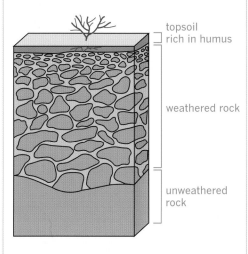

topsoil rich in humus

weathered rock

unweathered rock

**Mature soil**

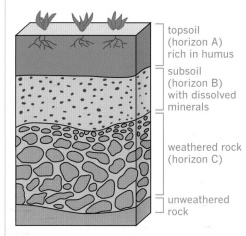

topsoil (horizon A) rich in humus

subsoil (horizon B) with dissolved minerals

weathered rock (horizon C)

unweathered rock

## Soil types

← movement of soluble material

**Humid climate**

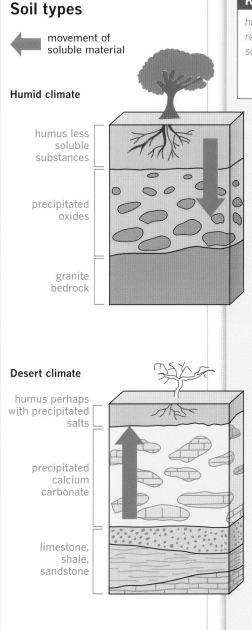

humus less soluble substances

precipitated oxides

granite bedrock

**Desert climate**

humus perhaps with precipitated salts

precipitated calcium carbonate

limestone, shale, sandstone

**Tropical climate**

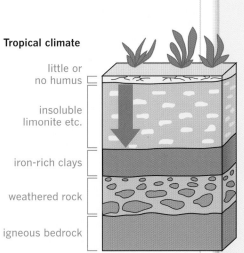

little or no humus

insoluble limonite etc.

iron-rich clays

weathered rock

igneous bedrock

## Soil

● *Soil* is composed of weathered rock fragments and rotting organic matter. The variety of organisms living in the soil ensures that it is an ever-changing dynamic material.

## Soil formation

● Prior to the formation of soil, a layer of partly weathered rock known as *regolith* lies above a much deeper layer of unweathered rock. The boundary between the two is known as the "basal weathering front."

● Over the years, a layer of organic material or "topsoil" forms over the regolith as plants grow, die, and decay on the surface. This topsoil gradually becomes rich in *humus*, a dark mass of rotting organic material formed when microorganisms digest plant and animal remains.

● Humus restores minerals and nutrients to the soil, a stage known as "immature" or "skeletal" soil.

● Eventually, a deep, humus-rich mature topsoil forms over a layer of subsoil poorer in humus but containing dissolved minerals washed down from above.

● Each layer of mature soil is known as a "horizon."

## Soil types

● Soil varies according to the climate it is formed in.

● In a humid climate, soil water washes soluble substances down and out of the soil.

● In a desert climate, soil water carries dissolved mineral salts upwards as water evaporates on the surface. These can form a hard desert crust on the surface.

● In a tropical climate, the soil has little or no humus.

**Key words**

*ped*

## Soil texture

- Soil texture depends on the size of the grains in the soil. The exact size of the three grains—clay (the smallest), silt, and sand (the largest)—varies according to which soil classification system is used.
- Because there are so many different soils in the world, no single system of soil classification has yet been adopted internationally.

## Soil classification

- Soils are roughly classified as clay soils, silty soils, and sandy soils. The percentage of clay, silt, or sand in the soil, either individually or in combination, determines its classification. A loam soil is a roughly even mix of all three grains.
- A clay soil is heavy, rich in nutrients, and retains water. A sandy soil is dry, light, but relatively infertile. A silty soil is fairly moist and fertile. A loam soil is the best for plant growth.

## Soil structure

- Soil grains stick together as clumps, known as *peds*. There are five main types of ped, and therefore five main types of soil structure: platelike peds; blocklike peds; crumbly or granular peds; prismatic peds, which are shaped into long, many-sided columns; and nuciform or formless peds.
- The structure of soil affects how easy it is to work and how porous and permeable it is.

# Soil textures

## Soil particle diameters

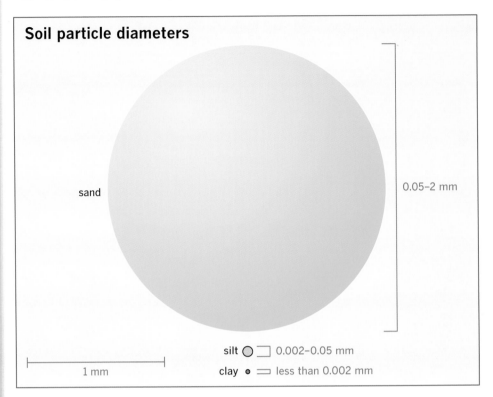

sand

0.05–2 mm

1 mm

silt ○ ▭ 0.002–0.05 mm

clay • ▭ less than 0.002 mm

## Texture classes

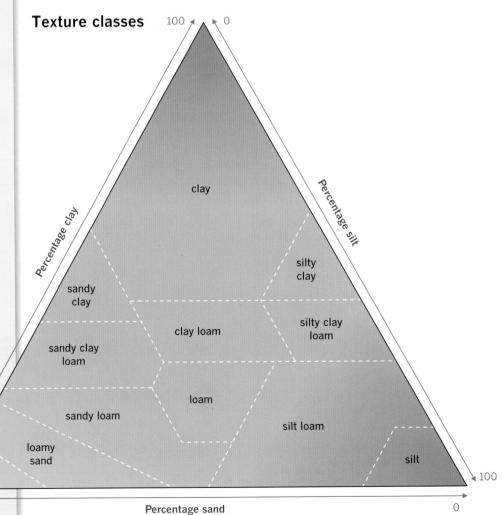

# Soils of the USA

**Key words**

*epipedon*

## Predominant soil types

### The contiguous states

Mountain and desert soils predominate in the mountainous west, grassland soils in the center, and forest soils in the east.

### Alaska

Arctic tundra soils dominate northern Alaska. Mountain soils fringe the Pacific coast. Between the two lie regions of forest soils.

### Hawaii

Mountain soils figure strongly on Hawaii itself. Forest soils feature on other islands in the group.

**Predominant soils**

 forest

 grassland

 desert

 mountain

 tundra

## U.S. soil types

- There are at least 10,000 different soil types in the USA, roughly classified according to the landscape in which they occur.
- The most detailed soil classification system used in the USA is the *Comprehensive Soil Classification System* (CSCS) or "Seventh Approximation System."
- The CSCS was devised by the Department of Agriculture and groups soils according to certain key properties and the existence of a particular horizon or surface humus layer called an *epipedon*.

**Key words**

*regolith*

## Mass movement

- Mass movement is the downhill movement of regolith—rock and weathered material—when it is detached from the underlying bedrock. There are five main types of mass movement.

## Rockslides and rockfalls

- Rockslides and rockfalls are both forms of landslide. They may be set off by an earthquake, heavy rainfall causing saturation of the rock, or waves crashing on them.
- A rockslide occurs when a mass of rock moves rapidly down a slope.
- A rockfall occurs when fragments of rock break away from a cliff or a steep slope. Rockslides are more dangerous than rockfalls because they take place on lower slopes and are therefore more likely to be closer to human habitation.

# Mass movement

## Rockslide

In rockslides, rock slips down a sloping fault.

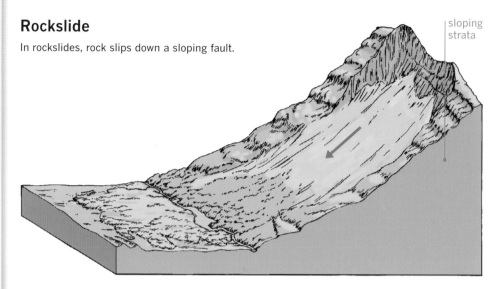

sloping strata

## Creep

In creep, soil or rock gradually creeps downhill, displacing trees and fences.

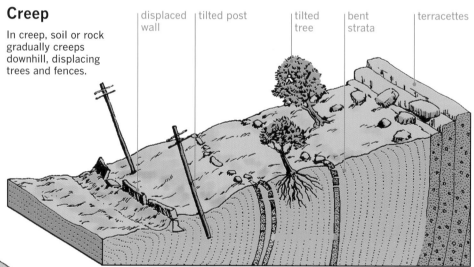

displaced wall | tilted post | tilted tree | bent strata | terracettes

## Rockfall

In rockfalls, fragments fall from cliffs.

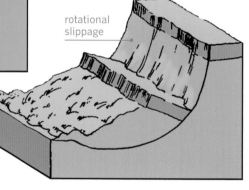

cliff

## Slump

Hillside rock or soil tilts back as it slips down a concave surface.

rotational slippage

## Mudflow

Mud charged with water flows down a slope.

# Slopes

## Slope decline

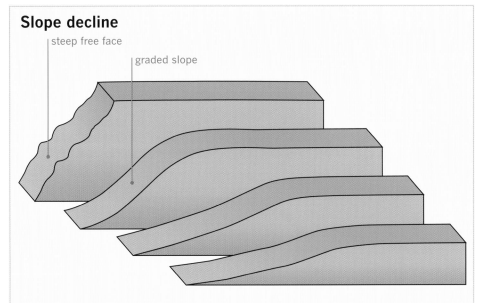

steep free face

graded slope

## Slope (or parallel) retreat

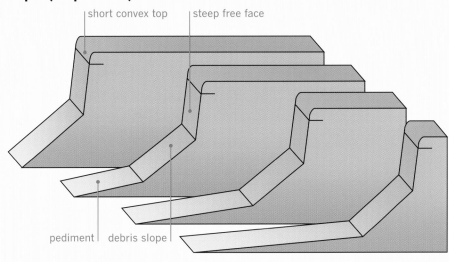

short convex top     steep free face

pediment | debris slope

## Slope replacement

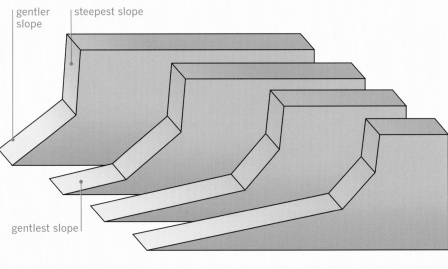

gentler slope     steepest slope

gentlest slope

**Key words**

*geomorphology*
*weathering*

## Slopes

- A slope profile is the shape of a hillside seen side-on. Hillsides are so varied in shape it is difficult to describe them accurately.
- Geomorphologists—scientists who study landforms—divide a slope into a series of slope units called straight and curved elements. There are three main theories of slope development in *geomorphology*: slope decline, slope or parallel retreat, and slope replacement.

## Slope decline

- Slope decline occurs when a slope gets gentler as it is worn away over time. This is because a slope's upper sections are weathered more than its lower sections.
- As a result, the old, steep face smoothes into a graded slope, convex toward the top and concave toward the bottom. The curvature of the slope gradually declines and the height reduces. This typically occurs in moist, temperate areas.

## Slope or parallel retreat

- In semi-arid regions, a slope might be worn back rather than worn away, thus retaining the same shape and staying at exactly the same angle.
- As it moves back, an angled slope of debris is formed below, while at the very bottom of the slope, a gentler pediment of debris forms and lengthens.

## Slope replacement

- Slope replacement occurs as the slope is worn back. The gentlest lower slope of debris gets longer and higher as it piles up against the steepest upper slope, which gets shorter.
- This replacement is typical of arid areas.

**Key words**

*precipitation*

## The water cycle

● Water is constantly recycled between land and sea. First, sea water evaporates (**1**), becoming invisible water vapor that rises in air. As the water vapor cools and condenses it produces droplets that form clouds (**2**). Windblown clouds travel inland. As they rise to cross mountains, they cool and their droplets coalesce, forming *precipitation*: raindrops or snowflakes that fall to the ground (**3**). Rainwater and melted snow feed lakes and rivers (**4**). Rivers flowing downhill return water to the sea (**5**). Water vapor rising from soil and plants and breathed out by animals (**6**) also forms part of the water cycle.

## Rainwater

● When rainwater hits the ground, some sinks into it, some flows over the surface as streams and rivers, some evaporates in the heat, and some is taken up by plants, later returning to the atmosphere.

# Water cycle

## The water cycle

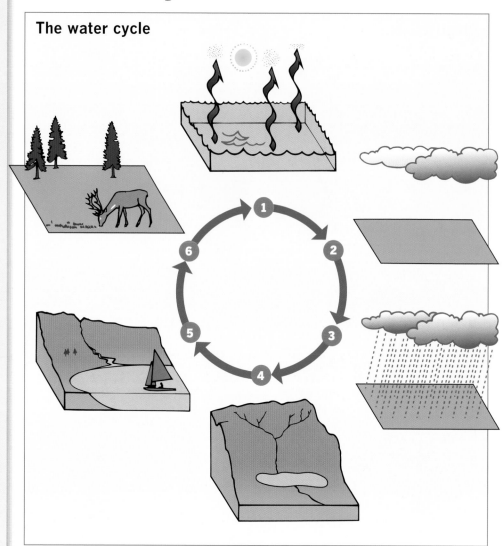

## Water recycled between land and sea

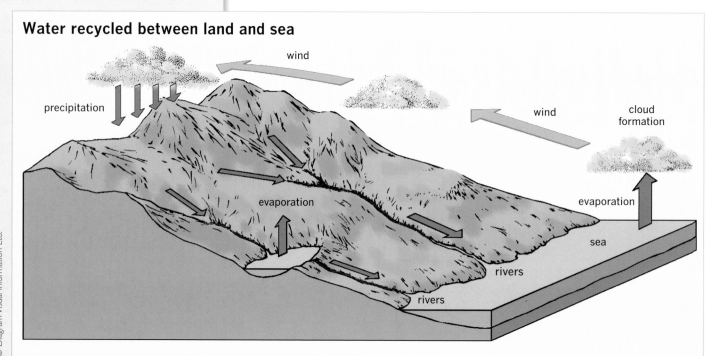

# Groundwater

**Key words**

aeration zone      water table
aquifer
artesian basin
artesian well
groundwater

## Aquifer

An aquifer is a water-saturated layer of permeable rock.

rock always saturated

impermeable rock

aeration zone

nonsaturated rock

water table

## Ground water

Water percolates between the grains of sand in sandstone, which is a porous permeable rock.

Water percolates only through joints in limestone, because it is a non-porous permeable rock.

## Artesian basin

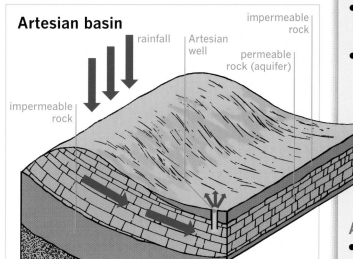

impermeable rock

rainfall

Artesian well

permeable rock (aquifer)

impermeable rock

## Spring

porous rock

impermeable rock

water table

spring

## Groundwater

- *Groundwater* is all the water that seeps into the many spaces between, and the pores or holes inside, rock.
- The *water table* is the level below which rock is always saturated. Water in this saturation zone can extend 3,300 feet (1,000 m) below the water table before it reaches impermeable rock.
- The *aeration zone* lies above the water table, where the rock is rarely completely saturated.

## Artesian basin

- An *artesian basin* is a rock structure that forms a natural reservoir for water. It occurs when layers of sedimentary rock are folded into a depression.
- An *aquifer* is a layer of permeable rock that can store water. If the aquifer lies between two impermeable rock layers, the water will be under high pressure.
- An *artesian well* is a hole bored down from the surface into the aquifer, allowing the water to gush up to the surface under pressure.

## Spring

- A spring is a natural emergence of water from the ground where the water table meets the surface, often at the foot of a slope.

# Chalk and limestone

**Key words**

carbonation
cuesta
karst

## Limestone landscapes

- Where limestone rock lies close to the surface, it is vulnerable to erosion by carbonic acid, a weak acid created when streams and rainwater absorb carbon dioxide gas from the air and soil. The action of this acid on the rock is called *carbonation*.
- Limestone landscape is often called *karst*, because the best-known example is the Karst Plateau in Bosnia.
- Karst landscape includes gorges, swallowholes, caves, limestone pavements, and other features. Such a landscape develops best in a wet climate.

## Chalk landscapes

- Although chalk is chemically similar to limestone, it is much softer, giving a chalk landscape a much more rounded appearance.
- If the beds or layers of chalk lie at an angle to the surface, they form a distinctive landscape known as a *cuesta*, with a steep escarpment or scarp slope on one side and a gentle dip slope on the other. This is caused by the softer beds of chalk and other rocks eroding faster to create a valley, while the harder beds resist erosion and form a ridge.
- Chalk landscapes include dry valleys, formed by rivers in times when the climate was much wetter.

## Mountain limestone landscape

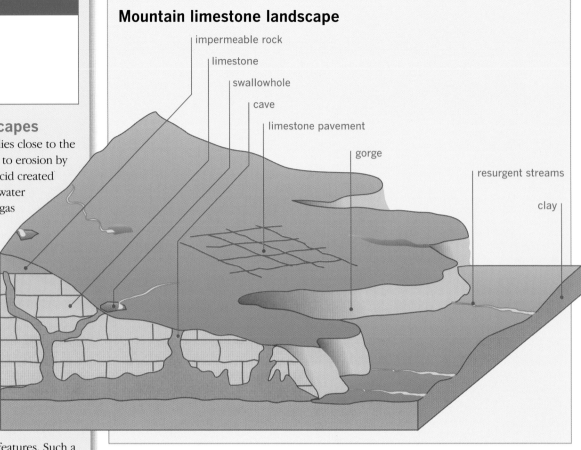

impermeable rock
limestone
swallowhole
cave
limestone pavement
gorge
resurgent streams
clay

## Chalk cuesta

A cuesta is a hill or ridge that has a steep scarp on one side and a gentle dip slope on the other.

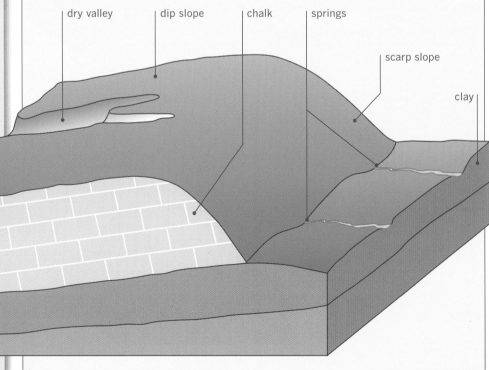

dry valley
dip slope
chalk
springs
scarp slope
clay

# Rivers

## Headward erosion

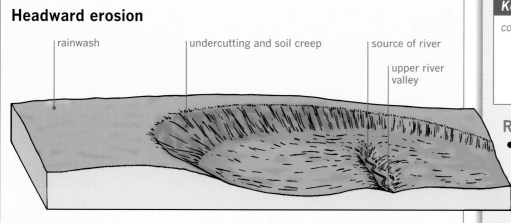

rainwash

undercutting and soil creep

source of river

upper river valley

## Pothole

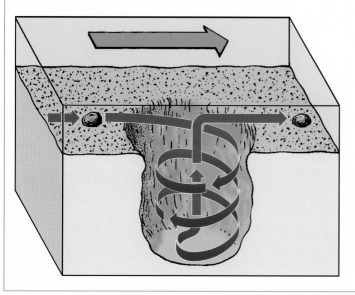

## V-shaped valley

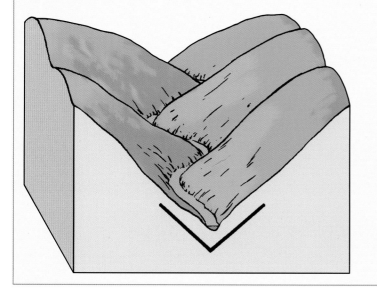

**Key words**

*corrasion*

### River erosion

- Rivers constantly and gradually sculpt the land around them, eroding rock and other material from some places and depositing it in others.

### Headward erosion

- A river cuts back into the hillside around its source through a combination of rainwash, undercutting, and soil creep.

### Pothole

- Potholes are holes in a rocky stream bed where lumps of waterborne rock have whirled around, deepening existing depressions in the stream bed. Potholes are features of fast-flowing mountain streams.
- The process of stream-channel erosion by fragments of rock is known as *corrasion*.

### V-shaped valley

- Where a stream erodes downward it produces a deep, steep-sided valley with a V-shaped cross section. Because it erodes the most land laterally on the outsides of bends, the stream carves a zigzag path between interlocking ridges, or spurs.
- V-shaped valleys with interlocking spurs are features of upland scenery.

# Rapids and waterfalls

## Resistant rocks producing waterfalls

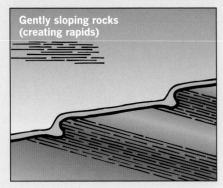

Gently sloping rocks (creating rapids)

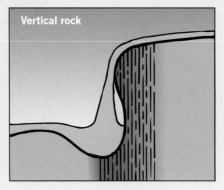

Vertical rock

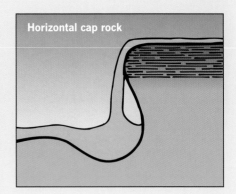

Horizontal cap rock

## Key words

*river*

## Waterfalls

- A waterfall is a vertical drop of water in a river or stream.
- Where the water flows over a gently sloping rock formation, it erodes the weaker rock layers, creating a series of rapids.
- Where it flows over a resistant horizontal or vertical rock formation capping a weaker rock, it creates a waterfall as the resistant rock forms a step that obstructs the river's normal action of smoothly grading its bed.

## Features of a waterfall

- Water speeds up over a waterfall because of reduced friction. It then erodes the soft rock below.
- Eroded rocks and boulders swirling round at the base of the waterfall undercut the rock and create a plunge pool.
- In places, this erosion might be extensive enough to create a ledge or cave behind the waterfall.

## Waterfall features

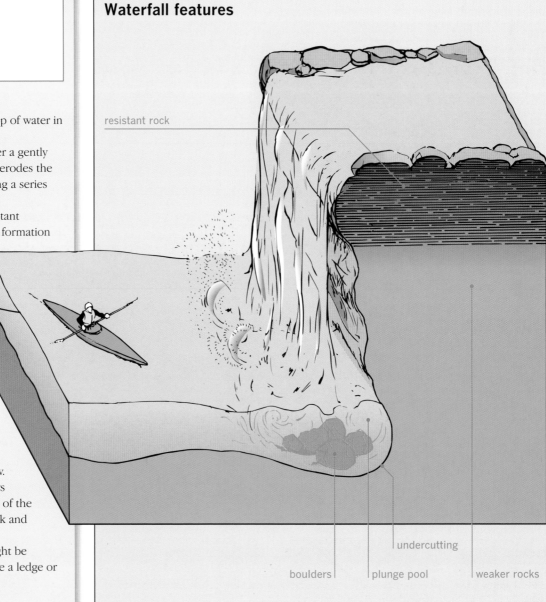

resistant rock

boulders    plunge pool    undercutting    weaker rocks

# River transport

### Suspension
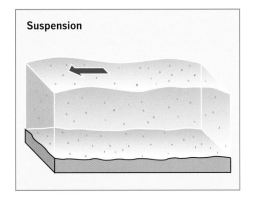

### Solution
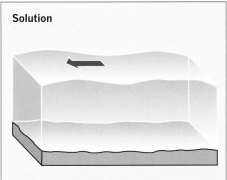

### Traction
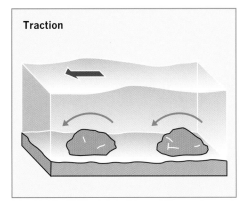

### Saltation (hopping)
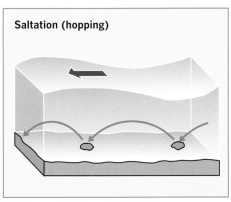

## Effects of stream velocity

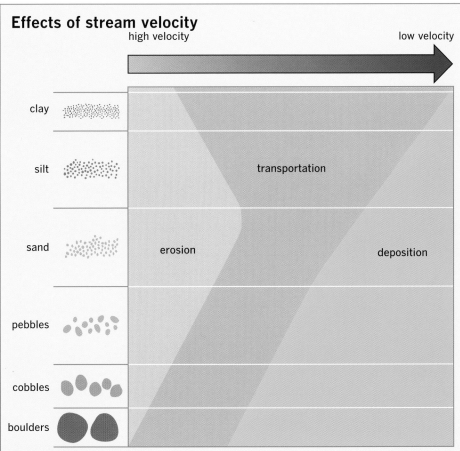

This diagram shows the effects that water flowing at different speeds has on different-sized objects, in ascending order from clay particles to boulders.

### Key words

*riverbed*
*saltation*
*traction*

## Load

- The material carried downstream by a river is called "load." The load varies according to the landscape the river flows through and the speed of its flow. Most load is only carried a short distance, during flooding or after a period of heavy rainfall.
- "Suspended load" is the lightweight material that is suspended or floats in the water.
- "Solute load" is the material dissolved in the water and carried in solution.
- *Traction* occurs when a river drags bedload—stones and larger particles—along the riverbed when it is in full flow.
- *Saltation*—hopping or bouncing—occurs when the flow of the river causes stones and larger particles of bedload to hop or bounce along the riverbed.

## Stream velocity

- Water flowing at different speeds along a river has a different effect on different types of load, eroding lighter materials such as silt and sand at high velocity and depositing heavier materials such as cobbles and boulders at low velocity.
- The river is better able to transport light materials at any velocity over a longer distance than heavier materials, which can only be transported at high velocity for a short distance.

© Diagram Visual Information Ltd.

**Key words**

*rapid*
*waterfall*

## River flow

- Flow is the way a river moves along its channel within its banks.
- As the volume of a river increases at any one point—causing the depth of the river to increase within its existing channel—its speed and the amount of sediment it carries both increase, the sediment load at a higher rate than the speed of the water.

## River capacity

- As the river runs downhill, the angle of slope at which it falls decreases from a steep to a shallow angle. The channel shape gets wider, although not always deeper, while both the speed of water and the sediment load increase.
- Streams and rivers run fastest downstream, as the friction is less where the river flows between banks of smooth silt. Upstream, the flow of a river is slowed by friction with the rough shallow bed. In places, however, the flow speeds up when it passes over rapids or a waterfall.

## Relative speed

- The fastest part of a river is near the surface in the middle of the stream, where the friction is least.
- The closer the river flow is to the sides or bottom of the bed, and thus the more friction it encounters, the slower it flows.

# River flow

## Capacity at the same point

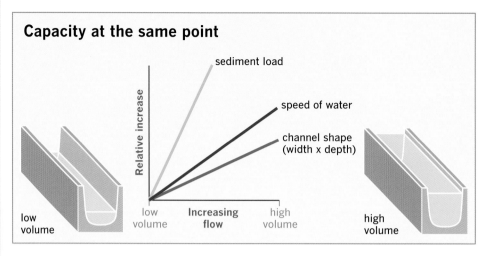

## Capacity upstream–downstream

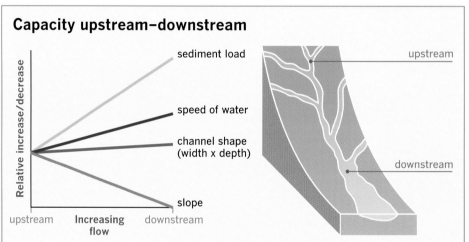

## Relative speed of water flow

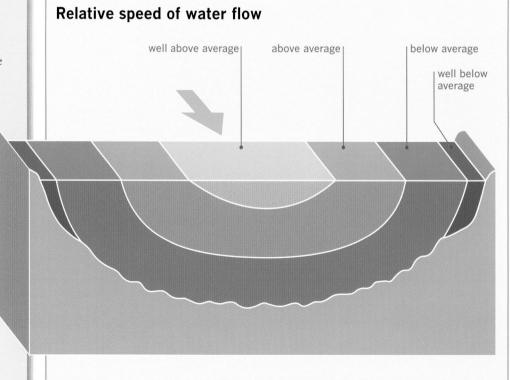

# River valleys

**a**

**Key words**

*erosion*
*sediment*

## River valley development and shape

● Water, in the form of streams and rivers, changes mountains by erosion. Three basic shapes of landscape and water channel are formed.

**❶**   Streams erode mountains by forming characteristic "youthful" V-shaped steep valleys (**a**), which divide the mountain landscape into ridges.

**❷**   River erosion gradually reduces mountains to mere low hills, and the valley then has the softer U-shape of a typical "mature" river valley (**b**).

**❸**   Eventually, river action bevels the hills to form a wide, low floodplain that is covered by river sediment. An "old" river valley has a flattened cross-sectional shape (**c**).

**b**

**❶**

**❷**

**c**

**❸**

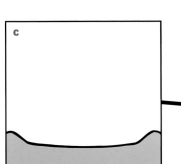

© Diagram Visual Information Ltd.

**Key words**

*anticline*
*confluence*
*syncline*
*tributary*

## Drainage patterns

- A *tributary* is a small river that joins a larger one. A *confluence* is where two streams join.
- River drainage patterns vary according to factors such as rock and soil types, climate, and human activity.
- Parallel drainage occurs when streams flow in a roughly parallel course due to the structure of the rock, perhaps due to its parallel folds.
- Dendritic drainage occurs in areas of uniform rock with little faulting or folding: it forms a branching network that looks like a tree. "Dendritic" comes from the Greek work *dendron*, meaning tree.
- Trellised drainage occurs when the rock structure causes streams to flow roughly parallel to each other and tributaries to join them almost at right angles, forming a trellis pattern. This occurs when streams flow along bands of softer rock or in line with the dip of the rock.

## Accordant drainage

- An accordant drainage pattern is directly related to the dip of the underlying rock strata, causing rivers to flow off anticlinal slopes and along synclinal troughs.
- Subsequent erosion lowers the anticlines to valleys and leaves synclines upstanding as mountains.
- A discordant drainage pattern is unrelated to the dip of the underlying rock.

## River capture

- Headward erosion by a river can lead it to capture the headwaters of a parallel or nearby river, thus shortening the latter river's length.
- The short valley left dry by the river capture is known as a wind gap.

# Drainage

## Types of drainage

**a** consequent stream
**b** subsequent stream
**c** obsequent stream

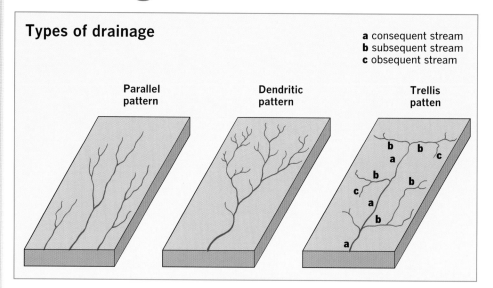

Parallel pattern

Dendritic pattern

Trellis patten

## Accordant drainage

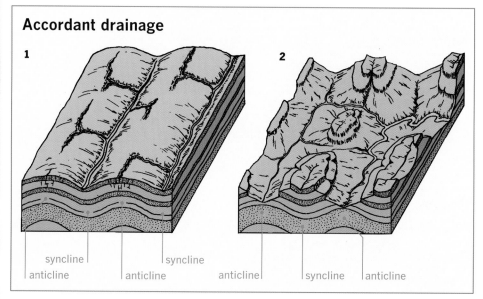

1

2

syncline
anticline

syncline
anticline

anticline

syncline

anticline

## River capture

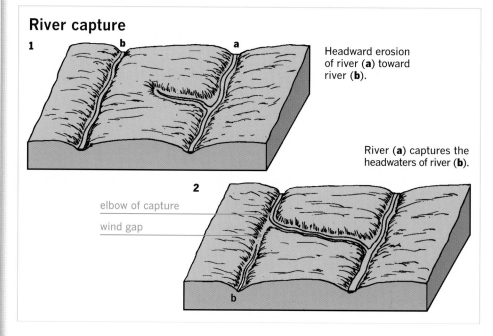

1

Headward erosion of river (**a**) toward river (**b**).

River (**a**) captures the headwaters of river (**b**).

2

elbow of capture

wind gap

# Watersheds

## Watersheds

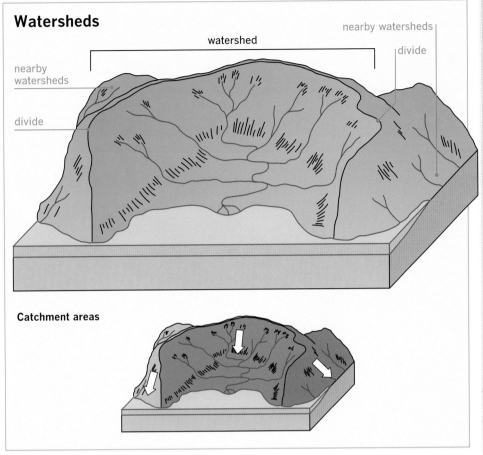

**Catchment areas**

## Mississippi watershed

**Key words**

*river*

### Catchment area

- A catchment area is the region from which a single river gathers all of its surface water.
- A watershed or drainage basin is the region from which all rivers flow into a single river.
- The boundary between two watersheds is called a divide.

### The Mississippi–Missouri watershed

- The watershed of the combined Mississippi–Missouri rivers covers most of the United States between the Rocky and Appalachian mountains, south of the Great Lakes. It measures 1,255,000 square miles (3,250,000 km²).
- This watershed is the biggest in North America and is the third largest in the world after the Amazon watershed in South America at 2,721 square miles (7.050,000 km²), and the Congo watershed in central Africa at 1,428,000 square miles (3,700,000 km²).

Rocky Mountains

Missouri

Platte

Mississippi

Arkansas

Ohio

Cumberland

Appalachian Mountains

Mississippi

Tennessee

Red

- - - - - divide

mountains

© Diagram Visual Information Ltd.

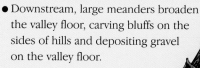

**Key words**

*erosion*
*meander*
*river*

## Meanders

- A *meander* is a marked curve or looplike bend in the channel of a river.
- Meanders form in any river valley, but are typical of the lower reaches of a river valley where the valley is broad and the slope of the river gentle.
- The largest meanders occur where the river is wide and the material on its bed and banks is soft and fine.
- Meanders form due to the way a river spirals between its banks, eroding material from a concave bank and depositing it on a convex bank. This process accentuates the curve of the river to form a meander.

## Valley broadening

- Meanders migrate down a river valley, widening the valley floor.
- In a steep river valley, the meander causes lateral erosion to start at the concave banks.
- In the middle reaches of a river, the meander widens, causing lateral erosion to lop off the spurs of hills.
- Downstream, large meanders broaden the valley floor, carving bluffs on the sides of hills and depositing gravel on the valley floor.

# Meanders

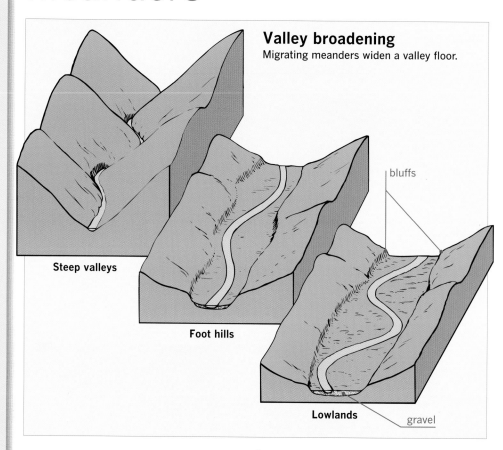

### Valley broadening
Migrating meanders widen a valley floor.

**Steep valleys**

**Foot hills**

bluffs

**Lowlands**

gravel

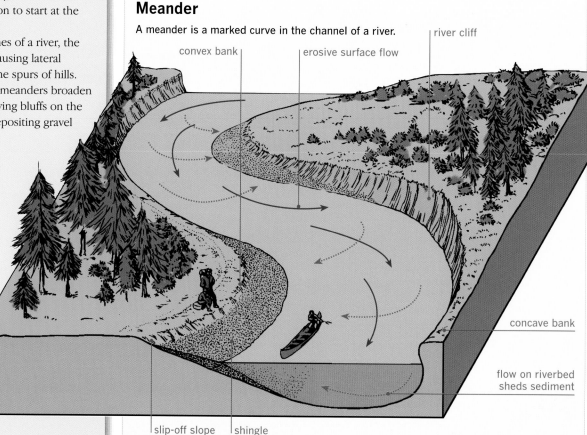

## Meander

A meander is a marked curve in the channel of a river.

convex bank

erosive surface flow

river cliff

concave bank

flow on riverbed
sheds sediment

slip-off slope

shingle

# Oxbow lakes

## Construction of an oxbow lake

**1** A meander develops in a river.

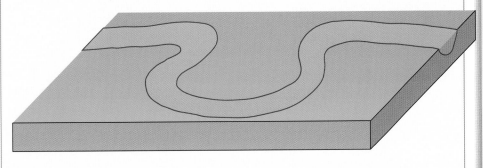

**2** The meander base is eroded.

narrow neck of land

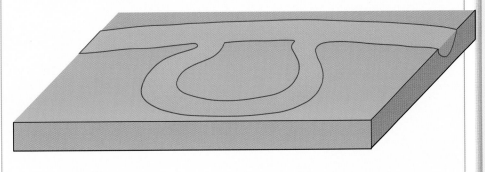

**3** The meander is bypassed by the river.

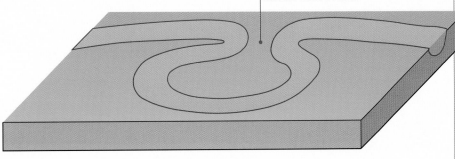

**4** Abandoned by the riverflow, the meander becomes an oxbow lake.

sediment "dams"

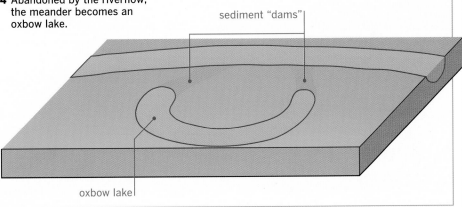

oxbow lake

### Key words

*floodplain*
*oxbow lake*
*river*

## Oxbow lakes

- An *oxbow lake* is a crescent-shaped lake formed on a river floodplain by a meander (**1**).
- As the meander increases in size, the river erodes away at the outside bend of the meander. As a result, the neck of the meander gets narrower and narrower (**2**).
- Eventually, the river breaks through the neck of the meander and straightens out, bypassing the meander (**3**).
- Dams of sediment build up between the river's new course and the old meander, sealing the meander off and creating an oxbow lake (**4**).
- A river crossing a long floodplain can create many meanders along its course.

© Diagram Visual Information Ltd.

### Key words

erosion
glacier
moraine
oxbow lake
rift valley

sediment
volcano

## Earth-movement lakes

- An earth-movement lake, such as those in deep *rift valleys*, forms as a result of movements in Earth's crust that create a natural basin or trough in which water can accumulate.
- The Dead Sea, a saltwater lake in the Great Rift Valley, is one of the best examples.

## Volcanic lakes

- A volcanic lake occurs when water fills up the crater of a dormant or extinct volcano, or when a volcanic eruption causes a lava flow to block up a river, creating a lake upstream.
- Lake Toba in Sumatra, Indonesia, is one of the world's largest volcanic crater lakes.

## Erosion lakes

- An erosion lake occurs in rock basins gouged out by ice sheets or in hollows worn away by wind in a desert.
- Lough Derg in Ireland shows the classic shape of an erosion lake.

## Deposition lakes

- A deposition lake occurs when a stretch of river has been cut off from the rest of the river through the deposition of sediment, as happens with the creation of an oxbow lake.
- Ice deposited by a glacier can also create a deposition lake, for example, Lake Vatnsdalur in Iceland.

## Erosion and deposition lakes

- Some lakes are formed by a combination of erosion and deposition.
- Glacial erosion can create a cirque, hollow, or U-shaped valley that is then blocked by moraine.
- Lake Seneca in New York State is the result of moraine damming a glacial valley.

# Lakes

## Earth-movement lakes

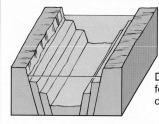

Deep rift valley lakes are formed by cracks in Earth's crust.

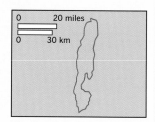

The Dead Sea (Israel, the West Bank, and Jordan)

## Volcanic lakes

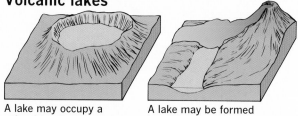

A lake may occupy a volcanic crater.

A lake may be formed by a lava flow damm.

Lake Toba, Sumatra

## Erosion lakes

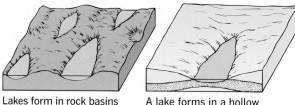

Lakes form in rock basins gouged by ice sheets.

A lake forms in a hollow worn by wind in a desert.

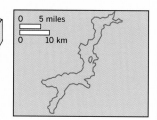

Lough Derg, Ireland

## Deposition lakes

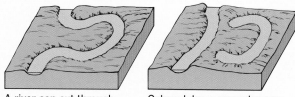

A river can cut through a meander.

Oxbow lake: a meander can be cut off by sediment or ice.

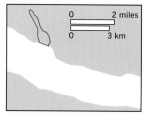

Lake Vatnsdalur, Iceland

## Lakes formed by erosion and deposition

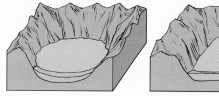

A lake can be formed by a moraine-dammed cirque.

Finger lakes are also formed by moraine damms.

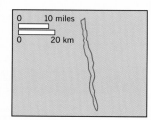

Lake Seneca, New York state

# Flood plains

## Raising riverbanks

Cross sections show how a river raises its banks.

**Flooding**

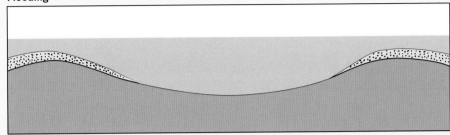

**Normal flow**

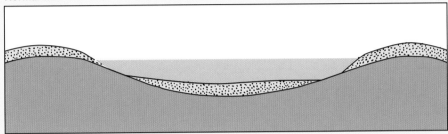

**Repeated flooding**

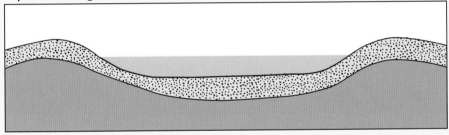

## Floodplains

- A *floodplain* is a broad, flat river valley at the lower reaches of a river.
- As a river flows downstream, it carries with it large quantities of *alluvium* or sediment, depositing much of it on the riverbed, thus raising its height.
- When the river floods, it deposits sediment on the riverbanks or levees as it spills over the top of its channel, increasing their height.
- The effect of both deposits—during normal flow and as a result of repeated flooding—is to raise the river and its levees high above the surrounding floodplain.

## Floodplain features

- Among the typical features of a river floodplain are meanders and oxbow lakes, raised levees, and hills eroded by the river into bluffs or river cliffs.
- The floodplain itself will be covered with a layer of mud, silt, sand, and other sediments washed down by the river.

## Floodplain features

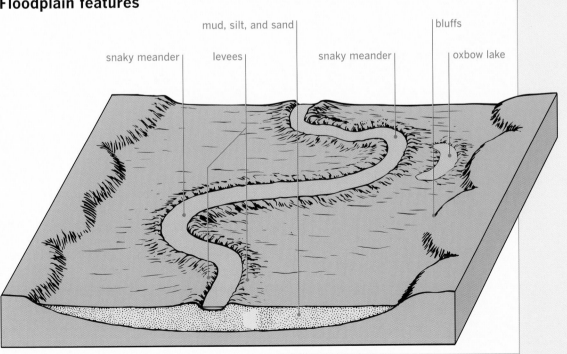

snaky meander    levees    mud, silt, and sand    snaky meander    bluffs    oxbow lake

**Key words**

| | |
|---|---|
| *delta* | *river* |
| *distributary* | *sediment* |
| *erosion* | |
| *lagoon* | |
| *levee* | |

## Delta formation

- A *delta* is a low-lying area of alluvial deposits lying at a river mouth.
- When a river enters the sea, it slows down, reducing its capacity to carry sediment. The heavier sediment is dropped immediately on the seabed, while the lighter sediment is carried further out to sea, slowly creating a fan-shaped delta.
- As the delta forms, the river often splits up into different branches called *distributaries*. Repeated flooding creates levees, often trapping pools of seawater behind them in lagoons.
- A delta can only form where the amount of river-deposited sediment exceeds that removed by coastal erosion.

## Delta expansion

- Over time, the delta slowly expands into the sea as the river deposits more layers of sediment. The river continues to divide into more distributaries, and the lagoons dry out and turn to saltwater swamps. Spits and bars of sediment form at the end of the delta.
- As the delta continues to expand, the swamps are filled with sediment during floods and become dry land.

## Types of delta

- Deltas take three main shapes: bird's foot deltas, such as the Mississippi; arc-shaped arcuate deltas, such as the Nile in Egypt; and kite-shaped cuspate deltas, such as the Tiber in Italy, where the sediments are deposited evenly either side of the main channel.

# Deltas

## River splits

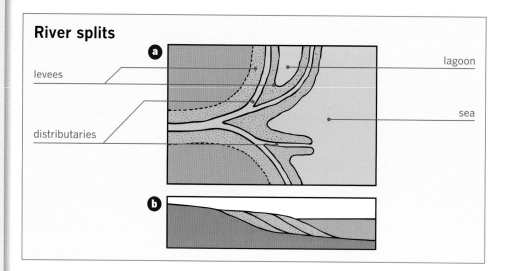

levees

distributaries

lagoon

sea

## Delta extends into sea

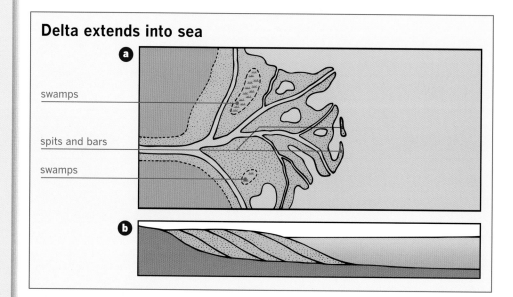

swamps

spits and bars

swamps

## Delta expands

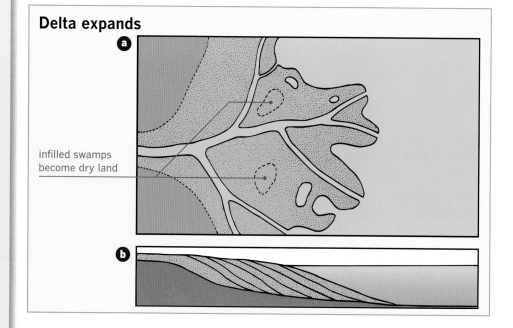

infilled swamps become dry land

# River profiles

## Original course

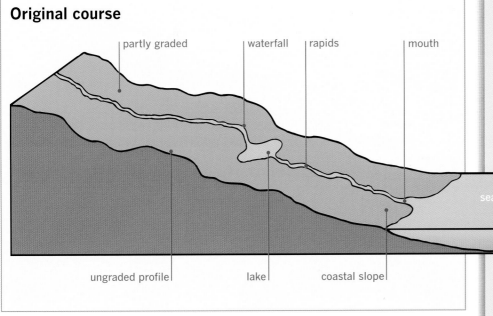

partly graded — waterfall — rapids — mouth

sea

ungraded profile — lake — coastal slope

## Later course

partly graded profile

sediment

## Mature course

graded profile

**Key words**

*deposition*
*erosion*
*river*

## Ungraded profile
● The original course of a river before erosion and deposition of sediments have taken place is of a steep stream near the source that flows more and more gently toward the mouth. Waterfalls, rapids, and lakes occur along its length.

## Partly graded profile
● As a river matures, it alters the shape of its channel, eroding it in some places and depositing the sediments in others. The balance between erosion and deposition therefore changes the shape of the channel by smoothing out or removing obstacles to its even flow.

## Graded profile
● Eventually, a river achieves a graded profile, one in which erosion and deposition are balanced along the course of the river. Once it has reached this stage, the shape of the river's channel only changes if this balance is upset.

## Key words

*deposition*
*erosion*
*nickpoint*
*river*
*river valley*

## Terrace formation

- The rejuvenation of a river occurs after a change to the land surrounding the river causes an increase in river erosion.
- When the land is lifted up, or the sea level drops, the river is rejuvenated and cuts vigorously downwards into the sediments lying on its flood plain.
- This sudden increase in erosion creates a sharp *nickpoint*, where the river suddenly steepens as it begins to cut downwards and backwards into the sediment.
- When rejuvenation occurs, the old valley floor is left behind as a river terrace. Later, lateral erosion will cut into the sides of this terrace.
- A second terrace may be cut if there is a further change if either the land rises or sea drops again.

## Long-profile development

- The rejuvenation of a river alters its "long profile"—the height and length of a river from its source along its entire length to its mouth at the sea.
- The creation of a nickpoint disrupts the even flow of the river and alters the profile. Erosion and deposition gradually move this nickpoint back up the course of the river until the original long profile is reformed.

# River rejuvenation

## Terrace formation

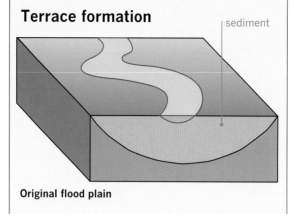

Original flood plain

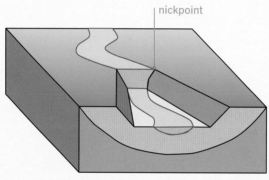

Terrace cut in sediment after land rises or sea falls

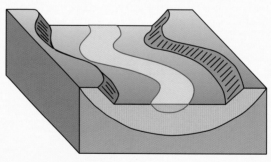

Later lateral erosion

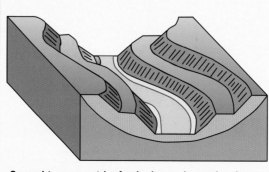

Second terrace cut by fresh change in sea level

## Long-profile development of rejuvenated river

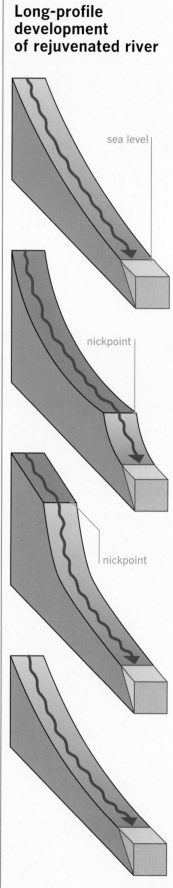

# Hills and valleys

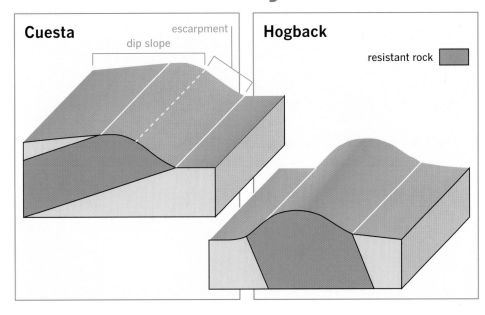

**Cuesta**

escarpment

dip slope

**Hogback**

resistant rock

**Plateau**

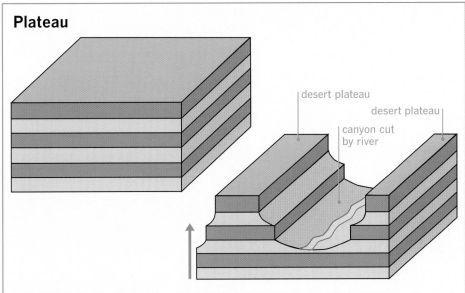

desert plateau

desert plateau

canyon cut
by river

**Anticline and syncline**

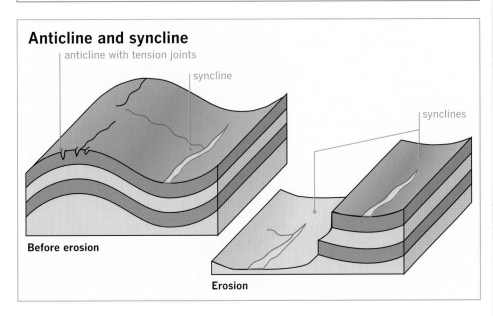

anticline with tension joints

syncline

synclines

**Before erosion**

**Erosion**

## Rock strata

● Rocks generally form in flat layers called *strata* (singular: *stratum*). However, movements in Earth's crust often twist and deform these layers into many different shapes and angles.

## Ridge hills

● A *cuesta* is a ridge that results from layers of rock folded at an angle to the surface. Erosion and weathering wear away the softer layers to create valleys, while the harder layers resist to form the long parallel cuestas. A cuesta has a dip or gentle slope on one side and an escarpment or steep slope on the other.

● If the layers dip very steeply, both sides of the ridge may be equally steep, forming a *hogback*.

## Plateaus

● A plateau or flat area of land surrounded by steep slopes is formed when a layer of resistant rock lies above other horizontal layers.

● After uplift and erosion, a river can cut into the plateau to create a valley with stepped sides of alternating weak and resistant rock layers.

## Anticline and syncline

● Layers of rock upfolded into an arch form an *anticline*. The downfolded layers form basins called *synclines*. Tension joints form in an anticline if the arch is too steep.

● Differential erosion can reduce an anticline to a basin lower than a syncline.

**Key words**

*ice cap*
*ice sheet*

## Ice

- An *ice sheet* covers a large area of land. An *ice cap* is a smaller dome of ice covering a mountain.
- "Pack ice" is an area of ice floating on the sea next to, but not necessarily attached to, an ice sheet.
- "Drift ice" is floating ice that has broken free of its point of origin and broken up into smaller pieces such that ships can still sail through.

## North Pole

- Most of the Arctic Ocean is covered by pack ice, while the islands of northern Canada and most of Greenland are covered by an ice sheet. Drift ice extends south toward North America and Siberia.
- During the winter months, drift ice can extend as far south as northern Norway, Russia, Siberia, and Alaska, and into the Atlantic and Pacific oceans.
- The Arctic ice sheet covers about 758,500 square miles (1,965,000 km²) of Greenland and northern Canada.

## South Pole

- The ice sheet at the South Pole lies on top of Antarctica and surrounding seas.
- Most of the Antarctic landmass is covered with ice, some of it below sea level. Only a small part of the continent is exposed land.
- During the summer months, narrow bands of pack and drift ice surround the ice sheet. A wider band of pack and drift ice surrounds the sheet in the winter.
- The Antarctic ice sheet covers about 5,340,000 square miles (13,830,000 km²) of Antarctica.

# Ice sheets

## Arctic ice sheet

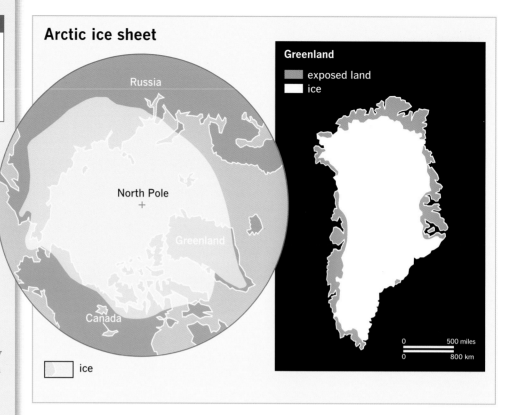

## Antarctic ice sheet

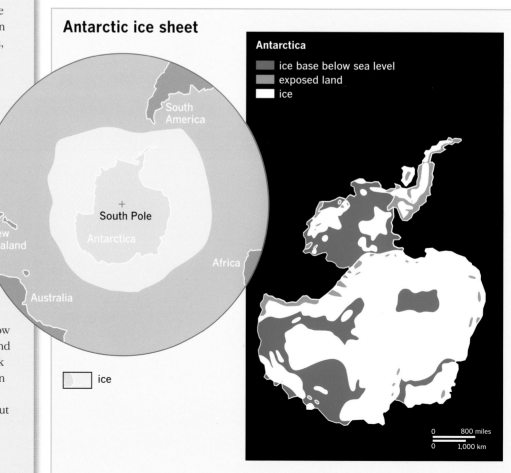

# Glacier features

## Ice-worn hummocks

**Roche moutonnée**

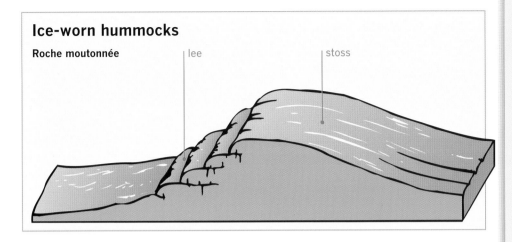

lee

stoss

## Crag-and-tail

protected tail of soft rock

ice-rubbed resistant crag

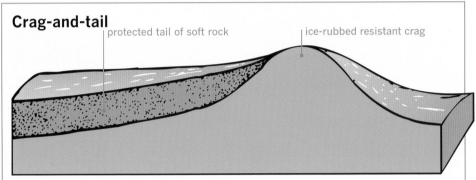

## Anatomy of a glacier

headwall

bergschrund

firn field

cirque floor

rock step

crevasses

subglacial moraine

ice fall

lateral moraine

medial moraine

subglacial stream

glacier snout

terminal moraine

### Key words

bergschrund
crevasse
erosion
moraine
volcano

### Ice-worn hummocks

- A "roche moutonnée" is a rock shaped and moulded by the action of ice. It has a smoothly polished, gently sloping upstream side called the "stoss," and a steep, rough downstream side called a "lee."
- A crag-and-tail is a mound of hard, resistant rock—such as the plug of a volcano—that protects the softer rock behind it from erosion by a moving glacier. This results in a distinctive formation of a crag of hard rock with a long, streamlined tail of softer rock. A famous example of this is the crag on which stands Edinburgh Castle in Scotland; the Royal Mile of churches, shops, and houses runs downhill from the crag.

### Anatomy of a glacier

- At the head of a glacier, a deep crack called a *bergschrund* opens up as the ice pulls away from the rock wall.
- As the glacier flows down the valley, it cracks into deep fissures known as *crevasses*.
- The moving ice deposits piles of moraine (debris).
- The lower end of a glacier is its "snout" or terminus. The terminal moraine here might be only a few feet high, but it can pile up to more than 1,000 feet (304 m).

**Key words**

*cirque*
*névé*

## Cirque (corrie) formation

- A *cirque*—also called a corrie, cwm, or kar—is a hollow scooped out by ice and is one of the most common features of a previously glaciated upland.
- A cirque starts to form where *névé* piles up in a small depression on a hillside. As the glacier develops, it cuts deeper into the rock, gouging out a large hollow with a steep backwall or headwall.
- Once the ice has gone, the raised rock barrier at the front known as the threshold traps water behind it, forming a small lake or "tarn."

## Gnawed by ice

- Glaciers can radically change the landscape, especially in a mountain valley with a V-shaped cross section.
- During glaciation, the ice cuts into the valley floor and scours the sides, carving out a deep, wide trough that widens, deepens, and straightens the valley.
- After the glacier has gone, the previously V-shaped river valley is now U-shaped, and the course of the river is far straighter.

# Glacial erosion

### Cirque formation

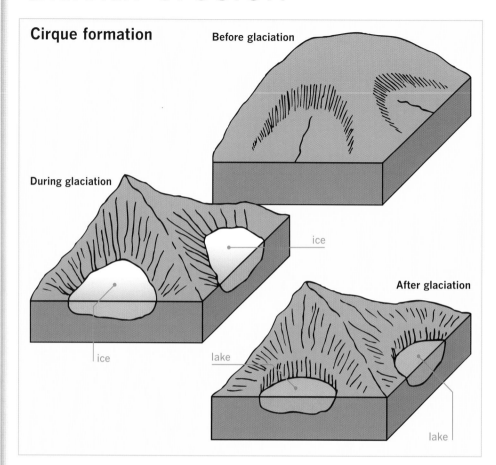

Before glaciation

During glaciation

ice

ice

After glaciation

lake

ice

lake

### Gnawed by ice

Three diagrams show the major changes wrought by glaciation in a mountain valley.

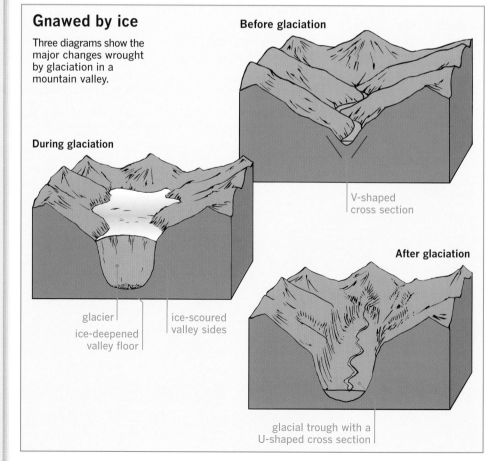

Before glaciation

During glaciation

V-shaped cross section

glacier
ice-deepened valley floor
ice-scoured valley sides

After glaciation

glacial trough with a U-shaped cross section

# Glacial deposits

**Key words**

*crevasse*
*esker*
*glacier*
*kame*
*till*

## Glacial valley

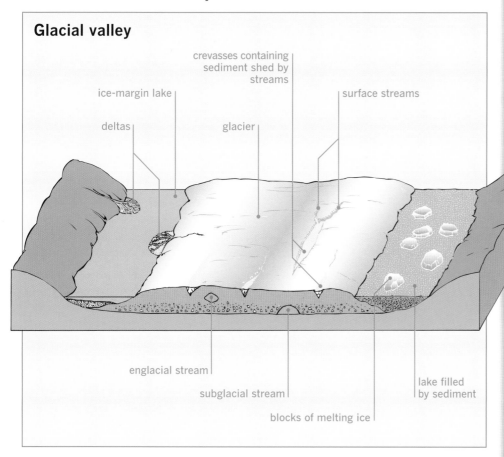

- ice-margin lake
- crevasses containing sediment shed by streams
- surface streams
- deltas
- glacier
- englacial stream
- subglacial stream
- blocks of melting ice
- lake filled by sediment

## Postglacial valley

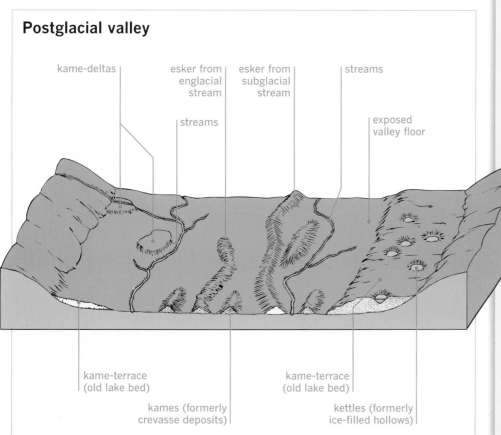

- kame-deltas
- esker from englacial stream
- esker from subglacial stream
- streams
- streams
- exposed valley floor
- kame-terrace (old lake bed)
- kame-terrace (old lake bed)
- kames (formerly crevasse deposits)
- kettles (formerly ice-filled hollows)

## Glacial valley

- As a valley glacier melts, its streams and lakes shed rock debris that the glacier has rasped from the walls and floor of the valley.
- Lakes appear at the edges of the ice and sediment is deposited at the bottom of the lakes.
- Crevasses form in the glacier containing sediment shed by streams.

## Post-glacial valley

- Even after the glacier has melted away entirely, traces of its path remain as features of the new landscape.
- As a glacier retreats or melts, it leaves behind a vast covering of glacial debris known as *till*. Till can lie up to 330 feet (110 m) thick and smooth out all the irregularities of the land.
- A glacier can leave behind small mounds of ice that become buried by glacial till. When these mounds finally melt, they leave behind a series of kettles or small hollows.
- Deposits left in a crevasse by meltwater flowing over the surface of the glacier are left as steep-sided mounds of sand and gravel known as *kames*.
- A subglacial stream flowing beneath the ice and an englacial stream flowing through it can both deposit a winding ridge of sand and gravel known as an *esker*.

### Key words

*periglacial*
*permafrost*
*pingo*
*soil creep*
*tundra*

## Periglacial landscapes

- A landscape formed next to an ice sheet during an ice age is described as *periglacial*.
- Periglacial landscapes are still being formed today.

## Patterned ground

- Periglacial landscapes are covered with stone patterns formed by frost heave, in which frost pushes stones up to the surface as the ground freezes. Areas of fine sediment are also pushed up into mounds. Large stones then roll to the bottom of these mounds to form rings called stone polygons 3 feet (1 m) or more across. If this occurs on sloping ground, parallel lines of stones are formed under the influence of *soil creep*.

## Pingo formation

- A *pingo* is a mound of earth with a permanent core of ice and can be up to 160 feet (50 m) high. The ice core may once have been frozen groundwater or part of a lake (**a**).
- As the ice expands underground (**b**), it pushes the dome up in the land surface (**c**). Tension cracks in the dome expose the ice (**d**). As the ice melts, it creates a pond (**e**) that deposits sediment (**f**).

## Ice-wedge landforms

- Cracks in a periglacial landscape often form when frozen ground contracts. Meltwater fills the cracks and expands when it freezes to create deep ice wedges.
- Ponds and raised rims are also common.

# Cold landscapes

## Patterned ground

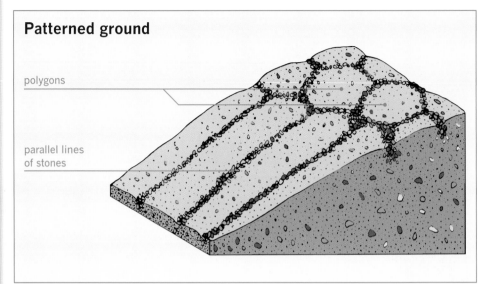

polygons

parallel lines of stones

## Pingo formation

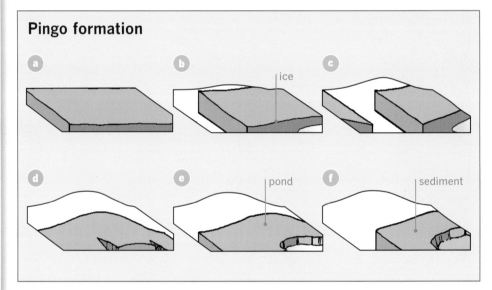

a

b — ice

c

d

e — pond

f — sediment

## Ice-wedge landforms

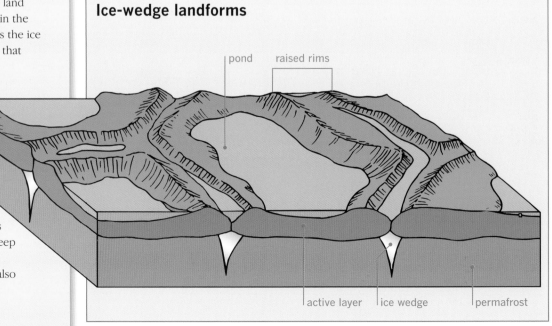

pond    raised rims

active layer    ice wedge    permafrost

# Permafrost

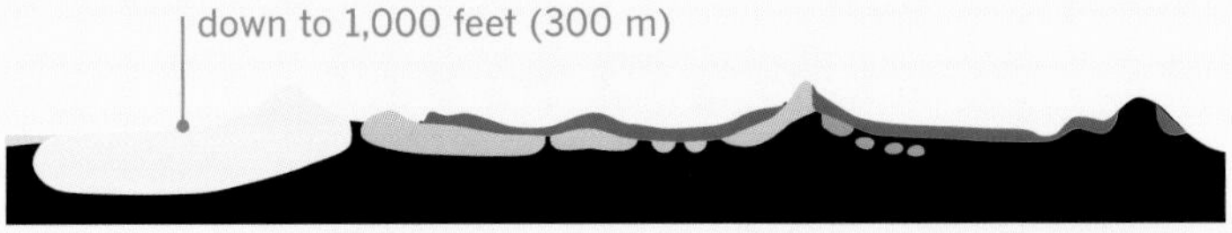

**Key words**

*ice wedge*
*periglacial*
*permafrost*

## Permafrost in the Northern Hemisphere

- ☐ continuous permafrost
- ▨ discontinuous permafrost
- ▨ sporadic permafrost
- ▨ active layer

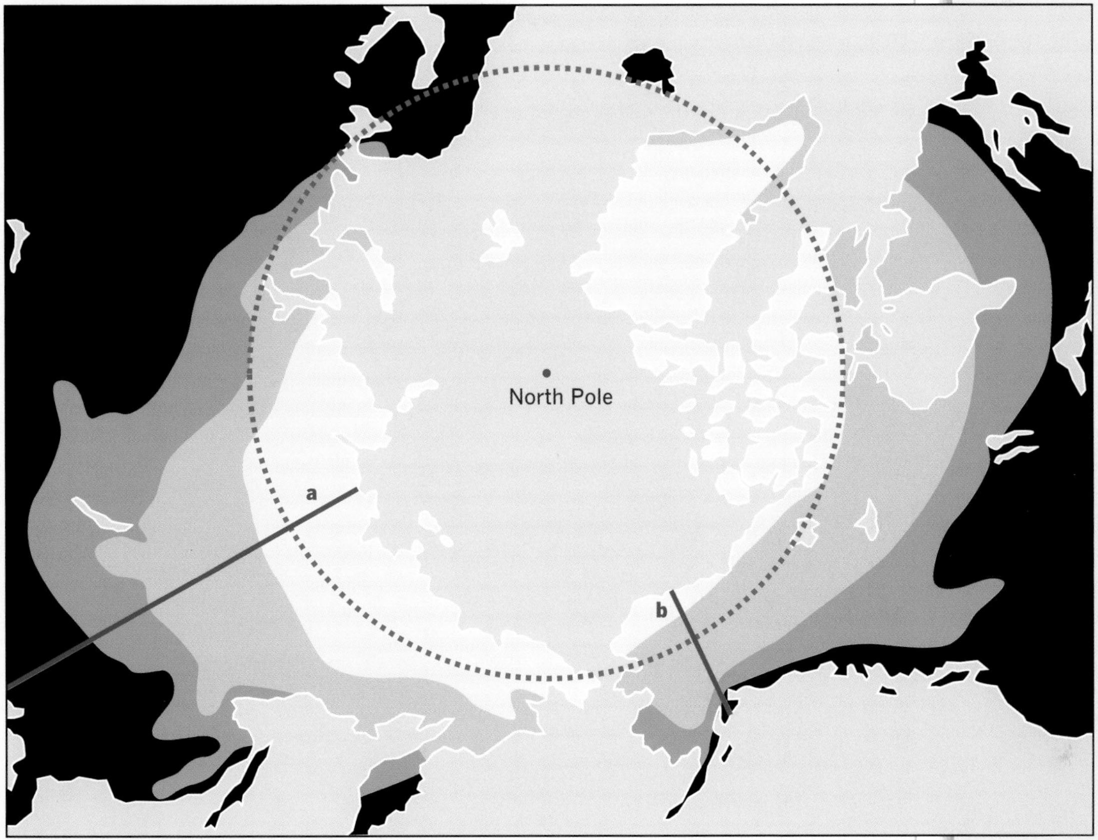

North Pole

a

b

## Permafrost

- *Permafrost* is permanently frozen ground and occurs in periglacial areas.
- In such areas, only the ice on or near the surface ever melts; the land beneath is permanently frozen.
- The distinctive landscape of periglacial regions occurs because the melting of the ice above the permafrost stirs up the ground in a process called "cryoturbation." This churns the soil into involutions, or buckled layers, which form ponds, bogs, and ice wedges.
- A periglacial climate has long cold winters where temperatures never rise above freezing and can drop to −58°F (−50°C).
- Summers are short and mild and allow the ice above the permafrost to melt. Only mosses, lichens, grasses, and small shrubs can grow. The absence of plants allows wind action to shape the landscape unimpeded.

## Sectioned landscapes

### a Section through North Asia

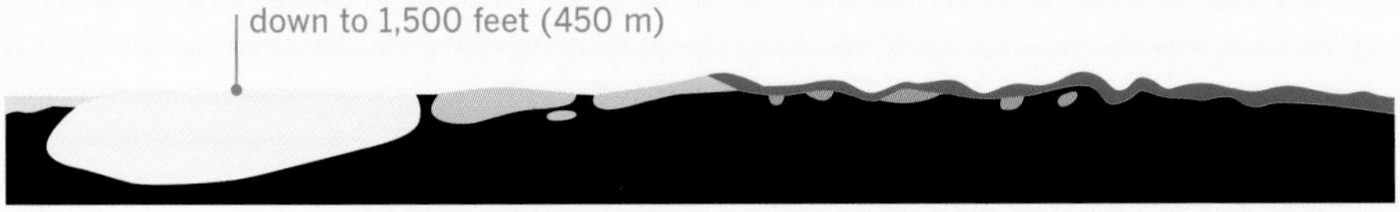

down to 1,500 feet (450 m)

### b Section through Alaska

down to 1,000 feet (300 m)

## Key words

*desertification*
*evapo-*
   *transpiration*
*precipitation*

## Deserts

- A desert is an area of land with little or no precipitation.
- Temperatures in deserts are often extreme, and many deserts are among the hottest places on Earth.
- What precipitation does occur is often less than the amount lost through *evapotranspiration*, a combination of evaporation from the surface and transpiration through plants.
- Because of the lack of rain, vegetation is sparse or entirely absent.
- Deserts can also be cold, such as the Antarctic ice desert, where precipitation is less than two inches (5 cm) per year, only a little higher than in the Sahara.

## The world's deserts

- The world's largest desert is the Sahara in North Africa, covering 3,500,000 square miles (9,000,000 km²). It is also one of the hottest and most arid of deserts.
- The world's six arid deserts are surrounded or adjoined by arid and semi-arid deserts, where there is more rainfall.
- An arid desert is one defined as having less than ten inches (25 cm) of rainfall per year.
- Semi-arid areas, such as the Sahel in Africa, are often in the process of desertification.

# Deserts

## Desert features

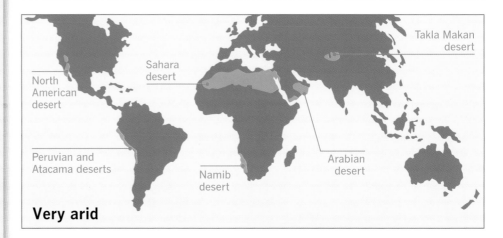

### Features of deserts
- Few plants cover the ground because there is so little water.
- Clear skies mean that the ground heats up quickly during the day, and cools down fast at night.
- The ground may be rocky or covered with sand.
- Loose sand is easily whipped up by the wind to form a sandstorm.

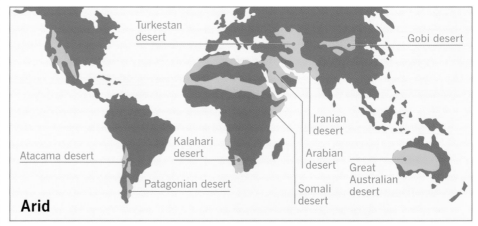

North American desert

Peruvian and Atacama deserts

Sahara desert

Namib desert

Takla Makan desert

Arabian desert

**Very arid**

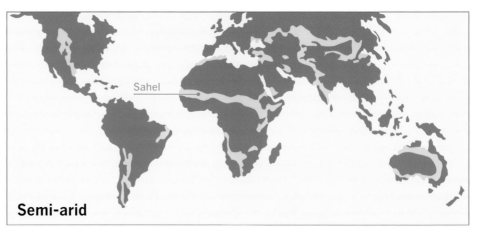

Turkestan desert

Gobi desert

Atacama desert

Kalahari desert

Patagonian desert

Iranian desert

Arabian desert

Somali desert

Great Australian desert

**Arid**

Sahel

**Semi-arid**

# Deserts of the USA

## Climate and U.S. deserts

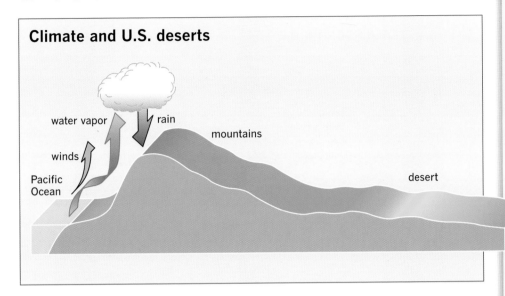

## North American deserts

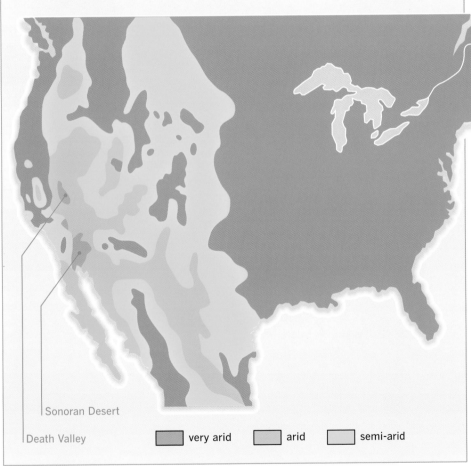

Sonoran Desert

Death Valley

■ very arid ■ arid ■ semi-arid

**Key words**

*desert*

## Climate

● The Coast Ranges and the Sierra Nevada on the west coast of the United States force rain-bearing winds from the Pacific Ocean to rise and cool, shedding their moisture before heading inland. The mountains therefore create a rain-shadow to their east in which the land stays dry or forms a desert.

## North American deserts

● There are two main deserts in the United States:
  ● The Sonoran Desert, on the border of California, Arizona, and Mexico, covers 70,000 square miles (180,000 km$^2$).
● The Mojave Desert in California covers 15,000 square miles (38,850 km$^2$) and includes Death Valley, one of the hottest places in the world.
● Both deserts lie within a vast region of arid and semi-arid land that stretches from Canada down through the western and midwestern states to Baja California in Mexico and across to the Gulf of Mexico.

## Key words

| | |
|---|---|
| *arroyo* | *mesa* |
| *bajada* | *pediment* |
| *butte* | *uplift* |
| *desert* | *wadi* |
| *inselberg* | |

## Mesas and buttes

- A *mesa* is an isolated, flat-topped, steep-sided desert mountain. A *butte* is a more eroded mesa.
- Mesas and buttes were once part of a plateau comprising horizontal rock layers laid down beneath the sea in which resistant rock layers sandwich easily eroded rock layers.
- As a result of uplift and dissection by downcutting rivers, the plateau is eroded into flat-topped mesas and rounded buttes.

## Desert features

- Weathering and flash floods produce a range of features in a desert landscape.
- An *arroyo* is a gorgelike dry valley in which a stream flows occasionally. A *wadi* is a narrow gorge formed over the years by torrential rainstorms causing flash floods to tear through the desert, cutting deep into the ground. A wadi is usually dry but can fill with water during such a flood.
- Flash floods wash alluvial material out of a wadi onto the desert plain to form a fan-shaped mound known as a *bajada*.
- A *pediment* is a shallow ramp of rock that often occurs at the base of a mesa or inselberg.
- An *inselberg* is an isolated, steep-sided mountain; Uluru in Australia is the most famous example.

# Desert landforms

## Origin of buttes and mesas

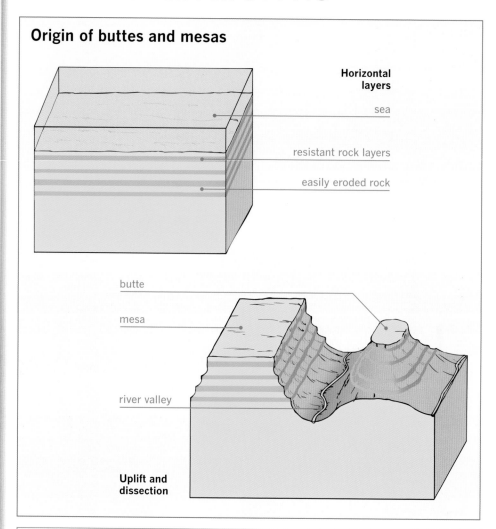

Horizontal layers

sea

resistant rock layers

easily eroded rock

butte

mesa

river valley

**Uplift and dissection**

## Desert landforms

Weathering and flash floods produce these features of arid mountainous regions.

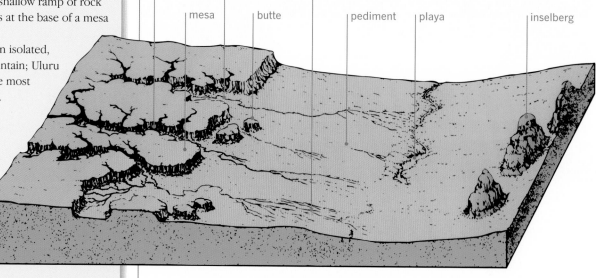

canyon  arroyo (wadi)  alluvial fan

mesa  butte  pediment  playa  inselberg

# Wind erosion

## Rock pedestals

Windblown sand whittles away the bases of desert rocks.

## Zeugen

→ wind direction

joint

zeugen | joint

hard rock

soft rock

**Rock beds before erosion**

**Rock beds after erosion**

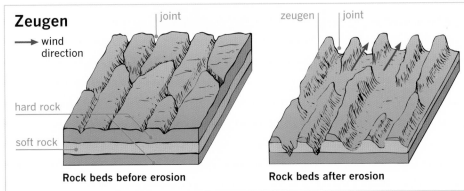

## Yardangs

→ wind direction

hard rock | soft rock | yardang

hard rock

soft rock

**Rock beds before erosion**

**Rock beds after erosion**

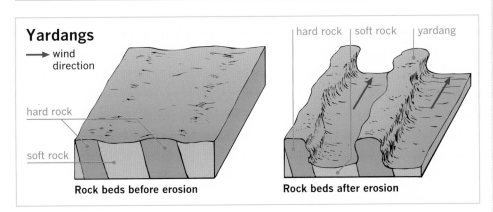

## Deflation hollows

prevailing winds

Qattara depression

sand removed by wind

0    100 miles
0    160 km

faulted rock layers | deflation hollow

**Northern Egypt**

**Hollow**

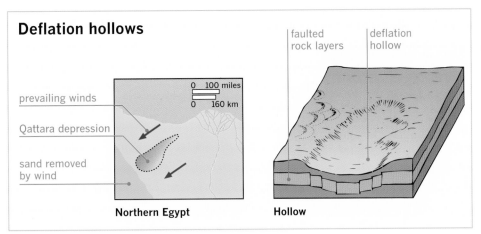

### Key words

| | |
|---|---|
| chemical weathering | rock pedestal |
| deflation hollow | yardang |
| erosion | zeugen |
| insolation | |

## Wind erosion

- Wind erosion is one of the major factors in the creation of desert landscapes, as there are few plants to slow down or deflect the wind and bind the dry, light surface materials together.
- The effect of the Sun's heat in breaking down rocks—the form of weathering known as "insolation"—and chemical weathering also have an impact.

## Rock pedestal

- A *rock pedestal* is caused by windblown sand whittling away the base of a solid rock.

## Zeugen

- *Zeugen* or mushroom rocks are formed when a combination of wind and chemical weathering erodes joints in the rock to create parallel rows of free-standing rock.

## Yardang

- A *yardang* occurs where alternating hard and soft rock beds are roughly perpendicular to the surface. Wind erodes the soft beds, carving out parallel ridges aligned with the prevailing wind that can be hundreds of feet high and many miles long.

## Deflation hollow

- A *deflation hollow* is a basin in faulted rock layers blown out by the wind. The wind can sometimes blow out a basin so deep as to reach the water table, thus creating an oasis.
- The Qattara Depression in Egypt—the world's fourth deepest depression—is 199 miles (320 km) long and 440 feet (134 m) below sea level.

## Key words

*barchan*
*desert*
*draa*
*sand*
*seif*

## Sand dunes

- A sand dune is a mound or ridge of windblown sand in the desert. Large dunes several hundred feet high and many miles long, often with smaller dunes on their summit, occur in the Sahara and are known as *draa* (or "dzraa").
- Dunes also occur above the high-water mark on sandy, low-lying coastlines.
- Desert dunes are generally free of vegetation, whereas coastal dunes are usually fixed by marram grass or coniferous trees.
- The main requirements for dune creation are a constant wind strength and direction, a continuous supply of sand, and an obstacle to trap the sand.

## Types of dune

- There are many different types of sand dune, often named for their shape.
- A head and tail dune has a short, steep windward slope and a long, gently declining leeward slope formed behind a rock or other obstacle impeding the flow of windblown sand.
- A *barchan* forms where sand is sparse and the wind direction is constant. The wind eddies over the top of the dune, creating a crescent-shaped dune with a gentle windward face and a steep leeward face.
- *Seif* or longitudinal dunes occur where sand is sparse and the wind comes from two directions or eddies from side to side, creating a series of long, parallel dunes
- When the wind shifts direction, it can slowly change a barchan dune into a seif.
- Other dunes include transverse dunes, where ridges form at 90 degrees to the strongest wind direction; and star dunes, where the wind blows in from all directions.

# Sand dunes

## Sand dune formations

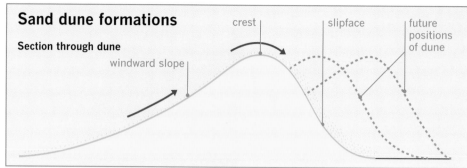

Section through dune

windward slope — crest — slipface — future positions of dune

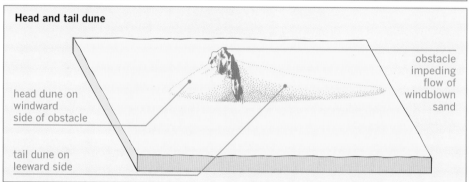

Head and tail dune

head dune on windward side of obstacle

tail dune on leeward side

obstacle impeding flow of windblown sand

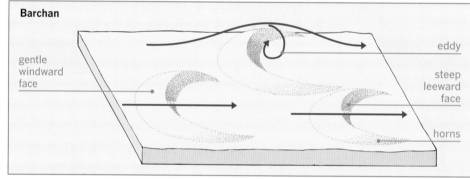

Barchan

gentle windward face

eddy

steep leeward face

horns

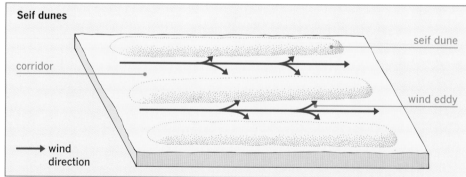

Seif dunes

corridor

seif dune

wind eddy

→ wind direction

Barchan dune to seif

**1** A barchan is shaped by a prevailing wind.

**2** The wind vacillates.

**3** The wind shifts; one horn lengthens.

**4** Later, a seif takes shape.

# Desertification

**Key words**

*desert*
*desertification*
*temperate*
*tropical*

## Deforestation

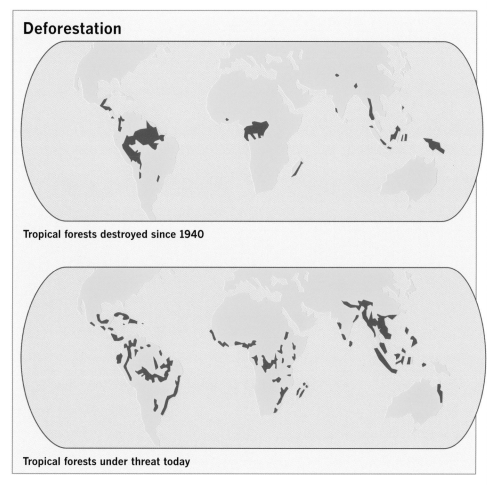

**Tropical forests destroyed since 1940**

**Tropical forests under threat today**

- Huge swathes of tropical rainforest have been destroyed by human activity in the last 60 years.
- Estimates vary about how much of the world's tropical rainforest has been destroyed, but it is at least half, occurring at the rate of about 50 million acres (20 million hectares) each year. Most of the damage has been done in the Amazon basin, central Africa, and in Indonesia and Papua New Guinea.
- About three quarters of the world's temperate forest has also been destroyed, although most of this clearance happened centuries ago: Europe had lost about 80 percent of its temperate forests by the end of the fourteenth century.
- Most of the trees have been cut for timber or to clear land for farming.
- The impact on the global environment will be irreversible, with fewer trees to convert carbon dioxide to oxygen, causing temperatures and sea level to rise worldwide.

## Desertification

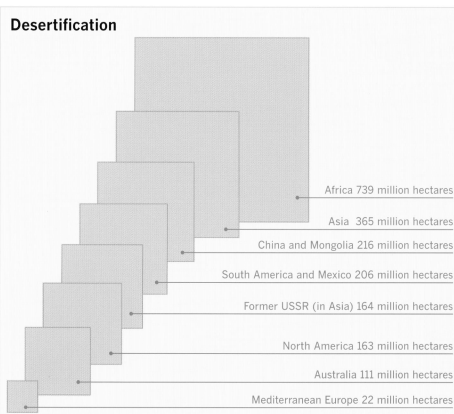

Africa 739 million hectares

Asia 365 million hectares

China and Mongolia 216 million hectares

South America and Mexico 206 million hectares

Former USSR (in Asia) 164 million hectares

North America 163 million hectares

Australia 111 million hectares

Mediterranean Europe 22 million hectares

- *Desertification* is the slow expansion of the world's deserts as fertile land is transformed into a dry wasteland.
- Desertification is caused by deforestation, overgrazing, and intensive farming, which strip the land of vegetation cover and thus allow the soil to dry out completely. Drought in the affected areas increases the speed of desertification.
- Most of the desertification has taken place in Africa, in the Sahel fringe south of the Sahara.
- The Indian subcontinent, China, and parts of South and Central America are also affected. Even previously unaffected areas, such as the southern regions of Spain and Italy, are now suffering desertification.

**Key words**

*continent*
*continental shelf*
*ice sheet*

## Seven continents

- A continent is a large landmass that rises fairly steeply from a deep ocean floor.
- The peripheral areas of a continent might be submerged as a continental shelf, a gently sloping area of the seabed between the edge of the continent and the deep ocean. The average depth of the water over a continental shelf is 430 feet (130 m).
- There are seven continents in the world, ranging in size from Asia down to Australasia. Most of Antarctica is buried beneath a massive ice sheet.
- The seven continents occupy almost one third of the world's surface, with the bulk of them—parts of South America, half of Africa, most of Asia, and all of Europe and North America—located in the Northern Hemisphere.

# Continents

## Continental landmasses

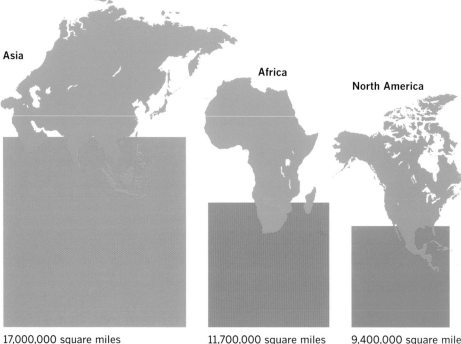

**Asia**

17,000,000 square miles
(44,000,000 km²)

**Africa**

11,700,000 square miles
(30,300,000 km²)

**North America**

9,400,000 square miles
(24,350,000 km²)

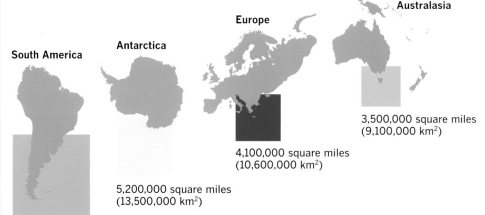

**South America**

6,900,000 square miles
(17,900,000 km²)

**Antarctica**

5,200,000 square miles
(13,500,000 km²)

**Europe**

4,100,000 square miles
(10,600,000 km²)

**Australasia**

3,500,000 square miles
(9,100,000 km²)

**The world as continental landmasses**
In this modified Mercator projection, only the land at the equator has accurate spatial representation.

# Lakes

## Locations of the largest lakes

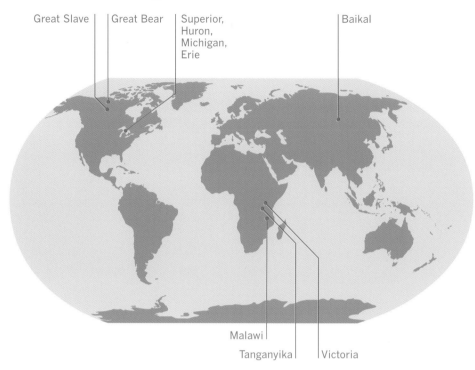

Great Slave | Great Bear | Superior, Huron, Michigan, Erie | Baikal

Malawi
Tanganyika | Victoria

**Key words**

*Northern Hemisphere*

### The world's largest lakes

- The world's ten largest lakes are Superior, Victoria, Huron, Michigan, Tanganyika, Great Bear, Baikal, Malawi, Great Slave, and Erie.
- Victoria, Tanganyika, and Malawi are in Africa, Baikal is in North Asia, and the rest are in North America. Most lie in the Northern Hemisphere.
- Four of the ten lakes—Superior, Huron, Michigan, and Erie—form, together with Lake Ontario, the Great Lakes system between the United States and Canada. Some geographers consider lakes Michigan and Huron to be branches of the same lake. If so, the joint lake would be the world's largest, at 45,410 square miles (117,600 km²).
- Although only seventh largest in area, Lake Baikal is the most voluminous lake, containing 5,518 cubic miles (23,000 km³) of water, because it is the deepest, with a maximum depth of 6,365 feet (1,940 m).

## Comparative shapes

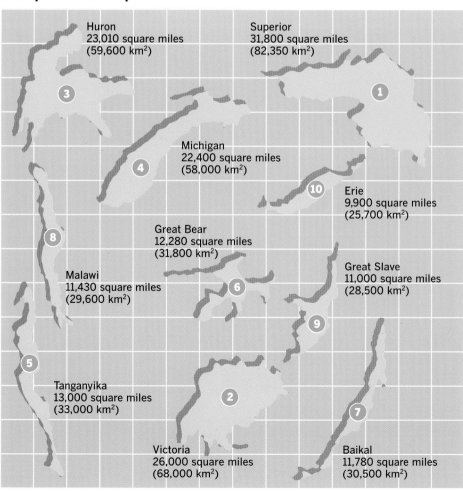

Huron
23,010 square miles
(59,600 km²)

Superior
31,800 square miles
(82,350 km²)

Michigan
22,400 square miles
(58,000 km²)

Erie
9,900 square miles
(25,700 km²)

Great Bear
12,280 square miles
(31,800 km²)

Great Slave
11,000 square miles
(28,500 km²)

Malawi
11,430 square miles
(29,600 km²)

Tanganyika
13,000 square miles
(33,000 km²)

Victoria
26,000 square miles
(68,000 km²)

Baikal
11,780 square miles
(30,500 km²)

## Comparative areas

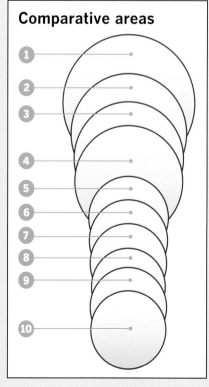

© Diagram Visual Information Ltd.

**Key words**

Northern
  Hemisphere
Southern
  Hemisphere

## The world's largest islands

● In descending order, the world's ten largest islands are Greenland, New Guinea, Borneo, Madagascar, Baffin, Sumatra, Honshu, Great Britain, Victoria, and Ellesmere.

● Four lie off the coast of North America, four close to Asia, and one each beside Africa and Europe. Six lie in the Northern Hemisphere, four in the Southern Hemisphere.

## Comparative areas

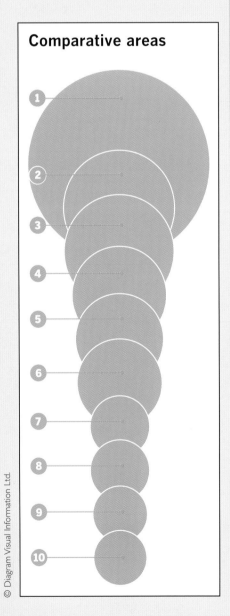

# Islands

## Locations of the largest islands

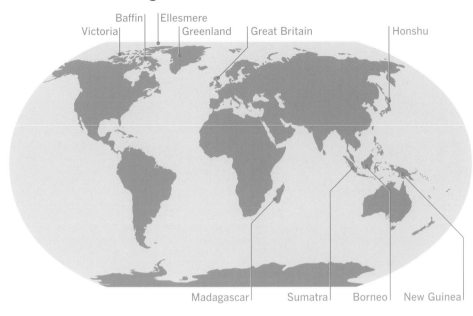

## Comparative shapes

The islands are shown against an outline of the contiguous United States—an area of 3,021,293 square miles (7,825,112 km²)—for comparison.

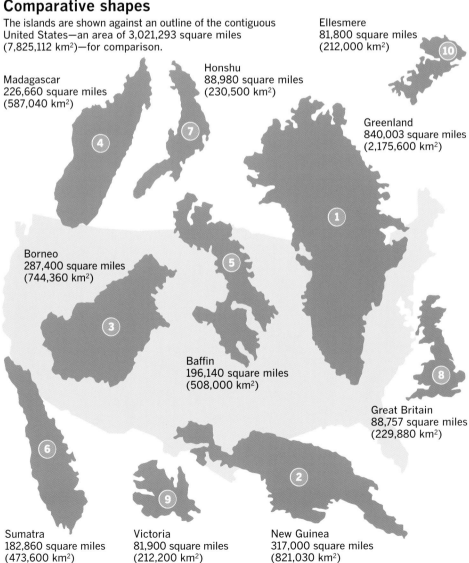

Ellesmere
81,800 square miles
(212,000 km²)

Madagascar
226,660 square miles
(587,040 km²)

Honshu
88,980 square miles
(230,500 km²)

Greenland
840,003 square miles
(2,175,600 km²)

Borneo
287,400 square miles
(744,360 km²)

Baffin
196,140 square miles
(508,000 km²)

Great Britain
88,757 square miles
(229,880 km²)

Sumatra
182,860 square miles
(473,600 km²)

Victoria
81,900 square miles
(212,200 km²)

New Guinea
317,000 square miles
(821,030 km²)

# Mountains

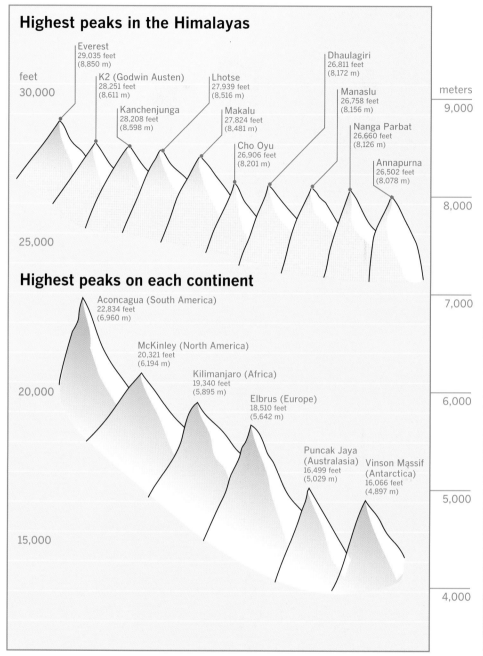

## Highest peaks in the Himalayas

feet
30,000

Everest
29,035 feet
(8,850 m)

K2 (Godwin Austen)
28,251 feet
(8,611 m)

Kanchenjunga
28,208 feet
(8,598 m)

Lhotse
27,939 feet
(8,516 m)

Makalu
27,824 feet
(8,481 m)

Cho Oyu
26,906 feet
(8,201 m)

Dhaulagiri
26,811 feet
(8,172 m)

Manaslu
26,758 feet
(8,156 m)

Nanga Parbat
26,660 feet
(8,126 m)

Annapurna
26,502 feet
(8,078 m)

meters
9,000

8,000

25,000

## Highest peaks on each continent

Aconcagua (South America)
22,834 feet
(6,960 m)

McKinley (North America)
20,321 feet
(6,194 m)

Kilimanjaro (Africa)
19,340 feet
(5,895 m)

Elbrus (Europe)
18,510 feet
(5,642 m)

Puncak Jaya
(Australasia)
16,499 feet
(5,029 m)

Vinson Massif
(Antarctica)
16,066 feet
(4,897 m)

7,000

20,000

6,000

5,000

15,000

4,000

**Locations of each continent's highest mountain**

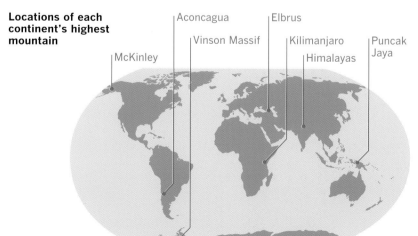

McKinley
Aconcagua
Vinson Massif
Elbrus
Kilimanjaro
Himalayas
Puncak Jaya

## Key words

*volcano*

## Top of the world

- The twelve mountains that are higher than 26,246 feet (8,000 m) are in the Himalayas or the related Karakoram and Hindu Kush ranges in southern Asia. Five of their subsidiary peaks are also more than 26,246 feet (8,000 m) high.
- The highest mountain in the world outside those ranges is Aconcagua in the Andes, South America.

## Highest feature

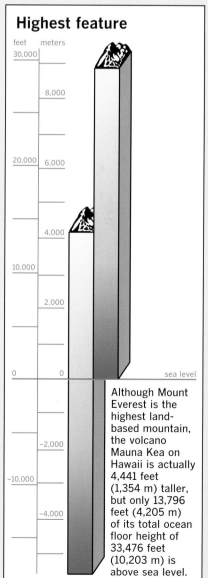

feet    meters
30,000

8,000

20,000    6,000

4,000

10,000    2,000

0    0
sea level

-2,000

-10,000

-4,000

Although Mount Everest is the highest land-based mountain, the volcano Mauna Kea on Hawaii is actually 4,441 feet (1,354 m) taller, but only 13,796 feet (4,205 m) of its total ocean floor height of 33,476 feet (10,203 m) is above sea level.

## Key words

*ocean*

## The world's oceans and seas

- The world's oceans and seas occupy 139 million square miles (361 km²): more than 70 percent of Earth's surface area. Their average depth is 12,240 feet (3,370 m).
- There are four true oceans: the Pacific Ocean is the largest, at 64,186,300 square miles (166,240,000 km²); followed by the Atlantic at 33,420,000 square miles (86,550,000 km²); then the Indian Ocean, at 28,350,500 square miles (73,427,000 km²). The Arctic Ocean is the smallest, at 5,427,000 square miles (14,056,000 km²).
- In 2000 the International Hydrographic Organization approved the description of the Pacific, Atlantic, and Indian oceans below 60° S as the *Southern Ocean* surrounding Antarctica. It occupies 7,848,300 square miles (20,327,000 km²).
- The Pacific Ocean covers almost half the world's ocean surface area, and the Atlantic and Indian oceans nearly a quarter each.
- By comparison, the world's seas are much smaller; for example, the Caribbean Sea at 971,400 square miles (2,515,900 km²) is less than a fifth the size of the Arctic Ocean.

# Seas and oceans

## World seas and oceans

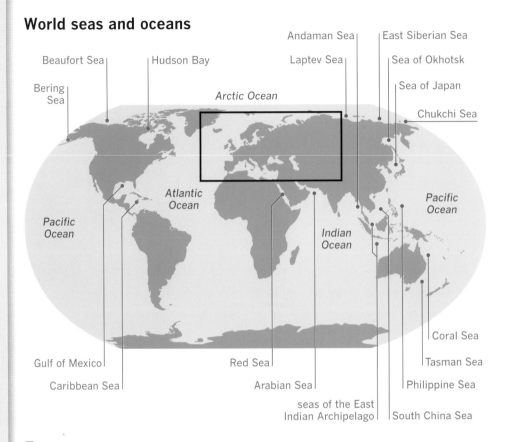

Andaman Sea
East Siberian Sea
Beaufort Sea
Hudson Bay
Laptev Sea
Sea of Okhotsk
Bering Sea
Sea of Japan
Arctic Ocean
Chukchi Sea
Pacific Ocean
Atlantic Ocean
Pacific Ocean
Indian Ocean
Coral Sea
Gulf of Mexico
Tasman Sea
Red Sea
Caribbean Sea
Arabian Sea
Philippine Sea
seas of the East Indian Archipelago
South China Sea

## European seas

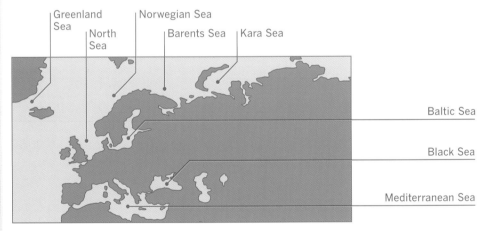

Greenland Sea
Norwegian Sea
North Sea
Barents Sea
Kara Sea
Baltic Sea
Black Sea
Mediterranean Sea

## Earth's surface water

### Water to land

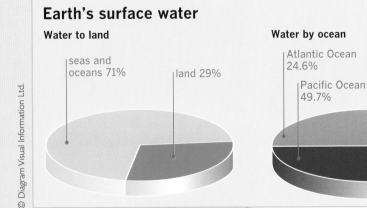

seas and oceans 71%
land 29%

### Water by ocean

Atlantic Ocean 24.6%
Arctic Ocean 3.6%
Pacific Ocean 49.7%
Indian Ocean 22.1%

### Comparative areas

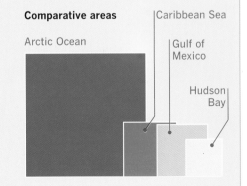

Caribbean Sea
Arctic Ocean
Gulf of Mexico
Hudson Bay

# Submarine features

## Locations of the major trenches and ridges

**Key words**

*ocean*
*trench*

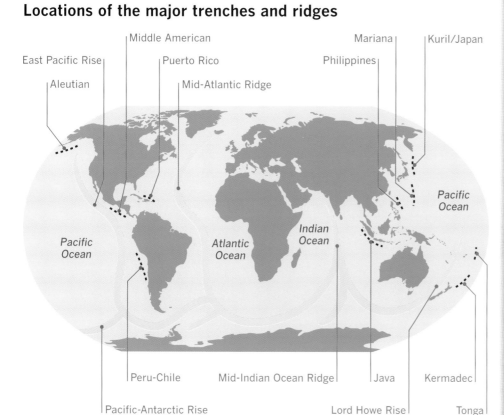

East Pacific Rise

Aleutian

Middle American

Puerto Rico

Mid-Atlantic Ridge

Mariana

Philippines

Kuril/Japan

Pacific Ocean

Pacific Ocean

Atlantic Ocean

Indian Ocean

Peru-Chile

Mid-Indian Ocean Ridge

Java

Kermadec

Pacific-Antarctic Rise

Lord Howe Rise

Tonga

 trench          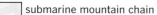 submarine mountain chain

## Submarine mountains

- A complex system of submarine mountain chains and trenches runs beneath the world's oceans.
- The mountain chains or ridges rarely stand more than 5,000 feet (1,500 m) above the ocean floor, but can snake along for thousands of miles: the Mid-Atlantic Ridge, for example, runs from the Arctic to the Antarctic.

## Submarine trenches

- Most deep trenches lie in the Pacific Ocean. The Mariana Trench is the deepest, at 35,840 feet (10,924 m). Four other Pacific trenches are of a similar depth.
- The deepest trench in the Atlantic Ocean is the Puerto Rico trench at 28,232 feet (8,605 m).
- The deepest trench in the Indian Ocean is the Java (Sunda) trench, at 25,344 feet (7,725 m).

## Depths of the major trenches

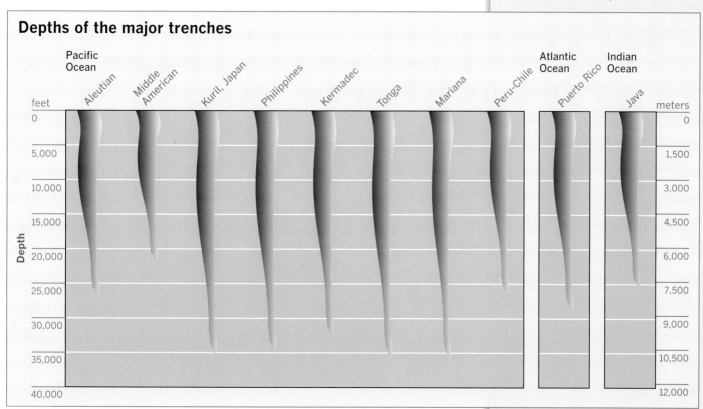

Pacific Ocean: Aleutian, Middle American, Kuril, Japan, Philippines, Kermadec, Tonga, Mariana, Peru-Chile

Atlantic Ocean: Puerto Rico

Indian Ocean: Java

| feet | meters |
|---|---|
| 0 | 0 |
| 5,000 | 1,500 |
| 10,000 | 3,000 |
| 15,000 | 4,500 |
| 20,000 | 6,000 |
| 25,000 | 7,500 |
| 30,000 | 9,000 |
| 35,000 | 10,500 |
| 40,000 | 12,000 |

Depth

## Key words

*earthquake*
*Richter scale*
*volcano*

## Volcanic eruptions

- The force of an erupting volcano can be considerable: the eruption of Tambora in Indonesia in 1815 was more than 300 times more powerful than the most powerful nuclear explosion to date, and sent up so much dust into the atmosphere that the Sun was obscured around the globe, causing poor summers for two years.
- Although volcanoes can explode with tremendous force, their death toll is rarely high since there are usually warning signs, such as the emission of clouds of ash and steam, before the eruption. Most volcanoes are also in relatively sparsely populated areas, reducing possible fatalities further.

## Earthquakes fatalities

- The most powerful earthquake ever recorded occurred in Chile on May 22, 1960, with a magnitude of 9.5 on the Richter scale.
- The highest death toll due to a recent earthquake was in Tangshan, China, on July 27, 1976, when the official figure was 255,000, though more than 650,000 people may have died.
- The deadliest earthquake on record also occurred in China, in Shaanxi, on January 23, 1556, when perhaps 830,000 people were killed by the earthquake, which is estimated to have been 8.0 on the Richter scale.
- The submarine earthquake off the coast of Sumatra that produced the devastating tsunami of December 26, 2004, measured 9.0–9.3 on the Richter scale and caused 283,000 deaths across the Indian Ocean region. A repeat in the same area on March 28, 2005, measured 8.5–8.7, though fatalities were barely more than 1,000 people.

# Volcanoes and earthquakes

## Volcanoes

| Dimensions of modern volcanoes | |
| --- | --- |
| Largest active volcano | Mauna Loa, Hawaii: dome 75 x 64 miles (120 x 103 km) |
| Largest crater | Toba, Sumatra: 685 square miles (1,775 km²) |
| Highest volcano | Aconcagua, Argentina: 22,834 feet (6,960 m) |

| Greatest volcanic eruptions in TNT equivalent | |
| --- | --- |
| Tambora, Indonesia (1815) | 20,000 Mt |
| Santorini, Greece (1628 BCE) | 7,500 Mt |
| Krakatau, Indonesia (1883) | 1,500 Mt |

1 megaton (Mt) = 1 million tons of TNT. The most massive nuclear explosion has been 60 megatons.

| Greatest volcanic eruptions: matter ejected | | |
| --- | --- | --- |
| Santorini, Greece (1628 BCE) | 12–16 cubic miles | (50–65 km³) |
| Tambora, Indonesia (1815) | 10 cubic miles | (40 km³, excluding collapsed material) |
| Krakatau, Indonesia (1883) | 5 cubic miles | (20 km³) |

| Most destructive nineteenth and twentieth-century eruptions | | |
| --- | --- | --- |
| Krakatau, Indonesia (1883) | 36,000 deaths | |
| Tambora, Indonesia (1815) | 12,000 deaths | |

## Earthquakes

| Severest earthquakes since 1900 (Richter scale intensities) | | | |
| --- | --- | --- | --- |
| Chile (1960) | 9.5 | Kamchatka, Russia (1952) | 9.0 |
| Kamchatka, Russia (1737) | 9.3 | Cascadia, California (1700) | 9.0 |
| Alaska (1964) | 9.2 | Colombia–Ecuador (1906) | 8.8 |
| Sumatra, Indonesia (2004) | 9.0–9.3 | Alaska (1965) | 8.7 |
| Alaska (1957) | 9.1 | Sumatra, Indonesia (1833) | 8.7 |

| Deaths in the most lethal earthquakes since 1900 | | | |
| --- | --- | --- | --- |
| Tangshan, China (1976) | 650,000 | Turkmenistan, USSR (1948) | 110,000 |
| Indian Ocean tsunami (2004) | 283,000 | Kashmir, Pakistan (2005) | 100,000 |
| Gansu, China (1920) | 200,000 | Messina, Italy (1908) | 70,000 |
| Qinghai, China (1927) | 200,000 | Gansu, China (1932) | 70,000 |
| Kwanto Plain, Japan (1923) | 143,000 | Northern Peru (1970) | 66,000 |

# Rivers

## Locations of the ten longest rivers

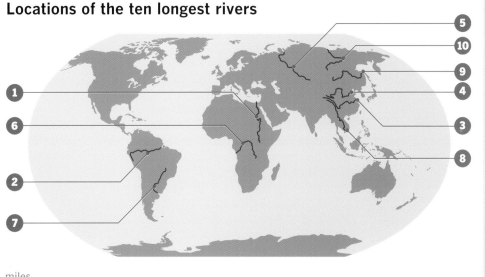

**Key words**

*delta*

### The longest rivers
- The world's longest river is the Nile, which rises in East Africa and flows north through Sudan and Egypt—"the gift of the Nile"—to the eastern Mediterranean, a total distance of 4,140 miles (6,670 km).

**miles**

| 0 | 1,000 | 2,000 | 3,000 | 4,000 |

| 1 | Nile, Northeast Africa 4,140 miles (6,670 km) |
| 2 | Amazon, South America 4,010 miles (6,450 km) |
| 3 | Chang Jiang (Yangtze), China 3,960 miles (6,380 km) |
| 4 | Huang He, China 3,395 miles (5,464 km) |
| 5 | Ob–Irtysh Russia, 3,360 miles (5,410 km) |
| 6 | Congo, Central Africa 2,900 miles (4,670 km) |
| 7 | Paraná-Plate, South America 2,800 miles (4,506 km) |
| 8 | Mekong, Southeast Asia 2,795 miles (4,498 km) |
| 9 | Amur, Northeast Asia 2,743 miles (4,416 km) |
| 10 | Lena, Russia 2,730 miles (4,400 km) |
| | Mackenzie, Canada 2,630 miles (4,240 km) |
| | Niger, West Africa 2,595 miles (4,180 km) |
| | Yenisey, Russia 2,540 miles (4,090 km) |
| | Mississippi, North America 2,350 miles (3,780 km) |
| | Missouri, North America 2,350 miles (3,780 km) |
| | Murray-Darling, Australia 2,330 miles (3,750 km) |
| | Volga, Russia 2,300 miles (3,700 km) |
| | Purus, Brazil 2,080 miles (3,350 km) |
| | Madeira, Brazil 1,990 miles (3,200 km) |
| | São Francisco, Brazil 1,800 miles (2,900 km) |

| 0 | 1,000 | 2,000 | 3,000 | 4,000 | 5,000 |
**kilometers**

- The mighty Amazon rises from tributaries across the north west of South America, flowing through equatorial Brazil into the Atlantic.
- The Chang Jiang (Yangtze) and Huang He rivers both rise in central China and flow into the Pacific, while the Amur forms most of the northeast border between China and Russia.
- The Ob–Irtysh, Lena, and Yenisey river systems all drain large tracts of Siberia into the Arctic.
- The Congo (formerly Zaïre) rises from tributaries across central Africa and flows westwards into the Atlantic.
- The Paraná rises in the Brazilian highlands and runs through Paraguay and Argentina to drain into the South Atlantic at Río de la Plata.
- The Mekong rises in and runs through Southeast Asia, forming a natural border between Laos and Thailand before flowing south through Cambodia. The Mekong delta then crosses southern Vietnam to exit into the South China Sea.

# Key words

**absolute humidity** The mass of water vapor present in a given volume of air.

**abyssal plain** The deep and mostly flat region that makes up most of the seafloor.

**accretion** (1) The process by which a rock or any other inorganic body grows in size by the addition of particles to its exterior. (2) The accumulation of a sediment. (3) The enlargement of a continent.

**advection fog** Fog that is formed when warm moist air is carried across a colder surface.

**aeration zone** The layer of rock and soil above the water table in which interstitial spaces contain both air and water.

**air mass** A large body of air that has approximately constant temperature and humidity throughout. The interaction of air masses with differing characteristics is one of the main causes of weather.

**alluvium** Silt, sand, or gravel deposited by moving water, either along the bed of a stream or on land that the water overflows.

**altocumulus** A variety of middle-altitude cloud composed of long thin elements and arranged in lines.

**altostratus** A variety of middle-altitude cloud that has the appearance of a thin veil or uniform sheet.

**andesitic lava** Lava with a silica content intermediate between those of basaltic and rhyolitic lavas. It is viscous and does not flow far.

**anemometer** An instrument that measures wind speed.

**angular unconformity** An abrupt change in the orientation of strata that results in horizontal strata overlying tilted strata.

**anthracite** A type of coal with a very high carbon content.

**anticline** A broad archlike upfold in layered rocks, caused by their compression. In anticlines, the oldest rocks are on the inside of the arch.

**anticyclone** A region in which atmospheric pressure is higher than in the surrounding area.

**aphelion** The point on a planet's orbit that is farthest from the Sun.

**aquifer** A water-bearing, permeable, and porous rock mass or layer through which ground water moves, and which is capable of storing considerable volumes of water.

**arroyo** A deep gully cut by an intermittently flowing stream in a generally dry landscape.

**artesian basin** Saucerlike sedimentary rock layers embedded in such a way that impermeable layers sandwich an aquifer.

**artesian well** A type of well in which the water is under hydrostatic pressure high enough to force it upwards naturally.

**asteroid** A natural object in space that is larger than 160 feet (50 m) in diameter, smaller than a moon, and mostly composed of rock rather than icy material.

**asthenosphere** A dense, plastic, semimolten layer of mantle just below the lithosphere.

**atmosphere** The envelope of gases gravitationally bound to Earth.

**atoll** A ring of coral reef around a subsiding volcanic island. Atolls enclose lagoons.

**atom** The smallest particle of an element that can exhibit that element's properties.

**aureole** The zone around an igneous intrusion in which the local rocks have been subjected to metamorphism.

**authigenesis** The crystallization of minerals within a sediment during or after its deposition.

**axis** (1) The imaginary line through the poles, about which a planet or moon rotates. (2) An imaginary line dividing a crystal symmetrically.

**backwash** Water flowing back to the sea from a wave that has broken as it surges up a beach.

**bajada** An extended deposit of sediment formed by the overlapping of alluvial fans from adjacent river valleys.

**bar** A ridge of mud, sand, or shingle lying across a river mouth or a bay.

**barchan** A sand dune shaped like a crescent, with its points blown forward by the wind.

**barycenter** The common center of mass around which two or more bodies orbit each other.

**basalt** A dark-colored, fine-grained type of extrusive, basic (as opposed to acid) igneous rock.

**basaltic lava** A basic lava low in silica. It flows far before hardening.

**basin** An area in which the rock has a natural concavity toward a lowest point.

**batholith** A large dome-shaped, deep-seated, intrusive body of igneous rock. Batholiths often consist of granite.

**bay** A wide inlet in a sea or lake, smaller than a gulf.

**bedding** The arrangement of sedimentary rocks into distinct layers.

**bergschrund** A deep crevasse in a glacier filling a cirque.

**berm** A sand or shingle shelf high up on a beach, formed from material thrown there by storm waves.

**bight** A broad crescent-shaped bay.

**blowhole** A passageway connecting the roof of a sea cave with the surface of the land above it.

**bolide** An extraterrestrial object that strikes Earth's surface or explodes in Earth's atmosphere.

**boulder** A rounded lump of stone more than about 10 inches (25 cm) across.

**breaker** A wave that breaks on a shore after rising and toppling forward on reaching the shallows.

**breccia** A coarse sedimentary or igneous rock consisting of angular broken fragments (clasts) held together by a natural cement.

**Burgess shale** A layer of Cambrian rock near Mount Burgess in Canada in which many unique fossils have been discovered.

**butte** A small, steep-sided hill with a flat top, formed when part of a mesa erodes away, leaving the butte, which is protected from erosion by a resistant top layer.

**caldera** A large bowl-shaped volcanic crater, typically several miles across, with a steep inner slope.

**carbonation** The chemical breakdown of rocks by carbonic acid.

**cast** A type of fossil that forms when the body of an organism dissolves leaving an impression in clay or other material known as a mold. Mineral material may later fill this mold to form a cast.

**cementation** The hardening of sediments into sedimentary rock by precipitated minerals filling tiny gaps between particles and cementing them together.

**chelation** The process by which rocks are eaten away by acids in soil humus.

**chemical weathering** The breakdown of rock by chemical processes.

**chromosphere** The lowest level of the Sun's atmosphere.

**cirque** A steep-walled mountain rock basin scooped out by freezing, thawing, and slipping ice formed from compacted snow.

**cirrus** A form of high-altitude cloud composed of ice crystals that has the appearance of narrow bands, diffuse filaments, or white patches.

**clast** Any weathered fragment of rock.

**coal** A carbon-rich rock that burns easily.

**coal forest** A wetland forest that gives rise to coal deposits.

**coal measure** A layer of rock that contains coal.

**coast** The region of land influenced by sea.

**comet** An irregular agglomeration of water ice, frozen gases, and other material in orbit around the Sun.

**compaction** The physical process brought about by the increasing pressure at the base of a thickening sediment.

**condensation** A change in state from a gas to a liquid.

**condensation nucleus** A microscopic solid particle in the atmosphere onto which water vapor easily condenses. Condensation nuclei allow the condensation of the water droplets that make up fog.

**confluence** The point at which two streams join.

**conglomerate** Any sedimentary rock containing smooth rounded rock fragments (clasts) greater than 0.08 inches (2 mm) in diameter embedded in the fine-grained matrix of, for example, sandstone or limestone.

**continent** One of Earth's major landmasses.

**continental drift** The hypothesis that continents have moved relative to each other over Earth's surface.

**continental rim** The rim of the continental shelf surrounding a continent that forms its true but submerged structural edge.

**continental rise** The gentle gradient at the bottom of the continental slope consisting of material that has slid down from the continental slope.

**continental shelf** The shallow seafloor that extends from the shore to the edge of the continental slope.

**continental slope** The steep gradient that descends from the continental shelf to the abyssal plain.

**convection** Heat transfer by movement of the medium heated, such as through the movement of air, water, or molten rock below Earth's crust.

**convectional rain** Rain that develops as a result of the transport of warm moist air by convection.

**convergence** A region where water masses with different properties (for example, temperature) merge.

**coral** A hard calcium carbonate made up of the exoskeletons of coral polyps.

**coral reef** Coral forming a shallow, submerged rock platform, with a steep outer slope and a gentler inner slope.

**core** The dense matter forming the center of a star, planet, or moon.

**Coriolis effect** The tendency for ocean currents and winds to be deflected to the west by the eastward rotation of Earth.

**corona** The Sun's gaseous outer layer.

**corrasion** The abrasive erosion of a solid rock surface by particles dragged over it by river water, glaciers, sea waves, or the wind.

**cosmic ray** Electromagnetic rays of extremely high frequency and energy.

**craton** An ancient part of a continent that has not been deformed by mountain-building activity.

**crest** The highest point of a wave.

**crevasse** A deep crack in a glacier.

**crust** The hard outer layer of a solid-surfaced planet or moon. Earth's crust consists mainly of crystalline rock and extends from the surface to the boundary with the mantle below.

**crystal** A solid of definite chemical composition, with a characteristically ordered geometrical arrangement of atoms and faces that form naturally with external symmetry.

**cuesta** A ridge with a steep scarp on one side and a gentle dip slope on the other.

**cumulonimbus** A form of cloud that may extend from low to high altitudes. It usually has a flat top and a rounded cloud base. The base is commonly dark gray while the body of the cloud is bright white.

**cyclone** An area in which atmospheric pressure is lower than the surrounding area.

**cyclonic rain** Rain associated with a cyclone.

**deflation hollow** A depression scoured in a desert surface by windblown sand and dust.

**degassing** The escape of gases from molten rock.

**delta** An area of low, flat, often fan-shaped land at a river mouth. A delta is built out into a lake or sea by sediments deposited by a river.

**denudation** The wearing away of the land surface by processes such as weathering and erosion.

**deposition** The laying down of dust, mud, sand, gravel, or other materials removed by weathering and transportation.

**desert** A region too dry to support many plants. Deserts may be defined as places with less than about 10 inches (25 cm) of rainfall per year.

**desertification** The transformation of fertile land into unproductive desert.

**diagenesis** The physical and chemical changes that occur in a sediment at normal temperatures and pressures to turn it into a rock.

**dike** A vertical sheet of igneous rock intruded through older rocks so that it cuts across their bedding planes.

**dip** The angle between the horizontal plane and a tilted rock bed or fault.

**disconformity** An unconformity where erosion has left a gap in the sequence of rock strata but, unlike an angular unconformity, those above and below it are horizontal.

**distributary** A stream diverging from a main river.

**draa** A large dune formation several hundred feet high and many miles long found in the Sahara desert.

**Earth** The solar system's fifth largest planet, third in distance from the Sun.

**earthquake** A violent shaking movement on Earth's surface caused by plate tectonics or volcanic activity.

**eclipse** The obscuring of one celestial body by another, usually the Moon or Earth obscuring the Sun.

**electromagnetic radiation** The entire range of wavelengths and frequencies of the electromagnetic spectrum.

**electron** A subatomic particle with a negative charge.

**element** A chemical substance containing only one kind of atom. An element cannot be chemically broken down into a simpler substance.

**ellipsoid** A surface that can be cut in any direction to produce ellipses or circles.

**eon** The largest unit into which geologic time is divided. Four eons have been identified.

**epilimnion** The layer of water above the thermocline in a body of fresh water.

**epipedon** The top layer of soil.

**epoch** A subdivision of a geologic period.

**equator** An imaginary line around Earth midway between the North and South poles.

**equatorial low** A persistent belt of low pressure at the equator.

**equinox** One of the two occasions each year on which the Sun crosses the plane of the equator. In the Northern Hemisphere the vernal (or spring), equinox occurs on or about March 21st and the autumnal (fall) equinox on or about September 22nd. These dates are transposed for the Southern Hemisphere.

**era** A time unit forming a major subdivision of geologic time. An era contains at least two periods.

**erosion** The wearing down, loosening, and transportation of features of the surface of the land by wind, water, gravity, and moving land and ice.

**eruption** An outpouring, especially of volcanic gas, lava, and ash from Earth's surface.

**esker** A long, winding ridge of sand and gravel. It consists of sediments shed by a stream flowing under a stationary glacier that has subsequently melted away.

**evaporite** Rock made of crystals precipitated by the evaporation of salt-saturated water.

**evapotranspiration** The combined processes by which water is transferred to the atmosphere from the surfaces of bodies of water or ice, from Earth's surface, and from the surfaces of respiring plants.

**exosphere** The highest part of Earth's atmosphere. The density of gases is so low that molecules rarely collide and some molecules escape into space.

**fault** A fracture zone where one rock mass has moved against another in the continental or oceanic crust.

**faulting** The fracturing and displacement of rock layers.

**feldspar** Any of a group of hard rock-forming minerals containing aluminum silicates of potassium, sodium, calcium, or barium.

**fetch** The influence of the wind on wave height over a period of time across a stretch of water.

**fissure** A deep, narrow depression.

**fjord** A long, narrow, steep-sided sea inlet invading a glaciated valley.

**floodplain** Low land flanking a river that is usually flooded when the river overflows.

**fog** A cloud with a cloud base at or close to ground level.

**fold** A bend in rock layers, formed when pressure has made them plastic.

**folding** The deformation of rock layers under pressure.

**fossil** The remains or trace of a prehistoric plant or animal, organism, footprint, or dropping, preserved in sedimentary rock.

**fumarole** A small hole in the ground, emitting steam and other hot volcanic gases.

**gabbro** A dense, dark, coarse-grained intrusive rock largely consisting of plagioclase feldspar and pyroxene; the intrusive equivalent of basalt.

**gas giant** A large planet that is mostly composed of elements that are gases on Earth (hydrogen and helium) rather than rocky material.

**geoid** The shape that would be formed by the surface of a body of water that covered the entire Earth.

**geologic time** The period from the formation of Earth to the present.

**geomagnetism** The influence of Earth's magnetic field.

**geomorphology** The study of the origin and evolution of the shape and structure of the landforms of Earth.

**geyser** A periodic fountain forced up through a hole in the ground by the pressure of steam produced by hot rocks heating underground water.

**glacier** A naturally accumulating mass of ice that moves downward in the process of discharging from a head or center to its terminal dissipation zone.

**Gondwana** The prehistoric southern supercontinent, which included what are now South America, Africa, India, Australia, and Antarctica.

**granite** An intrusive igneous rock rich in quartz and feldspar, often with mica or hornblende.

**grassland** Open countryside where the main vegetation is grass.

**gravity** The quality of an object with mass that results in gravitational attraction.

**groin** A wall or sturdy fence jutting out across a beach from the land designed to stop longshore drift moving sand and shingle away from the beach.

**groundwater** The water in soil and rock, which is largely rainwater that filters down through permeable and porous rock until it reaches impermeable rock.

**gulf** A region of an ocean enclosed on three sides by land and usually larger than a bay.

**guyot** A flat-topped submarine mountain formed when a seamount is eroded.

**gyre** A roughly circular ocean current.

**headland** A cape or promontory jutting into the ocean, especially one bounded by cliffs.

**hogback** A long, narrow ridge formed from very steep or vertical rock layers.

**hot spot** A small area of Earth's crust heated by a mantle plume rising below it.

**humidity** The (variable) amount of water vapor in the atmosphere.

**humus** The dark upper part of soil, consisting of dead plants, organisms, and animal remains and droppings that have lost their original structure and undergone decomposition.

**hurricane** A severe tropical cyclone occurring over the North Atlantic, the Caribbean, the Gulf of Mexico, or the eastern North Pacific.

**hydration** The breakdown of rocks as they absorb water.

**hypabyssal** A form of igneous rock that solidifies near Earth's surface as relatively small strips or sheets rather than as massive blocks.

**hypolimnion** The bottom layer of water in a body of freshwater.

**ice cap** A permanent ice mass smaller than an ice sheet.

**ice sheet** An immense mass of ice covering a large land area. Ice sheets cover much of Antarctica and Greenland.

**ice wedge** A wedge-shaped mass of ice up to 100 feet (30 m) deep, projecting down into the ground of periglacial regions. Ice wedges form from summer meltwater filling cracks that gape open when the ground shrinks in winter.

**igneous rock** Rock formed from cooled, solidified magma.

**impact crater** A crater formed by the impact of a meteorite rather than by volcanic activity.

**inner planet** Any of the four planets closest to the Sun.

**inselberg** An isolated, steep-sided hill rising abruptly from a tropical plain.

**insolation** The amount of solar radiation reaching Earth's surface.

**intrusion** A mass of igneous rock that solidifies before it reaches the surface.

**ionosphere** The region of the atmosphere containing the highest concentrations of ions and electrons.

**island arc** A line of islands associated with a geologic feature, such as a trench or a hot spot.

**isostasy** The equilibrium state of lithospheric plates floating on the asthenosphere.

**isotope** An atom of an element sharing the same atomic number as other atoms of that element but differing in atomic mass.

**jet stream** A narrow band of strong wind in the upper troposphere or lower stratosphere.

**kame** A steep-sided mound of sand and gravel formed from deposits left by meltwater flowing over the surface of a glacier.

**karst** A limestone or dolomite landscape with a largely bare, rocky surface and rivers that flow through underground caves.

**kopje** A torlike landscape feature found in the tropics.

**lagoon** A shallow area of water partly or wholly cut off from the sea by a low-lying strip of sand, shingle, or coral that forms a spit, bar, or atoll.

**Laurasia** The prehistoric northern supercontinent formed about 200 million years ago after the global landmass Pangaea began breaking up.

**lava** Molten rock when it appears at Earth's surface from a volcano through vents and fissures.

**layer** A sheetlike expanse of material with generally homogeneous characteristics.

**levee** The naturally raised bank of a river crossing a floodplain. It consists of alluvium deposited when the river overflows its banks.

**lignite** Coal formed from peat.

**limestone** Sedimentary rock mainly made of carbonates of calcium and magnesium and laid down in the sea.

**linear mobile belt** A belt of rock formed from an island arc or a submarine plateau swept up against a preexisting microcontinent and forming a line of mountains.

**lithification** Processes that change sediments into solid rocks; for instance, compaction due to compression combined with the precipitation of a mineral cement.

**lithosphere** Earth's crust, both continental and oceanic, together with the rigid upper mantle above the asthenosphere.

**lode** An extended vein of minerals or a system of veins. The term is sometimes limited to a productive vein.

**longitude** Location measured in degrees east or west of the Greenwich or prime meridian.

**longitudinal coastline** A coastline featuring a mountain range that parallels the coast.

**longshore drift** A tendency for sediment to be carried along a shore by waves breaking at an angle to that shore.

**magma** Liquid or semiliquid molten rock beneath Earth's surface.

**magnetic pole** A location in the world's far north or far south to which a magnetic compass needle points. They do not coincide with the geographical poles, and their locations vary through time.

**magnetometer** An instrument used to measure the strength of a magnetic field.

**magnetosphere** A roughly doughnut-shaped region in space containing Earth's magnetic field.

**mantle** The intermediate and largest layer of Earth, the mantle is a zone of dense hot rock, 1,800 miles (2,900 km) thick, lying between the crust and the core and extending roughly halfway to the center.

**mare** (plural: **maria**) The Latin word for lunar sea.

**meander** A curve in a river in which the water channel swings from side to side in a series of loops.

**meridian** A line of longitude between Earth's North and South poles.

**mesa** A steep-sided plateau capped by resistant horizontal rock layers.

**mesosphere** Earth's atmosphere between the stratopause and mesopause, where temperature falls with increasing altitude.

**metamorphic rock** Sedimentary or igneous rock altered by great heat or pressure.

**metamorphism** The changes brought about in preexisting rock masses by temperature, pressure, and the loss of any volatile content, but not by weathering or sedimentation.

**meteor** A meteoroid that enters Earth's atmosphere.

**meteorite** A meteoroid that impacts Earth's surface.

**meteoroid** A naturally occurring cohesive lump of material in space that is larger than a molecule but smaller than 160 feet (50 m) in diameter.

**microcontinent** A type of large island such as those that probably preceded, and formed the nucleus of, the first continents.

**mineral** A natural inorganic substance with a distinct chemical composition and internal structure.

**mofette** A small vent emitting gases.

**Mohs' scale** A scale showing the relative hardness of different minerals by their scratch resistance.

**monsoon** A seasonal shift in the prevailing wind direction caused by the greater seasonal variation in temperature over landmasses than over adjacent oceans. Monsoons also correspond to large seasonal variations in the quantity of rainfall.

**moon** A natural satellite kept in orbit around a planet by gravitational force.

**Moon** Earth's largest natural satellite.

**moraine** Rock debris moved by a glacier or ice sheet; also, such rock debris left behind when a glacier or ice sheet melts.

**mud volcano** A low mud cone deposited by mud-rich water escaping from a vent.

**neap tide** The tide with the smallest range between high and low tide. Neap tides occur twice per lunar month at most locations.

**neutron** A type of subatomic particle with no electric charge.

**névé** Snow that has been partially melted then refrozen. Névé which survives from one winter season to the next may become the basis of a glacier.

**nickpoint** A sudden drop in the elevation of a stream.

**nimbostratus** A variety of middle- to low-altitude cloud that often produces heavy precipitation. It generally appears as a formless, dark gray layer.

**nitrogen cycle** The continuous circulation of nitrogen through the biosphere, hydrosphere, lithosphere, and atmosphere.

**nonconformity** An unconformity where sedimentary rock overlies granite or another igneous or metamorphic rock.

**Northern Hemisphere** The half of Earth north of the equator.

**North Pole** An imaginary point at latitude 90° N—the northern end of Earth's axis.

**nuclear fusion** The fusion of lightweight atomic nuclei to form nuclei of a heavier element; large quantities of energy are released in the process.

**nucleosynthesis** The process of generating heavier elements from lighter elements in a star.

**ocean** The continuous body of saltwater that covers about 70 percent of Earth's surface.

**oceanic crust** Earth's crust beneath the ocean basins. Oceanic crust is thinner and denser than continental crust.

**orbit** The path taken by one body around another, usually more massive, body determined by gravity.

**ore** A mineral-rich deposit worth mining.

**orogeny** A mountain-building phase.

**orographic rain** Rain from cloud that forms when air is forced to rise by the topography of Earth's surface.

**outer planets** One of the five planets farthest from the Sun.

**oxbow lake** A small, curved, narrow lake that forms where a river cuts through the narrow neck of a meander and the ends of the bypassed cutoff silt up.

**Pangaea** Earth's single primeval landmass. The name is from the Greek for "all land."

**peat** A soft, dark mass of partly decayed plants that grow in marshes.

**ped** A naturally occurring clump of soil.

**pediment** The gentle slope at the foot of a desert mountain. Loose material eroded from the mountain may cover its surface.

**peninsula** A tract of land extending out into a sea or a lake.

**penumbra** An area cast in partial shadow during an eclipse.

**perigee** The point on an orbit around Earth that is closest to Earth.

**periglacial** Describing a cold landscape or climate, such as that found in regions near ice sheets.

**perihelion** The point on a planet's orbit that is closest to the Sun.

**period** A geologic time unit within an era.

**permafrost** The permanently frozen ground of polar and subpolar zones and of any area in which the temperature remains below freezing point for several years.

**photosphere** The visible surface of the Sun.

**pingo** A hillock produced in periglacial regions by an underground ice blister pushing up the surface materials.

**planet** Any large body in orbit around a star that does not generate its own light.

**planetesimal** The miniature planets that are believed to have coalesced and matured into planets such as Earth.

**plate** One of the solid, but distinct, segments that make up Earth's outer surface.

**plateau** A large area of high land with a fairly flat top.

**plate tectonics** The theory that Earth's crust consists of moving lithospheric plates lying above a weaker semiplastic asthenosphere and that their interactions build and destroy continents and oceans.

**platform** An eroded shield overlain by younger rocks.

**pluton** A general term for any large mass of igneous rock, such as granite formed from magma that cooled deep in Earth's crust.

**point** The end of a headland furthest out to sea.

**polar high** A persistent belt of high pressure around a polar region.

**pole** One of either end of Earth's axis—the northernmost or southernmost points.

**precipitation** The transfer of water, in any form, from the atmosphere to the land or the ocean.

**prime meridian** (or **Greenwich meridian**) The zero degree meridian from which longitude is calculated.

**promontory** An elevated piece of land, particularly one that is projecting into the sea.

**proton** A positively charged type of subatomic particle.

**pyroclast** Fragments of volcanic rock produced by the explosive action of expanding volcanic gases.

**radiation fog** Fog that forms as a result of heat being radiated from the surface of Earth into the atmosphere.

**radioisotope** A radioactive isotope.

**radio wave** An electromagnetic wave with a frequency between 100 and 3,000,000 MHz.

**rain shadow** A region of drastically reduced rainfall on the lee side of a raised topographical feature, such as a mountain range, compared to the windward side.

**rapid** A stretch of turbulent water flowing quickly over a stream bed that suddenly steepens.

**reef** A ridge of rock or coral always or sometimes just submerged by the sea.

**regolith** A layer of loose material covering bedrock.

**relative humidity** The ratio of water vapor in a given volume of gas and the maximum amount of water vapor that volume of gas at the same temperature could contain before reaching saturation point.

**rhyolitic lava** An acid lava with a high silica content. It is viscous and hardens before flowing far.

**ria** A deep, funnel-shaped inlet of the sea occupying a drowned river valley in a submerged upland coast.

**Richter scale** A scale measuring the energy released by an earthquake.

**rift valley** A long, steep-sided, flat-bottomed depression formed when a slab of continental or oceanic crust slips down between two or more parallel faults.

**river** A large, natural freshwater stream flowing downhill through a long channel to another river, lake, or sea.

**riverbed** A channel that contains or has contained a river.

**river valley** A valley that has been formed primarily by the action of a river.

**rock** Any mass of mineral particles forming part of Earth's crust. The three major types of rock are igneous, metamorphic, and sedimentary.

**rock pedestal** A mushroom-shaped rock, its base whittled away by the sandblasting effect of windborne sand.

**salinity** A measure of the quantity of dissolved salts in seawater.

**saltation** The rolling and bounding motion of individual grains of sediment propelled by water or wind.

**salt dome** A massive, vertical underground cylinder of rock salt that has risen through sedimentary rocks, forcing the rock layers above it up into a dome.

**sand** Rock particles with sizes between those of gravel and silt. Most sand consists of quartz.

**sclerometer** An instrument used to measure hardness.

**scree** (or **talus**) Pieces of rock that have fallen from a cliff face or steep mountainside and formed a steep slope of loose debris at the base of the cliff or mountain.

**sea level** The mean altitude between high and low tides.

**seamount** A volcanic mountain with a peak that lies below sea level.

**sediment** Any fine or coarse material deposited by water, ice, or wind.

**sedimentary rock** Rock formed at or near the surface of Earth from compacted sediments, often deposited in layers (strata) and hardened by natural cements.

**seif** A long sand ridge with a sharp crest, shaped by and aligned with the prevailing wind.

**shield** A geologically stable region of ancient (Precambrian) rocks, often forming a continent's core.

**shield volcano** A volcano with a broad, gently sloping cone formed from flows of low-viscosity lava.

**sial** The upper part of Earth's crust consisting of rocks rich in silicon and aluminum.

**silica** A silicon-oxygen compound, also known as quartz, that comprises 59 percent of Earth's crust.

**silicate** Any of the most plentiful group of rock-forming minerals, usually consisting of silicon and oxygen combined with a metal.

**sill** A horizontal sheet of igneous rock intruded between sedimentary rock layers.

**sima** Rocks rich in silicon and magnesium that predominate in oceanic crust.

**smoker** A submarine hot spring at an oceanic spreading ridge.

**soil** A mixture of mineral fragments, organic matter, air, and water that forms the surface layer of most land.

**soil creep** The gradual downslope movement of soil over an extended period of time.

**solar wind** A stream of energetic particles emitted by the Sun.

## KEY WORDS

**solfatara** A vent emitting steam and sulfurous gas.

**solstice** One of two occasions each year on which the Sun reaches its furthest point north or south of the plane of the equator.

**Southern Hemisphere** The half of Earth south of the equator.

**South Pole** An imaginary point at latitude 90° S—the southern end of Earth's axis.

**spit** A low strip of sand or shingle with one end joined to land and the other extending into the sea or across a bay.

**spreading ridge** A submarine mountain chain built by magma that rises to plug a widening gap between two diverging lithospheric plates.

**spring tide** The tide with the greatest range between high and low tide. Spring tides occur twice per lunar month at most locations.

**star** A celestial body that emits radiation derived from nuclear fusion reactions.

**storm beach** A band of sand and shingle thrown above a high-tide mark by storm waves.

**stratosphere** A region of the atmosphere above the troposphere and below the mesosphere.

**stratum** (plural: **strata**) A distinct layer of sedimentary rock.

**strike** The compass direction of a horizontal line at right angles to the dip of a layer of rocks or a fault.

**subduction** The sliding of one lithospheric plate downward at an angle under another that remains stationary.

**submarine plateau** An extended area of land raised above the general elevation of the ocean floor.

**Sun** The star at the center of the solar system.

**superposition** The principle that, in undisturbed layered rocks, the higher a stratum lies, the younger it is.

**swash** The surge of water up a beach after a sea wave breaks on a shore.

**syncline** A downfold in sedimentary rocks, creating a basin or trough in which the strata slope toward the vertical.

**talus** *see* **scree**

**temperate** Refers to the regions or the climate typical of the regions between the tropics and the polar circles in both the Northern and Southern hemispheres.

**terrestrial** (1) Of or from the planet Earth. (2) Of or from the land rather than the atmosphere or the ocean.

**thermoclastic erosion** Erosion that results from the repeated heating and cooling of rocks.

**thermocline** The narrow band in the water column where the temperature gradient is at its maximum.

**thermosphere** The outermost region of the atmosphere extending from the top of the mesosphere to space.

**tide** The periodic rise and fall of sea level under the gravitational influence of the Moon and the Sun.

**till** Sheets of sediment dumped by ice sheets and glaciers: its ingredients range from boulders to rock flour—clay formed from finely ground rock particles.

**tillite** Rock formed from consolidated till.

**tilting** A displacement in the angle of a layer away from the horizontal.

**time zone** One of 24 longitudinal regions of the world based on the prime meridian within which the time is the same. Clocks are set back one hour with each zone entered to its west. Clocks are set forward one hour with each zone entered to its east.

**tombolo** A spit linking an island to the mainland.

**tor** An exposed weathered mass of heavily jointed rocks crowning a hilltop.

**tornado** A rapidly rotating column of air in contact with the ground.

**traction** The movement of boulders and other heavy sediment by a river in full flood.

**trench** A long narrow depression in the seafloor created where one lithospheric plate slides beneath another.

**tributary** A stream flowing into a larger stream.

**tropic** Either the Tropic of Cancer, the Tropic of Capricorn or the area that lies between them.

**tropical** Relating to the region south of the Tropic of Cancer and north of the Tropic of Capricorn.

**troposphere** The region of the atmosphere closest to Earth's surface. Almost all weather phenomena occur in the troposphere.

**trough** The low part of a wave between crests.

**tsunami** A large sea wave generated by a seismic event.

**tundra** A cold treeless Arctic zone where the subsoil remains permanently frozen.

**typhoon** A severe tropical cyclone occurring over the western Pacific Ocean.

**umbra** The conical shadow cast by one celestial body upon another in an eclipse.

**unconformity** An interruption in a succession of rock layers, where one stratum overlies others that are tilted at a different angle. These are revealed where erosion has removed an older rock surface.

**uplift** A movement that raises land.

**volcanic** Produced or related to a volcano.

**volcano** Commonly a steep-sided, or cone-shaped mountain or hill, formed by the accumulation of hardened magma pierced by a hole or fissure from which lava and/or hot ash and gases erupt from deep underground.

**wadi** A normally dry desert watercourse.

**waterfall** A stream flowing over a sudden drop in elevation.

**waterspout** A rising and rotating column of water and spray generated by an air vortex.

**water table** The upper limit of rock saturated by groundwater.

**weathering** The decay and breakup of rocks on Earth's surface by natural chemical and mechanical processes.

**Wilson cycle** The processes by which ocean basins form, widen, and then shrink.

**yardang** A narrow rock ridge in a desert.

**zeugen** A tabular rock formation in a desert.

# Internet resources

There is a lot of useful information on the internet. Information on a particular topic may be available through a search engine such as Google (http://www.google.com). Some of the sites that are found in this way may be very useful, others not. Below is a selection of Web sites related to the material covered by this book.

The publisher takes no responsibility for the information contained within these Web sites. All the sites were accessible in March 2006.

### Berkeley Geochronology Center
A research institution concentrating on the history of Earth and the solar system.
http://www.bgc.org

### British Geological Survey: Education
Educational resources to popularize geology.
http://www.bgs.ac.uk/education/

### BUBL: Earth Science
An index of bibliographical resources for Earth science from the UK's Bulletin Board for Libraries.
http://bubl.ac.uk/link/e/earthsciencelinks.htm

### Cambridge Cosmology
Discusses the academic concepts and hypotheses on the origins and nature of the universe in a way that remains accessible to the general reader.
http://www.damtp.cam.ac.uk/user/gr/public/
    cos_home.html

### Chemistry: Web Elements Periodic Table
An authoritative reference resource updated as discoveries in the world of chemistry are made.
http://www.webelements.com

### Columbia University, Earth Institute: Center for International Earth Science Information Network (CIESIN)
Working at the intersection of the social, natural, and information sciences, CIESIN provides online data and information management essential to Earth science researchers.
http://www.ciesin.org

### Common Ground Database
A database of rock and mineral samples from around the world.
http://commonground.mines.edu

### The Geography Site: Physical Geography
An introduction for school students.
http://www.geography-site.co.uk/pages/physical.html

### Geological Survey of Canada
The Canadian national information and research center for Earth science.
http://gsc.nrcan.gc.ca

### Geology.com
Useful resources for geologists, some commercial.
http://geology.com

### Google Earth
A remarkable Web resource that attempts to provide high-resolution digital mapping of the entire globe.
http://earth.google.com

### International Seismological Centre
A nongovernmental organization concerned with the collection, analysis, and publication of standard earthquake information from all over the world.
http://www.isc.ac.uk

### Mission to Geospace
An educational resource from NASA that locates the study of Earth in the wider context of the solar system.
http://www-istp.gsfc.nasa.gov/istp/outreach/

### NASA: Destination Earth
NASA's stated goal in Earth science is to observe, understand, and model Earth system to discover how it is changing, to predict change more accurately, and to understand the consequences for life on Earth.
http://www.earth.nasa.gov

### National Geophysical Data Center: Natural Hazards
Online resources and information about natural hazards and disasters, including searchable databases.
http://www.ngdc.noaa.gov/seg/hazard/

### National Oceanic and Atmospheric Administration (NOAA)
NOAA conducts research and gathers data about the global oceans, atmosphere, space, and the Sun for practical use by governmental agencies.
http://www.noaa.gov

INTERNET RESOURCES

## National Speleological Society
The Web site of the organization that promotes the study, exploration, and conservation of cave and karst resources in the United States.
> http://www.caves.org

## Natural Disaster Reference Database
A bibliographic research resource for the use of satellites in the analysis and mitigation of natural disasters.
> http://ndrd.gsfc.nasa.gov

## Natural Resources Conversation Service: Soils
Scientifically-based information about soils from the Department of Agriculture.
> http://soils.usda.gov

## Nature
News from the leading science journal.
> http://www.nature.com

## Open Directory Project: Earth Sciences
A comprehensive listing of internet resources grouped as Earth sciences, and categorized by subdisciplines.
> http://dmoz.org/Science/Earth_Sciences/

## Open Directory Project: Physical Geography
A comprehensive listing of internet resources for physical geography.
> http://dmoz.org/Science/Social_Sciences/Geography/
> Physical_Geography/

## Paleographic Atlas Project
Reconstructions of prehistoric maps of Earth's surface, from the Department of Paleogeography at the University of Chicago.
> http://pgap.uchicago.edu

## Physical Geography
Internet resources for the study of physical geography.
> http://www.uwsp.edu/geo/internet/
> physical_geog_resources.html

## Planet Earth: An Introduction to Earth Sciences
An online introduction hosted by Columbia University.
> http://www.ldeo.columbia.edu/res/pi/4d4/planet/

## United States Geological Survey (USGS)
The federal portal for the science of Earth, its resources, and its hazards.
> http://www.usgs.gov

## University of California, Berkeley Library: Earth Sciences Collection
Includes an extensive collection of maps, some available online.
> http://www.lib.berkeley.edu/EART/

## University of California, Berkeley: Museum of Paleontology: Plate Tectonics
Provides animations that condense the geologic time of continental drift into a few seconds.
> http://www.ucmp.berkeley.edu/geology/tectonics.html

## USGS Geography
Uses satellite mapping to provide some of the best geographic information available on the Web.
> http://geography.usgs.gov

## USGS Geologic Time
An online publication explaining the science underlying concepts such as geologic time.
> http://pubs.usgs.gov/gip/geotime/

## Volcano World
A central reference point from the University of North Dakota for information on volcanoes worldwide.
> http://volcano.und.nodak.edu

## World Soil Information
An center of information about the world's soils and their importance for humanity.
> http://www.isric.org

## World-wide Earthquake Locator
Daily updated reports and maps on earthquakes around the world from Edinburgh University Geography Department.
> http://www.geo.ed.ac.uk/quakes/

# Index

Index of subject headings.